Praise for
AWAY WITH ALL GODS!
Unchaining The Mind And Radically Changing The World

"Bob Avakian has written the first book in years that makes me actually want to re-read the Bible, but this time as freaky horror show, weirded out fiction and gothic nightmare.

"Everyone should read *Away With All Gods* because it is necessary, critical and timely, but also because it is a book written with joy and humor. Avakian has a whole lot of fun mocking the absurdities of those who should be called 'god-botherin fools'—never better than when he retells old Richard Pryor routines about Cleveland or reminds us of the hypocrisy of Ronald Reagan as Christian leader while wife Nancy reads the tarot. The trouble is that the people who go in for this religious-fantasy foolishness are serious, and they must be stopped. Avakian shows how and why.

"Pointing out that the myth that Zapata had not been killed and would return to fight again some day was flawed because it overlooked the fact that he was just as dead as was the resurrected Jesus; showing that Mel Gibson's 'Passion of the Christ' movie perpetuates an anti-Jewish slander that the mob killed the son of God; equally critical of contortions such as the one where the Quran is as fair to women thieves as it is to men ('cut off their hands' if they do not repent); and skewering Christopher Hitchens' whose critique of religion is just as much an anti-Muslim tirade ('God is not great') as is the US War on Terror; Avakian eviscerates all manner of soft thinking on issues that have a mysterious afterlife in popular thought today.

"Avakian has answers as to why religious fundamentalism (Christian or Islamic) is on the rise, and he does this not with candles and mirrors, dark robes and incense, but rather a philosophico-political analysis and a program for change. These are things we really need to hear."

Professor John Hutnyk, Professor, Academic Director, Centre for Cultural Studies, Goldsmiths, University of London; author of *Bad Marxism: Capitalism and Cultural Studies*

"While Bob Avakian comes from a decidedly different perspective on religion than myself, there are many shared views on the need for human emancipation. His new book opens up a much needed conversation about the role of religion and spiritual belief in the overall fight for justice, along with questions of morality and what it will take to bring about an end to white supremacy and patriarchy."

Rev. Lennox Yearwood, Jr., President, Hip-Hop Caucus

"Forceful, scathing, and timely. While I did not personally agree with everything Bob Avakian has to say in this book, I found his arguments cogently articulated and provocatively put forth. Angry, humorous, provocative, and hopeful in equal measure, this was an enjoyable and engaging read."

Phil Zuckerman, Associate Professor of Sociology, Pitzer College; author of *Society Without God* (NYU Press, 2008)

"'God' has been used to justify every kind of atrocity for thousands of years. Bob Avakian says, 'god does not exist and here's why.' This proposition is so radically different from what people around here are told. It makes me want to get a deeper understanding of communism and how everything could be different for humanity."

22 year old Black man from Harlem

"Bold, wide-ranging, down-to-earth, provocative. One needn't be a Marxist to learn a lot from this work. I especially like the forthright critique of the obfuscating epistemology of religion, and of religion's appalling consequences for women."

Laura Purdy, McCullough Distinguished Visiting Professor of Philosophy, Hamilton College, 2007-08; Ruth and Albert Koch Professor of Humanities, and Professor of Philosophy, Wells College

"When I joined the Black Panther Party we had mandatory readings. This book needs to be mandatory reading for everybody, especially young people, and definitely not put away somewhere in a left-wing literature section. This world is upside down–topsy turvy–and lots of people haven't actually studied what that Bible says. Bob Avakian has. He exposes the hypocritical bullshit. He brings it down hard and plain, cold and simple. He goes into history *and* morality. This book is serious reading."

Eric G., former Black Panther member

"Whether readers enthusiastically embrace or reject its claims and arguments, Away With All Gods! is a book that cannot be ignored. This is especially so at a time when religion continues to negotiate a sweetheart deal with leviathan capital, when the Christian Reconstructionist/Dominionist movement tries to seize the helm of the corporate-state-military-media complex, when the apocalypticism of the American empire lurches perilously forward and when religion and capitalism/imperialism become more tightly woven together than ever before."

Peter McLaren, Professor, Graduate School of Education and Information Studies, University of California; author of *Che Guevara, Paulo Freire, and the Pedagogy of Revolution.*

"Bob Avakian's "Away With All Gods" is more than an apologia for humanism. Well and engagingly written, Mr. Avakian succeeds once again in confronting his reader with authoritative, fact-based challenges to our most basic beliefs. With this kind of thinking and writing, Avakian may just spearhead a return to the Age of Reason."

Harry Lennix, actor, instructor

AWAY WITH ALL GODS!

Unchaining the Mind and Radically Changing the World

Bob Avakian

Insight Press • Chicago

Published in 2008 by Insight Press.
Printed in U.S.A.

FIRST EDITION

Paperback:
ISBN 13: 978-0-9760236-8-5
ISBN 10: 0-9760236-8-7

Hardcover:
ISBN 13: 978-0-9760236-9-2
ISBN 10: 0-9760236-9-5

CONTENTS

PUBLISHER'S NOTE

This book is based on two talks by Bob Avakian, one in 2004, entitled "God Does Not Exist—We Need Liberation Without Gods"; and a more recent talk, "Communism and Religion: Getting Up and Getting Free—Making Revolution to Change the Real World, Not Relying on 'Things Unseen,'" (part of 7 Talks given by Avakian in 2006). For the purposes of publishing this as a book, the texts of the two talks have been combined (along with the text of a portion of the remarks by the author at the conclusion of the 7 Talks in 2006). This involved a significant amount of editing on the part of the author—rearranging parts of the combined text, rewriting certain passages to effect smoother transitions and greater continuity and clarity, and removing redundancy where it did not seem helpful. In addition to citations for material quoted or referenced (most of which is included within the body of the text), footnotes have been added by the author to further clarify and in some cases to elaborate on certain points.

At the same time, while what is published here is a written text (and while it is not possible to reproduce in this form the effect in the places where, in the course of these talks, Avakian sings lines from a song or enacts a comedy routine), an effort has been made to retain not only the essential content and substance but also, as much as possible, the style and flavor of the original, spoken material (including by indicating, in brackets within the text, the responses of the audience at various points). On the whole we believe the result, as with Bob Avakian's talks and writings in general, is a work that is both substantial and lively, controversial and challenging—combining, to paraphrase a passage in another book by Avakian, a solemn sense of purpose with a lively and penetrating sense of humor.

Part One:

WHERE DID GOD COME FROM...

AND WHO SAYS WE NEED GOD?

"God Works in Mysterious Ways"

Day after day we learn of terrible tragedies that would make no sense if there were an all-knowing, all-powerful and loving god looking over and looking out for human beings. Here are just a few stories taken from the news in recent years:

A family loses five children and two other relatives in a terrible bus crash, and then a grandfather of the children dies of a heart attack after hearing the news of this terrible accident.

But—we are told—God works in mysterious ways.

In a plane crash in Nigeria, 60 Jesuit college students are killed.

But, God works in mysterious ways.

A fiery auto accident and explosion takes the lives of six children of devoutly Christian parents.

Indeed, God works in mysterious ways.

A woman works long and patiently to help her husband in need of a lung transplant to get in physical condition to qualify for the transplant, and, finally, he does. And then, after receiving the good news, they are involved in an auto accident in which the woman is killed and the man is injured.

But, again, God works in mysterious ways.

People suffer all kinds of tragedies and atrocities, big and small, more personal and society-wide or even world-wide—car crashes, bus crashes, train crashes, plane crashes, earthquakes, floods, hurricanes and tsunamis—wiping out thousands, tens and hundreds of thousands.

Generation after generation, down through the centuries, millions of people were sold into slavery, often worked to death in inhuman conditions (and in some places this continues today). Genocide after genocide is carried out, wiping out or nearly wiping out whole peoples.

Wars are waged in which tens of millions of people have been massacred through the use of weapons of massive slaughter and destruction, all the way to nuclear atrocities, such as the U.S. devastation of two Japanese cities with atomic bombs in the second world war.

Thirty to forty thousand children die every day in the Third World from starvation and preventable disease.

Epidemics throughout history strike down large sections of humanity.

Women are raped in huge numbers throughout the world, and then often they are subjected to shaming and even literally murdered by members of their own family because *they*—in being the victims of rape—have not only been devalued, but have supposedly soiled the honor of the family.

But, through all this, always there is the refrain: "God works in mysterious ways."

A Cruel and Truly Monstrous God

How much of this has to go on, and how long does it take, before it becomes clear that if such a god existed, it would indeed be a cruel, vicious, sick, twisted, and truly monstrous god? That no sane and decent person would want to bow down to or follow such a god. And that it is very fortunate that no such god exists—and very liberating to finally come to that realization.

In case this is not enough, to see yet another dimension to the murderous nature of God as presented in the major monotheistic (one-god) religions—to see how this God is capricious, volatile and seemingly even schizophrenic in his cruelty—let's turn to the "Judeo-Christian" scriptures. Let's begin with the story in the Bible, in the book of Second Samuel (chapter 24), of how it came about that King David brought the wrath of this God down on his people.

David, we are told in Second Samuel, ordered a census of the people of Israel and Judah, his kingdom, and (as a footnote in one version of the Bible offers as a possible explanation) it seems that David did this particularly to get a count of men eligible for military service. But, in conducting the census in the way he did, David made a big mistake, because, as this footnote explains, soldiers on active duty were subject to a strict regimen of ritual procedures in ancient Israel, and were especially vulnerable therefore to cultic dangers. (See *The HarperCollins Study Bible, New Revised Standard Version, with the Apocryphal/Deuterocanonical Books, A New Annotated Edition by the Society of Biblical Literature*, pp. 506–07, annotation to 2 Samuel 24:3. All citations in this text in reference to the Bible [except where they are contained in a quote from another author] are from this *Harper-Collins Study Bible* edition.)

And what results from all this? Readers of the Bible may be able to anticipate: a terrible plague is sent by God. 70,000 people died, we are told. But then, finally, the loving God relented and declared, "It is enough," and the plague was ended when David, following God's instructions, built an altar "and offered burnt offerings and offerings of well-being." (See 2 Samuel 24: especially verses 15–25.)

But that is not all there is to the story. According to the author of Samuel, it was God who ordered David to carry out this census in the first place. As it says Second Samuel 24, verse 1: "Again the anger of the Lord was kindled against Israel, and he incited David against them, saying, 'Go, count the people of Israel and Judah.'" Then, in-furiated with David for carrying out the census that God ordered him to carry out (or perhaps angry at how David carried it out), God turns around and sends a plague to slaughter 70,000 of his "chosen people" who, by any logical reckoning, had no fault in the matter of the census.

Now, apparently, this was too much for the author of another book in the Bible, Chronicles. For, in First Chronicles, Chapter 21, in speaking of the very same census, we are informed that it was not God but *the devil* who made David do it: "Satan stood up against Israel, and incited David to count the people of Israel." (1 Chronicles 21:1.) Now, this is hardly a minor matter. Which was it—God or the devil? [Laughter] Here, again, we see an illustration of the not-so-inerrant word of the lunatic, maniacal and murderous god of the Bible.

And this—it is important to note—is not one of those much-invoked "isolated incidents." As one sees in reading the Bible, and as I will come back to shortly, a plague is one of God's most frequent means of bringing down devastation and suffering on human beings, on vast numbers of people, not least his own "chosen people," including many whom any reasonable person would have to regard as completely innocent. And some people, including religious people—and even many religious people who are generally progressive—have the nerve to talk about the alleged horrors of communism?! Whatever you want to say about the errors that have been made in the experience of socialist societies and by communist leaders, no leader of the international communist movement, or of a socialist state, has ever even *advocated* the things that this God repeatedly *insists* must be done.

But...**God works in mysterious ways**.

Once again, if all this—and much, much more in the way of cruelty, agony, devastation and atrocity—is "God working in mysterious ways," *who needs* such a god?

Stepping back for a minute, just to inject a little reality into this, insofar as there was any historical and factual basis for this plague, the reality was not as the Bible presents it; the reality was that a plague happened and then somehow it had to be explained and rationalized. All these people are dying—why, what's the reason? In order to hold the society together, it was no doubt necessary to provide some explanation for why this was happening, why there was this terrible suffering. As long as you believe in God, the explanation can't put the ultimate blame on this God, so it has to be found in some human action. And the explanation that is given in the Bible reflects the social and economic-production relations—and the corresponding institutions, ideas, customs and values—that characterized and predominated in the society in which the authors of this part of the Bible lived and of which they were advocates.

Now, this was not necessarily, and may well not have been, a matter of conscious invention and deception. Those who wrote this part of the Bible may have actually believed the explanation they gave for this plague. Or it may have been a combination of actual belief and conscious calculation on their part, in line with and to serve the prevailing and predominant social forces, institutions and relations of their own time and place. But, in any case, the time has long since passed when humanity has to be enslaved by those kinds of relations, institutions, customs, values, ideas and beliefs, and the ignorance, fear and oppression that they embody, advocate and reinforce.

Along with what is pointed to here, as well as in previous talks and writings of mine, in regard to the murderous nature and acts of the Biblical God, not long ago there was an important series of articles, "God the Original Fascist," by A. Brooks, which appeared in our Party's newspaper, *Revolution*. This series provides further glaring examples of the absolutely ruthless and viciously *demented* nature of the God of the Bible, and the particular fixation this God seems to have on the use of plagues as a weapon of mass retribution and destruction. So (with the permission of the author) I would like to include here some of the more striking passages found in "God the Original Fascist."

First, in reference to the ordeal of the ancient Israelites in Egypt, Brooks writes:

> Instead of subjecting his own "chosen" people to horrible suffering and enslavement for centuries and then freeing them, why not just prevent them from being enslaved in the first damn place?
>
> Well, reading on in Exodus, we get our answer. God hints to Moses that this whole process by which the Israelites become slaves to the Egyptians and then are freed is to him nothing more than a sick game—an opportunity to "shock and awe" everyone with his power:

"You shall repeat all that I command you....But I will harden Pharaoh's heart, that I may multiply my signs and marvels in the land of Egypt." (Exodus 6) The "you shall repeat all I command you" portion of this passage refers to the instructions God provides to Moses where he tells Moses to tell the Pharaoh to release the Israelites from captivity or else God will punish Egypt. The next few passages of Exodus follow a basic pattern: Moses threatens the Pharaoh that unless he releases the Israelites from captivity, God will unleash plagues on the Egyptians—including blood, lice, frogs, locusts, swarms of insects, and inflammation of the skin, among other things. The Pharaoh witnesses one of these plagues, and immediately agrees to free the Israelites if the plagues are stopped. God halts the plagues, but then also hardens Pharaoh's heart so that he recants on his promise to free the slaves, and thus God "has no choice" but to inflict more plagues on the Egyptians. ("God The Original Fascist," Part 3A, *Revolution* #017, October 9, 2005. In relation to the above, see especially chapters 3 through 14 in Exodus. This entire series, "God the Original Fascist," is also available online as one document at revcom.us)

Brooks writes further:

What does it say about this "God" that, even though he is "all-powerful" and could easily have prevented the Israelites from being enslaved in the first place, and then subsequently could have freed them once they were enslaved, he would instead choose to intentionally prolong the suffering of both the Israelites and the Egyptians merely so that he could show off his—powers? Is that God any kind of God to uphold or believe in? ("God the Original Fascist," part 3A, *Revolution* #017, October 9, 2005)

Then, from another passage in this series, "God the Original Fascist":

> The book of Numbers describes how the armies of God's people begin assembling and then marching towards Canaan, prepared to battle and annihilate those who are already dwelling on the land.
>
> But at a certain point, hard times fall upon the armies and troop morale becomes low. The troops begin lamenting to Moses that their conditions are dire, that they do not have enough food to eat. So what is God's response? Well, being the "compassionate God, slow to anger" that is mentioned in Exodus 34, the Lord undoubtedly responds by blessing the Israelites with food so that they are no longer starving, right? WRONG! God instead responds by initially giving his people food, but then, "The meat was still between their teeth, nor yet chewed, when the anger of the Lord blazed forth against the people and the Lord struck the people with a severe plague." (Numbers 11) All this perpetrated on a people who did nothing more than simply complain that they were starving! ("God the Original Fascist," Part 3B, *Revolution* #018, October 16, 2005. Notice that when God promises this land to his "chosen people," there are already other people living there, so something has to be done about them. As we shall see, they have to be slaughtered and driven off the land, and those— or in particular those virgin women—who escape the slaughter must be taken as slaves.)

Brooks also observes that

> Eventually, some of the Israelites became so exasperated with the tyrannical rule of Moses that they launch a rebellion against his tyranny. God responds to this rebellion by annihilating the rebels—he opens the earth and swallows them whole, consuming 250 men in a great fire. (Numbers 16) The next day, the entire Israelite

community is up in arms about what God, acting through
Moses and Aaron, has done to them. So God, being "a
compassionate God, slow to anger," naturally responds
by profusely apologizing, recognizing his brutality, and
promising never to repeat it, right? WRONG AGAIN!
God responds with more brutality: He kills 14,700 Israelites in (you guessed it) a plague! ("God the Original Fascist," Part 3B, *Revolution* #016, October 16, 2005)

As Brooks points out: "Apparently, God has some kind of fetish
for plagues." Brooks notes that

In Leviticus, God refers again to one of his favorite
practices—inflicting plagues as a punishment on those
who do not follow him: "When you enter the land of
Canaan that I give you as a possession, and I inflict an
eruptive plague upon a house in the land you possess,"
God begins, before outlining the proper procedure for
cleaning a house that God Himself infected with the
plague! (Leviticus 14). In Leviticus 20, God again offers
his supposed justification for the brutality he is inflicting upon the inhabitants of Canaan: That justification,
once again, is that the inhabitants of the land deviated
from or resisted his ways: "You shall faithfully observe
all my laws and all my regulations, lest the land to
which I bring you in to settle spew you out. You shall
not follow the principles of the nation that I am driving
out before you. For it is because they did all these things
that I abhorred them and said to you: 'You shall possess
their land, for I will give it to you to possess.'" (Leviticus 20). ("God the Original Fascist," Part 4A, *Revolution*
#019, October 23, 2005. In relation to the conquest of
Canaan see, in addition to Leviticus: Numbers, chapters
13 and 14; Exodus, chapter 23; Deuteronomy, chapter 9;
and Genesis, chapter 15.)

One more time from "God the Original Fascist"—whose title
should be resonating more and more at this point. Brooks refers

to Numbers, chapter 25, where we learn that some of the Israelites had fallen under the sway of Midianite women and not only had sex with them but also—even worse abomination!—had been seduced by these woman into worshipping their gods. And so, as Brooks recounts:

> Upon discovering this, God became so enraged that he struck down 24,000 Israelites in (any guesses, anyone?)...yes, a plague! ("God the Original Fascist," Part 4B, *Revolution* #020, October 30, 2005)

By now the answer to the question Brooks poses, after depicting one of these horrors perpetrated by the God of the Bible, should be even more clear: "Is that God any kind of God to uphold or believe in?"

But we have not yet seen the full bloodthirstiness of this God, and his servant and enforcer Moses. For that, let's turn to Numbers 31. Perhaps no other part of the Bible contains as open a celebration of unrepentant and merciless conquest, slaughter and rape as that found in this chapter of Numbers. This part of Numbers recounts the battle of Moses and the Israelites against the Midianites. As we recall, Moses and the Lord, according to the Bible, were furious with the Midianites, as well as with many of the Jewish people because they were sleeping with the women of Midian and being seduced into worshipping their gods, instead of "the one true God" of Israel. Thus, the Lord commanded Moses, and Moses commanded the people: go out and slaughter the Midianites. And so they did. You can read this in Numbers 31, verses 13 to 18 and 31 to 35. Here I'm going to focus on verses 17 to 18.

The leaders of the Israelite army went out and slaughtered the Midianites. Then they came back and reported to Moses what they had done, and Moses became very angry. Did he get angry because they had massacred the Midianites? No. He got angry because they were *too lenient*: they only killed off the adult males and took some of their cattle and other possessions. And Moses said, Goddamn it!—well, he may not have said that [Laughter], but he told them: you go back there and not only kill every adult male who might have escaped, but also kill every male child among the Midianites and every female who is not a virgin. And those women who are virgins, Moses said, you may take as prizes of war, as concubines—sex slaves.

If you don't believe this, here is the passage, word for word, in Numbers—this is Moses speaking, on behalf of "The Lord":

> Now therefore, kill every male among the little ones, and kill every woman who has known a man by sleeping with him. But all the young girls who have not known a man by sleeping with him, keep alive for yourselves. (Numbers 31:17–18)

And what about Joshua and the battle of Jericho? We've all heard about Joshua and the battle of Jericho. Many people have heard the spiritual that was written about it, which tells us how the walls of Jericho "came tumbling down." Well, what we're not so often told is what happened *after* "the walls came tumbling down." According, once again, to the commandment of the Lord, the followers of this Lord went into Jericho and slaughtered everybody. If you look, for example, at Joshua, chapter 6, verses 17 to 19 and then especially verse 21, you will find that, after "the walls came tumbling down": "Then they devoted to destruction by the edge of the sword all in the city, both men and women, young and old, oxen, sheep, and donkeys." So, on this occasion as well, the *little children* among "God's enemies" did not escape the "justice" of this God and his messenger, Joshua.[1]

---

1. As for the story of how, in another battle, Joshua made the sun and the moon stand still while the Israelites "took vengeance on their enemies," that of course is a myth with no basis in reality: along with the fact that it is actually the earth that moves around the sun, and not the other way around (a fact which Christian Church authorities suppressed for as long as they could, through the use of torture and other means, because this basic fact contradicts what is said in the Bible), if the motion of the sun, the earth and the moon had been affected in the way the Bible alleges, in the book of Joshua, there would have been catastrophic consequences, and we would not be here to read this tale in the Bible. (See Joshua 10:10–13.)

Or, if you read through the book of Isaiah, which was supposed to be one of Jesus's favorite parts of the Jewish scripture, you will see (for example, in chapters 11 through 14) how Isaiah goes on and on about the revenge that is going to be taken on Babylon, for oppressing the Jewish people, and on other nations who are opposed to and practice different religions than that of "the one true God." Once again, the women of Babylon and these other nations are going to be raped, the babies are going to have their heads bashed in, and all the men are going to be slaughtered. Over and over and over again, this is proclaimed, sung about in hymns almost, by the prophet Isaiah.

Or, we often hear about the Psalms in the Bible and how they are expressions of god's love, mercy, and other admirable qualities. Well, let's look at Psalm 137. There was actually a reggae song that was based on this, which began [Singing:] "By the rivers of Babylon, where we sat down, and there we wept, when we remembered Zion." Well, those are the first verses of Psalm 137. But what are the last verses? Here are verses 8 and 9 which conclude that Psalm:

> O daughter Babylon, you devastator! Happy shall they
> be who pay you back what you have done to us! Happy
> shall they be who take your little ones and dash them
> against the rock!

In fact, if you accept what the Bible says, God is no better than Dracula. The only problem is, God is more powerful than Dracula. The character Dracula in literature and in the movies was based, at least loosely, on an historical figure in Romania several centuries ago, who was called Vlad the Impaler. And for his enemies, like those from Turkey who practiced Islam, as well as the peasants who rose up against his rule in Romania, his favorite form of punishment was to impale them—drive stakes through their body, and let them sit out rotting until they died. That is the historical basis for the character Dracula.

Well, in the Bible, not only does Moses, acting on the Lord's behalf, kill thousands of his own people, the Israelites, because they worshipped an idol (see Exodus chapter 32, especially verses 25 to 29); but, later, when the Lord learns that the men of Israel—here we go again—are having sexual relations with the women of Moab, and are being seduced by these women into worshipping their gods instead of "the one true God," then that "one true God" orders Moses to "take all the chiefs of the people of Israel and impale them in the desert sun." (This is once again from the book of Numbers, chapter 25, verses 1 to 5.)

According to the Bible itself, this kind of slaughter, pillage and rape was carried out over and over again in accordance with the commandments of the Lord. And the first five, so-called "Mosaic" books of the Bible (as well as the book of Joshua that follows) are full of instructions from the Lord, and his representatives and spokesmen like Moses and Joshua, insisting that pillage, rape and slaughter—including the mass murder of babies and infants—be carried out thoroughly and without mercy. But then, today, one sees these zombie-like Christian fundamentalists at abortion clinics, wrapping themselves in the Bible, accusing the women who have abortions and the medical personnel who perform them of being "baby-killers"—distorting what actually happens with an abortion, obscuring the reality that more than 90% of abortions take place during the first three months of pregnancy when the fetus is very small and not highly developed, and is far from being capable of life on its own. These Christian fundamentalist fanatics try to portray things as if fully developed and independent little children are being killed when fetuses are aborted. But, along with the gross ignorance that they are expressing and promoting, there is the profound hypocrisy and irony that the very Bible which they are wielding as a weapon against women with unwanted pregnancies—that very same Bible calls over and over again for slaughtering *actual* babies and infants.

The Bible, Taken Literally, Is a Horror

All this is why, with profound reason and justification, it must be said that the Bible, taken literally, is a horror. And the fundamental question demands to be posed: Is what the Bible portrays about people and their relations—how those relations ought to be, how, according to the decrees of God, they *have* to be—is that really the kind of world we want?

From what has been shown so far, and what will be gone into further in the course of this book, it becomes unmistakably clear that the following are some of the extremely oppressive relations and beliefs that are upheld—and not just upheld, but advocated, commanded and celebrated—in the Bible:

Slavery and other forms of ruthless exploitation.

The domination and degradation of women by men, including the so-called right of male conquerors to carry off women, especially virgins, as prizes of war, rape them, and make them concubines—sex slaves—of the conquerors.

The killing of women who are not virgins when they get married.

The execution of women alleged to be witches.

The condemnation of homosexuality as not just a sin, but an abomination deserving of death.

The right, and indeed the duty, as commanded by God, to plunder and slaughter people—including the babies and infants of people—following other religions.

The slaughter of people *of* the one true faith who displease that God.

Killing of children who rebel against their parents.

Belief in superstition and fear, and fear-inspiring ignorance, such as demon possession and exorcism.

The cruel notion that disease is caused by sinfulness.

The condemnation to eternal damnation and unbearable suffering in hell for all those who do not accept "the one true God"—and, in the case of Christianity, Jesus as the son of God who was crucified but then raised from the dead.

All of this, along with many other atrocities and outrages, is upheld and promoted in the Bible. If you believe in the Bible—and especially if you believe and insist that it is the divinely-dictated, or divinely-inspired word of God and all of it must be taken literally—then all of these atrocities and outrages are things that you must say are right and good because the Bible says they are right and good. And that is precisely the case with the right-wing Christian fundamentalists who can be very accurately characterized as Christian Fascists.

Christian Fundamentalists, Christian Fascists

Now, right away, the question may arise: "Why do you call these right-wing Christian fundamentalists Christian Fascists?" Well, the simple and basic reason is that they are Christians, *and* they are *fascists*. [Laughter] They are the present-day American version of the Nazis in Germany, headed by Hitler, in the period before and during World War 2. They want to impose a fascist *theocracy* on society— an openly repressive form of reactionary rule, in the interests of the capitalist class and the capitalist-imperialist system of exploitation, in which law and the exercise of political power will be based on and justified on the basis of Christian scripture and "Biblical law"—as interpreted by authoritative figures recognized as legitimate by these Christian Fascists.

These Christian Fascists are forever talking about, and insisting upon, "traditional morality." So let's examine further what traditions and traditional morality they are actually insisting on and want to force on all of society. What is this actually all about and what does it really represent?

One of the things that is very striking is that when these Christian Fascists are confronted with the kinds of horrors that I've mentioned, many of which are based in the Old Testament of the Bible, they will say: "Oh, that was the Old Testament which God had with the ancient nation of Israel. That's the old covenant. Now we have a new covenant, a New Testament, based on the life and teachings, and the death and resurrection, of Jesus."

Well, as a matter fact, the *New* Testament upholds such things as slavery and the subjugation of women. Paul's letters throughout the New Testament, for example, do this rather emphatically. Paul insists repeatedly that slaves should be loyal to and obey their masters (see, for example, Colossians 3:22–24). The *New* Testament, in the person of Paul—who, as I will return to later, really is the most influential figure in the New Testament—tells people to obey earthly authority, without regard to how oppressive that earthly authority may be, because, as Paul puts it, such earthly authority is ordained by God (see Romans 13:1–7). The *New* Testament insists, in the words of Jesus himself (as in John 14:6 and John 15:6), that if you do not follow him and accept what he teaches, you will not be able to get into heaven and instead will be damned to horrible suffering in hell for all eternity.[2] So, if you believe in and insist on taking the Bible literally, as the inerrant and unchallengeable word of God, you have

---

2. It is also worthwhile looking at Jesus's parable of the Ten Pounds, in which a nobleman gives ten pounds to ten of his slaves and then, after a time, rewards or punishes them according to how they used this money—whether they wisely invested it or foolishly squandered it. At the end of this parable—which is supposed to be about the coming of the Kingdom of Heaven and what will happen to the righteous and to the evil ones when that time comes—the nobleman in the parable says: "But as for these enemies of mine who did not want me to be king over them—bring them here and slaughter them in my presence." (See Luke 19:1–27—what is quoted here is verse 27.) And, not without any reason, Christian Fascists in the U.S., including in the U.S. military, interpret this parable, and in particular its concluding verse (Luke 19:27), as a declaration that those who do not recognize Jesus as Lord and savior will face merciless destruction when the Kingdom of Heaven arrives. As reported in the newspaper of our Party, *Revolution* (issue no. 98, August 13, 2007), in an interview with *Tikkun* magazine Mikey Weinstein of the Military Religious Freedom Foundation describes the outlook of the Christian fundamentalists in the U.S. military: "They often quote Luke 19:27 when I speak to them. That's the Parable of the Pounds in which Jesus says: 'go out among the people, and bring back to me those who refuse to accept me as King over them, and slaughter them.'"

to believe that everybody who follows another religion—and even children who die at any early age, without knowing anything about religion, one way or the other—must be condemned to eternal damnation because they haven't accepted Jesus as their personal savior.

Seeing Jesus in a True Light

With all the mystical and sacred "aura" surrounding Jesus, it is important to look at him, and examine what he stood for, in its true light. According to the Bible, Jesus encounters somebody who has epilepsy, and how does he supposedly cure the epilepsy? Through *exorcism*—by casting out a demon. Apparently, the all-knowing God, in the person of Jesus, hadn't been paying attention to the field of medicine. Even though people back then didn't know what was the actual cause of epilepsy, if God existed, then *God* should have known. There are many things that people didn't know about in those times, and so (as still happens far too often today) when they didn't understand things, they made up rationalizations and explanations for them—explanations which often, and in fact generally, ended up blaming the people themselves for their own misfortunes. That's the whole point about sicknesses being caused by sin: Jesus, the Bible tells us, goes around curing sickness by casting out demons and casting out sin. This is all in the New Testament.

And it's not just that Paul, in his letters—again, in the New Testament—upholds slavery; but Jesus himself, in his parables, accepts slavery as a given. There is the parable of the weeds among the wheat, the parable of the unforgiving servant, the parable of the wicked tenants, the parable of the wedding banquet, the parable of the talents—all these parables accept the idea that slavery and oppression will exist in this world, and use these as a way of drawing lessons for life. Look at Matthew 10:24-25: there Jesus says, "A disciple is not above the teacher, nor a slave above the master; it is enough for the disciple to be like the teacher, and the slave like the master."

And, with regard to the status of women, Jesus once again accepts as given the relations of male domination that run through—and in fact are foundational to—the whole of the Bible, in the New Testament as well as the old. Often, those who seek to find in Jesus—and to present Jesus as—a champion of the downtrodden, oppressed and marginalized, argue that Jesus allowed women who were outcasts and condemned as sinners to approach him and even to become part of his close circle, and therefore Jesus provides a model and a way for achieving equality between men and women and overcoming thousands of years of the subordination and degradation of women.[3] But the truth is that from the Bible it is clear that

---

3. Not only in the West, where Christianity has been the dominant religion for more than 1500 years, but in Asia as well there have been attempts in recent times to (re)fashion Jesus as the advocate of the oppressed and his teachings as the basis for a kind of "liberation theology." One of the more interesting of these is contained in the book *Jesus the Dalit, Liberation Theology by Victims of Untouchability, an Indian Version of Apartheid*, by M.R. Arulraja. In the "Introduction" to this book, its essential thesis is summarized:

"The Dalits who reread the Bible in the context of their struggle for liberation were in for many surprises.

"They found that the struggle of Jesus was precisely against the practice of untouchability prevalent in his place and time. Jesus was not exactly giving an example for Dalits to carry their cross meekly unto death. He was rather asking them to fight caste discrimination even if it would cost them their lives! His struggle became directly relevant to them. They discovered in Jesus their hero, their leader, their God who died for their liberation." (p. VII)

And again in the "Epilogue," it is argued:

"Jesus affirms by his word and deed that untouchability is a myth. He touches the Dalits and says they are as much children of God as he himself is. All human beings are children of the one Father. The same Father cannot have children belonging to different castes..." (p. 210)

What Arulraja is referring to are the instances in the Bible where Jesus reaches out to and embraces people denounced as sinful and treated as pariahs, and his willingness (and at times even insistence on) breaking with a dogmatic adherence to the strict Mosaic laws, as well as the way in which Jesus calls for mercy and compassion for the poor and afflicted. Arulraja also seeks to build his thesis on the fact that Jesus in some instances acknowledged the faithfulness or other positive traits among non-Jewish people, and that Paul, much more so and as a matter of policy, spread the Christian message and organized Christian communities increasingly among non-Jews (gentiles). But, as Arulraja

Jesus *never challenged* but instead incorporated into his teachings the view of women as inferior in their relations with men, and indeed as essentially the property of men—a view deeply rooted in the scriptures and religious traditions to which Jesus himself adhered. Nowhere does this find a more concentrated expression than in the question of *virginity*.

Not only does the Bible place a great emphasis on Jesus's supposed "virgin birth" and the image of Jesus's mother, Mary, as someone who had not "lain with man" before her marriage and who, furthermore, we are told, conceived Jesus not through intercourse with her husband, Joseph, but through the embrace of the holy spirit; but, again, the teachings of Jesus assume that virginity and chastity are qualities that are essential for women—this is reflected, for example, in the parable of the ten virgin bridesmaids (Matthew 25:1–13) as well as in Jesus's discussions of marriage (and divorce). So, it is important to understand what this whole concept of virginity—and the great importance attached to it—rests on, and in turn what it reflects.

Once human societies, thousands of years ago, evolved and changed in such a way that the wealth that was produced by society was taken for the most part by a small group of people who dominated and exploited the rest—once private property and wealth of individuals emerged and developed—then not only was the basic role of a woman increasingly reduced to being a breeder of children,

---

acknowledges (and as will be discussed more fully later in this book), Jesus saw his efforts as being aimed essentially and overwhelmingly among Jews—his religion was a version of Judaism, and Christianity developed initially as a sect within Judaism—and Paul's decision to focus mainly and increasingly among gentiles came about not out of devotion to the principle of rejecting "untouchability," but rather as a necessity that was imposed because of the rejection of Christianity by the overwhelming majority of Jews and the growing openness to it among a number of gentiles in the larger Mediterranean area. Even more fundamentally, as has already been illustrated, and will be further elaborated on through the course of this book, the teachings of Jesus and Christianity do not, in fact, aim to overcome or provide a basis for overcoming relations of oppression in this, real, world; on the contrary, they embody, propagate and reinforce such relations, including some of the most egregious expressions of them.

but it also became crucial to ensure that her children would be those of her husband, so that he could pass his property on to *his* heirs—and in particular his *male* heirs—and *not somebody else's*. So then women's sexual activity had to be very carefully controlled.

What were the means through which this was done? Well, in a society of private ownership of wealth and property, a female child, when she was a girl and then grew into a young woman, was the property and possession of her father. Sometimes, he used his wife, or his mother (the wife's mother-in-law) to carry out direct control over his daughter, but in any case it was he, the father, who ultimately controlled her. And, in keeping with the requirements of these patriarchal, male-dominated social relations, he was responsible for guaranteeing that when she got married, she was a virgin. We see this tradition continuing down to today, and not just in Islamic cultures where young women are often killed, by members of their own family, if they have "lost their virginity"—even if they have been raped—because this is considered to bring dishonor on their family (these are the so-called "honor killings"). Look at the whole "abstinence" campaign, being promoted from the highest levels of government in the U.S. today. While boys as well as girls are encouraged, and coerced, into making pledges of "abstinence" (virginity until marriage), there is no question that, as it always has, such an emphasis on virginity falls most heavily on girls and young women. And, as we shall see, if the Christian Fascists were to have their way, the punishment, particularly for girls and women, who did not "abstain"—who were not virgins when they were married—would be *death*: that is what a literalist reading of the Bible would demand, and these Christian Fascists are very serious about making a strict adherence to "Biblical commandments" the law of the land.

And look at the renewed emphasis in America in recent decades on the traditional wedding ceremony: here comes the bride in her "beautiful white wedding gown." How come it has to be *white*? Because white is the color representing virginity. And who "gives the bride away?" The *father*. In effect, and with whatever degree of consciousness may be the case with particular individuals, what is objectively happening is that the father is carrying forward the patri-archal tradition of bringing his property up to the altar and handing it over to the husband who will now take it over as *his* property.

If we go back to the "Judeo-Christian tradition," which embodies and promotes this whole view and practice of marriage, it is very clear that the question of virginity—the virginity of the *bride*—is a deadly serious matter. For example, if you read Deuteronomy, chapter 22 verses 13 through 21, you will see this *very graphically* spelled out. There, under the heading "The Accused Bride," it speaks to what happens if "a man marries a woman, but after going into her he dis-likes her and makes up charges against her, slandering her by saying, 'I married this woman; but when I lay with her, I did not find evi-dence of her virginity.'" Well, then, what is supposed to happen, if the husband accuses his wife in this way? As the Bible, in Deuteronomy, sets forth, the parents of the bride are to provide proof of the virgin-ity of the bride to the (male) elders of the community. What is the proof? They have to bring a bloody sheet from the wedding night before the town, and hold up the sheet and say: here is the evidence that she was a virgin. And, according to Deuteronomy, if such evi-dence can be provided, then the husband who has falsely accused his bride has to pay a fine—to the bride's *father*. On the other hand, "If, however, this charge is true, that evidence of the young woman's virginity was not found, then they shall bring the young woman out to the entrance of her father's house and the men of her town shall stone her to death, because she committed a disgraceful act in Israel by prostituting herself in her father's house. So you shall purge the evil from your midst." (Deuteronomy 22: 20–21)

It would be hard to ask for a more clear-cut statement of the fact that what is involved in all this is *relations of property ownership*—in which *the young woman is property*: first she is the property of her father (which is why false accusations against her for not being a vir-gin will result in a fine paid to her *father* and why, if the accusations are true, her *father*, along with the *other men* of the town, must take part in killing her); and then, upon her marriage, and assuming she passes "the virginity test," she becomes the property of her husband and the breeder of further property for him (children—again, especially *male* children).

Think of all the oppression and brutality bound up in this, and all the ways in which this has led not only to physical abuse of women, in many forms, but also unbearable mental anguish and torment for women—right down to today.

This is the tradition in which Jesus was deeply steeped—a tradition with which he never ruptured, but in fact propagated and fostered.

As another illustration of this, consider what Jesus says about divorce. According to Jesus (for example, in Luke 16:18, and Matthew chapter 5:31–32), getting a divorce and remarrying is committing adultery—is a sin. Imagine, and unfortunately we do not have to imagine, what the effect has been of this "teaching" down through the ages, through thousands of years of male-supremacist social relations. Think of the effect of this especially on women who are trapped in marriages that are oppressive and abusive—the idea that if they leave an oppressive and abusive husband, that is a sin, a sin equal to adultery. Think of all the truly horrific suffering this has caused and reinforced down through centuries and centuries and centuries—people, and women in particular, having this preached at them by the religious authorities, citing the Bible and the words of Jesus himself. And today, in 21st century America, we find Christian Fascists, inspired by—and wielding—these "teachings," working to make it more much difficult to get a divorce, with the ultimate aim of outlawing and criminalizing divorce altogether (witness key steps in that direction, with the "covenant marriage" provisions that have been adopted in more than one state in the U.S.).

Still some people say: "Yes, but there's something about Jesus." [Laughter] They insist: "Despite all these things in the Bible—and, alright, they're in the New Testament and not just the Old Testament—there is something about Jesus, his message of love and the essential mission of Jesus, that we still have to hold onto." Well, once again, let's look at what Jesus does and says, in its actual content and its actual implications and effect. Let's go back to what Jesus does in the so-called miracles of healing in the Bible, to the ways in which Jesus attributes people's suffering to possession by the devil or demons, or to the sin of those who are sick and afflicted. For example, in Matthew 17:14–20, as I referred to earlier, there is the story of Jesus supposedly curing an epileptic boy by casting out a demon. Or there is the story in Luke 5:17–26 where sickness is associated with sin and Jesus heals someone and forgives his sin. In Luke 8, verses 26–39, we find that Jesus cures a mentally ill man by casting a demon out of him. But in this case, Jesus is a little bit nasty and he hurls the demon into a bunch of pigs, and the pigs go off a cliff—and I'd imagine the owner of the pigs wasn't very pleased with that. [Laughter]

Here a question has to be asked: If Jesus went around supposedly curing people in this way, why did Jesus not know better? If this is supposed to be the son of God (a part of the same essence of God, according to the dominant Christian doctrine of the Trinity) how come Jesus didn't know that epilepsy is caused by real material things—problems with electrical and chemical processes in the brain? How come he thought it was a demon or the devil? Or, if someone wants to argue that Jesus *did* know better but he chose to speak to people in the terms of those times, then I have another question: Why not tell people the truth, and help them understand reality as it actually is, including the real causes of sickness and affliction? Why did Jesus, who supposedly loves humanity, instead of telling people the truth, reinforce ignorance and superstition—and, along with that, guilt and fear?

And if you think the superstition and ignorance that is promoted by this religious tradition associated with Jesus is harmless, think again—think of the images of peasants in Mexico crawling on their bellies to the shrine of the Virgin, tearing off their flesh, asking forgiveness for their sins because they are sick and crippled. All this does a tremendous amount of harm.

Or let's talk more generally about what was really Jesus's vision and program for humanity. Jesus himself said that you could boil the commandments of the Old Testament down to two main commandments (see Matthew 22:34–40). The first of these commandments, he said, is: "You shall love the Lord your God with all your heart, and with all your soul, and with all your mind." And the second is: "You shall love your neighbor as yourself." Now, it could be said that this second "commandment" represents something that is better than telling people they should have hatred for and should slaughter and plunder their neighbors. But the fact is that these "commandments" cannot be—and, more than that, *should not* be—applied in human society. Why not?

Well, let's take the first of these commandments: "You shall love the Lord your God with all your heart, and with all your soul, and with all your mind." Right away, there is a problem here. The problem is that God doesn't exist—and for this fundamental reason, it is not possible to carry out this commandment. But, for the sake of argument, and for the sake of pursuing this further, let us for the moment set aside the fact that there is no god. If there were a god, the only god that Jesus could be talking about is the god of the Old Testament, the Jewish scriptures. That is the god, and the only god, Jesus was familiar with, and those are the scriptures he makes reference to repeatedly. Well, a person who is seeking to do good in the world could not, and *should not*, love a god like that—for all the reasons I've been speaking to so far (and which I will get into even more fully as we go along).

As for the second commandment, it is not really possible to love all your neighbors, after all. In a world marked by profound divisions of class and by great social inequalities, in reality it is not possible to love, and to act out of love, for everyone, regardless of the class position they occupy and the role they play in society and in relation to other classes and groups of human beings. If you love the slavemaster, how can you really love the slave? If you love the exploiters and oppressors, you cannot really love those they exploit and oppress. If you act out of love for the one, you cannot really, objectively act out of love for the other, *because their needs and interests are fundamentally and antagonistically opposed to each other.* The slaves want to be free of slavery, and the slavemaster wants to keep them chained. How can you love them both? There can be no reconciliation between them, on the basis of love or any other basis, because in the real world, they will be compelled to act in ways that are opposed to—and, in a definite sense, harmful to—the needs and interests of the other.

The slaves will repeatedly seek ways to rebel against the slavemaster. When they rebel, they aren't polite and nice and loving. They want to throw off their oppression. When Nat Turner led a rebellion of slaves in the southern U.S. in the 19th century, those slaves killed all kinds of white people—including children, which maybe they shouldn't have done, but often things like that happen when people who have been long and bitterly oppressed are rising up and trying to find a way out of their oppression. Of course, they need leadership to do this in the best way, but when they rise up, you can't say: "Oh, now, wait a minute, you should love your master." And if *you* love the master, then you are going to preach to the slave to be docile and obedient to the master, because that is what the master needs the slave to do.

So, as a matter of fact, seeking reconciliation will only aid the oppressors and exploiters, because they hold a position of domination, and they are very happy to have reconciliation preached to those under their domination. And in general, they are happy to have the situation as it is, the *status quo* preserved, which is where such attempts at reconciliation will lead, when they do not lead to even worse brutality being brought down on the oppressed.

As I referred to earlier, with all the talk of love and peace that is attributed to Jesus, after all, he says, in the end, if you don't believe in me, you are going to be condemned to the torments of hell forever. So this is not a vision and a program that is good for humanity or that should be carried out by people trying to strive for the betterment of the oppressed and of humanity in general.

Another question that gets at something very basic is this: Why was Jesus wrong in his predictions about certain decisive events? According to the Bible, Jesus, as well as Paul, was very clear in insisting that the Second Coming would arrive very soon. For example, if you look at Matthew, chapter 16, verses 27 and 28, you will see that Jesus says:

> For the Son of Man is to come with his angels in the glory of his Father, and then he will repay everyone for what has been done. Truly I tell you, there are some standing here who will not taste death before they see the Son of Man coming in his kingdom.

This could hardly be more clear-cut. And 2000 years later, it could hardly be more obviously wrong!

What this shows, once again, is that Jesus was not a supernatural being, part of the same substance of God, the Father, and at the same time the son of God.[4] Jesus's ideas and visions, and what they will lead to, need to be evaluated just like those of any other human being, which is what Jesus was and all that he was. And I have already spoken at some length to why those ideas and that vision cannot and will not lead to another world, a radically new and better world, a world without oppression and exploitation, right here on earth, in this material reality—which is the only reality there is.

---

4. Here I won't attempt to further explore the arcane Christian doctrine of the Trinity (God the Father, the Son, and the Holy Spirit), which nobody can really explain—although it is important to note that arguments and struggles relating to this doctrine led, especially in the early centuries of Christianity, to a great deal of struggle and extremely violent conflict among opposing Christian sects, literally torturing and slaughtering each other. Accounts of this can be found, among other places, in Edward Gibbon's major work, *The Decline and Fall of the Roman Empire.*

What About the Ten Commandments?

Besides the fact that the New Testament itself—and the teachings of its two main figures, Jesus and Paul—can be shown to embody and insist upon all kinds of exploitative and oppressive relations, and the corresponding ideas, often in extreme form, the reality is that those who profess Christianity do not want to base themselves on the New Testament alone—nor could they. This applies above all to the fundamentalist Christian Fascists. And in this light we can see, sharply illuminated, the hypocrisy of those who, when confronted with the very real horrors that are upheld, and insisted upon, in the so-called "Mosaic" books and elsewhere in the Old Testament of the Bible,[5] seek to evade this by insisting: "That is the *Old* Testament; now, through Jesus, there is a *New* Testament." Well, if that is the case—if the Old Testament has been replaced and superseded by the New Testament—then what about the Ten Commandments? Why are you bothering everybody about the Ten Commandments—demanding that they be propagated everywhere as a "moral guide and standard"?

Where are the Ten Commandments in the Bible? You won't find them in the New Testament. The Ten Commandments are in the heart of the Old Testament. They're in the Torah of the ancient Jewish scriptures, in the "Mosaic books" of the Old Testament of the Christian Bible. They are a crucial part of the old covenant, the Old Testament.

What about Judge Moore in Alabama—a big hero of the Christian Fascists, who has talked about running for governor of Alabama (it seems that he is seeking to become the George Wallace of this era)? Why did he insist on putting the Ten Commandments in the

---

5. The term "Mosaic books" refers to the first five books of the Bible, which it has been claimed, were written by Moses. Biblical scholarship has clearly indicated that these books were, in reality, not written by the character referred to in the Bible as Moses—and this is further suggested by the fact that, in the fifth of these books (Deuteronomy), the author tells us that Moses has died! (See Deuteronomy 34:5)

courthouse in Alabama? Didn't somebody tell him: "Oh, that's the *Old* Testament. Forget about it. We have a *New* Testament now. Get rid of those Ten Commandments." Why do Pat Robertson and other prominent Christian Fascists keep repeating: "Remember now, it's the Ten *Commandments*, not the Ten *Recommendations*?" Why do they never tire of saying—and citing Biblical authority for their position—that the Ten Commandments have to be upheld and carried out? Why do they talk about the Psalms supposedly written by King David and the wisdom of King Solomon? That's all in the Old Testament.

Well, Robertson and others like him are right about one thing: The Bible, specifically in the Old Testament, does insist that the Ten Commandments, and the other parts of the "Mosaic Law," must indeed be carried out *to the letter, and without exception or qualification*. We are told this, for example, in chapter 5 of Deuteronomy—and, in fact, repeatedly throughout Deuteronomy. Not only is it very clear here (and in other parts of the Old Testament particularly) that all this has to be carried out to the letter, but the Bible goes on, after enumerating the Ten Commandments, to specify very definite penalties—cruel and vicious penalties—for not carrying out the Ten Commandments. These are most definitely not ten "recommendations" or "requests." And what are these penalties? Well, violators of these Commandments must be put to death not only for things like committing murder, but also for worshiping other gods (besides "the one true God") or blaspheming the name of the Lord. They must be put to death for working on the Sabbath. Children must be put to death for not honoring their father and their mother: In other words, if you are a rebellious child and you strike your parents, or even if you are disrespectful to them, according to the Bible you should be *executed*.

And the Bible insists that people be put to death for many other things, which most people in the world today do not even view as crimes, let alone crimes that should carry the death penalty. All this is spelled out particularly in Exodus, Leviticus, and Deuteronomy.

What is wrong with the Ten Commandments? How could it do any harm to instill these values in people, and in particular the youth today? Well, one thing is that these Commandments *uphold slavery*. Let's look at the tenth commandment. The tenth commandment says what? "Thou shall not covet..." And here we discover something very revealing. When Judge Moore in Alabama—and William Bennett,[6] who wrote *The Book of Virtues*, promoting Biblically-based traditional values—when they propagated the Ten Commandments, all they included of the tenth commandment were the initial words: "Thou shall not covet." What were they leaving out? Well, if you go to the Bible itself, it tells you *what* you're not supposed to covet— what you're not supposed to envy and wrongfully desire among your neighbor's possessions. You are not supposed to covet your neighbor's house, your neighbor's ox or his donkey; *and* you are not supposed to covet his *slaves*, or his wife—and here again we can see that in the social relations embodied here, and elsewhere, in the Bible, when "thy neighbor" is spoken of, it is the *man* of the household who is being referred to, and his *wife* is listed among his *possessions*, as well as his house, his oxen and asses, and his slaves. So, along with enshrining patriarchal relations of oppression, the Bible is saying slavery is fine, just don't try to take away from your neighbor the slaves who are rightfully his. (The Ten Commandments can be found in Exodus chapter 20, verses 1–17.)

What's wrong with the Ten Commandments? Plenty. What harm would it do to have the Ten Commandments put up everywhere, including in all kinds of public places—wouldn't that be good moral instruction for our children? No, it would *not*—not when you recognize what it is these commandments are actually talking about and when you see what penalties are demanded for going against these commandments.

---

6. For a critique of Bennett's *The Book of Virtues*, from a communist standpoint, see my book *Preaching From a Pulpit of Bones, We Need Morality But Not Traditional Morality*, Banner Press, 1999, in particular the first essay in that book: "Preaching From a Pulpit of Bones: The Reality Beneath William Bennett's 'Virtues.'"

No New Testament Without the Old

As a matter of fact, and as the Christian Fascist leaders know very well, the Old Testament is the foundation for the New Testament. For example, and very importantly, the Old Testament is the basis for the claim that Jesus is the Messiah. This is why the book of Matthew begins the way it does, with the genealogy of Jesus (all the "begats" in the classical English version of this scripture). It appears, by the way, that God got confused in dictating this genealogy—or He had too much wine on the Sabbath or something—because different lineages are presented in Matthew and in Luke (see Luke 3:23-38, in contrast with Matthew 1:1–17). But the essential point here is that this gene-alogy is all about establishing the fact that Jesus is from the line of the Biblical figure David. Why is that important? Why is that in the *New* Testament? Because, according to the ancient Jewish scriptures (which constitute in large part, or are essentially equivalent to, the Old Testament of the Christian Bible), the Messiah had to come from the line of David. Without that authority from the Old Testament, the whole claim that Jesus was the Messiah would have no foundation.

Christianity arose as a sect within Judaism, and then became a separate religion after the time of Jesus. It was totally rooted in the Old Testament. Jesus frequently refers to scriptures from the Old Testament—and, as we'll see, sometimes does so incorrectly, which is yet another problem with the "inerrant word of God" (apparently, among other things, there is some miscommunication between the Father and the Son parts of the Trinity).

One of the things I've pointed out before that is very interest-ing, and revealing, about this lineage (in the classical English version of Matthew: "so and so begat so and so, begat so and so, begat so and so...") is that when it gets to establishing Jesus's bona fides and legitimacy as the Messiah, the lineage is traced to whom? To *Joseph*, his father. But what does Joseph have to do with it? Joseph's "seed" is not involved. Remember, Jesus came from a *virgin* birth. Mary was impregnated by the Holy Spirit. Joseph and his lineage have noth-ing to do with Jesus's supposed special character. So why is Joseph mentioned in the context of providing Jesus's genealogy? This is a reflection of the patriarchal, male-dominated nature of the society in which Jesus lived—and of the religion that reflected that society. *That* is why, despite Jesus's supposed virgin birth, his lineage is traced through a series of patriarchs. And, again, all of this—and the claim of Jesus's legitimacy as the Messiah—goes back to the Old Testament.

Further, the Old Testament scriptures were repeatedly cited by Jesus as the foundation for what he believed and preached. The New Testament could not have anything to stand on without the Old Testament, which is why the Old Testament is still included in the Christian Bible, after all.

Fundamentalist and "Salad Bar" Christianity

Really, the attempt to avoid acknowledging and (to use a phrase that is so current these days) "taking responsibility" for the horrors and atrocities that are advocated in the Old Testament—this dodge about how "that was the Old Testament, now we have a New Testament"—is, after all, just another version of the "salad bar Christianity" that is so often and so vehemently condemned by the fundamentalist Christian Fascists, as part of their insistence that the Bible is absolutely accurate and true, is the inerrant word of God, and must be believed in and followed, to the letter and in every detail. This is something these Christian Fascists consistently insist on—except when they get caught with a passage from the Bible that they find difficult to explain away and see as an impediment (at the time) to their objectives. And then they themselves go for "salad bar Christianity."

What these fundamentalist reactionaries are referring to when they speak of and denounce (in others) "salad bar Christianity," is the phenomenon of liberal theologians and others who generally identify with the Christian religious tradition but who advocate a kind of multi-culturalism, who argue that there are many ways to get to the divine, so let's not insist that our way is the only way and that accepting Jesus as your savior is the only path to a righteous life. Well, is there truth to the claim that these people are practicing what could be called "salad bar" (or "buffet") Christianity? Yes. There is a phenomenon where they "pick and choose" from the Bible and Christian religious tradition—embracing what they want to believe and are comfortable believing, while passing over or putting aside that which makes them uncomfortable or strikes them as wrong, or outdated, and so on. It is very much like being at a buffet or salad bar and going down the line: "I want this, but I don't want *that*; ok, I'll take some of this, but I really don't like that—I don't like all that stuff in the Bible about killing children who are rebellious against their parents—I'm gonna put that to the side, I'm gonna take this part over here, about love and peace." This is a common phenomenon among liberal and progressive Christians these days. But then the very basic question arises: Once you have in effect denied that the Bible and Christian religious tradition is true and valid for all times and in all circumstances, once you have objectively made it a matter of what *human beings* say is right and valid in all this, then where is the "divine authority" for any of this, and how is it any different from any other set of beliefs and principles that human beings have come up with, including ones that do not claim any divine authority? Why should *your* beliefs be privileged over others by being invested with some special magical power or "aura?"

This is an important question to which I will return later. But the fact is that, in the world today and in American society specifically, *everybody* who claims to be a Christian practices "salad bar" (or "buffet") Christianity, in one form or another. Even the Christian fundamentalists practice it—while denying that they do and attacking others for doing it. They insist that they believe every word in the Bible, that it must all be taken literally, that it's the absolute truth, handed down from God in every syllable; but they themselves put to the side and don't talk about things which, if they openly upheld them, would more obviously reveal them to be the monstrous lunatics they are.

For example, if you really upheld everything in the Bible, you'd have to believe it was your duty and responsibility to sacrifice animals. Most people, even most Christian fundamentalists (at least in the U.S.,) don't do that, so far as I know. And, as we have seen, you'd have to insist not just on beating children to punish them—which is called for in the Bible: "spare the rod and spoil the child"—but on *killing* children who are rebellious. You'd have to believe and advocate that homosexuals should not just be condemned as sinners, but should be put to death. That women when they have their period are unclean, and men should avoid all contact with them. That women who are accused of being witches should be put to death. You'd have to believe in and extol raping women and carrying off women as prizes of war and sex slaves when fighting a holy war against people who believe in a god other than "the one true God." You'd have to believe that people who practice other religions should be slaughtered.

It is a legitimate and very important question, which must be put to these Christian Fascist fundamentalists: Which is it? One way or the other—either you believe that the Bible, all of it, is the "inerrant word of god," and every word is absolutely true and must be believed in and followed, or you don't. If you are not going to uphold all if it—including the kinds of outrages to which I have referred here—then admit that you don't believe in every word and every part of it, and that this cannot be the absolute word of god. And if you do believe that all of this must be upheld and acted upon, then come out and say so. These people have to be forced into the open more fully, so that it becomes more clear what they are really all about. They must not be allowed to waffle and sidestep what, in the Bible and Christian religious tradition, is inconvenient for them at the time. At the same time, it is very important to understand that things which they don't want to uphold and advocate openly today, they may very well insist upon, and seek to enforce, tomorrow. And, even today, while the more highly-placed leaders among the Christian Fascists—those who hold powerful positions in government (and there are today quite a few of them) or those who in any case have powerful connections with the highest levels of government, those who are frequent guests and commentators in the mainstream "news" programs, where they are treated as not only legitimate but respected voices—while *they* may seek to avoid, or explain away, at least some of the most egregious examples of the barbarism that is advocated in the Bible, there are *others* who right now are openly and unapologetically promoting this and proselytizing on the basis of this.

It is very important to understand that all of this is deadly serious. These people—not just the more obvious lunatics out on the streets, and the ones who have no obvious ties to the highest circles of power, but also the more "respectable" types who at times seem to talk in reasoned tones and who often package their fascist program in seemingly innocuous adjectives like "family" (the "Family Channel" [formerly the Christian Broadcasting Network], the "Family Values Coalition," and so on)—actually want a literal reading of the Bible, as *they* interpret it, to be the basis on which the whole country is run—and anybody who doesn't follow that will be persecuted, and even put to death in many cases. They actually believe, right up to George W. Bush, that not only do they have a personal relationship with god, but that they are being given a mandate and instructions from god, including in ordering the invasion and occupation of Iraq and in carrying out "the war on terror" overall.

Now, a lot of people, who aren't George W. Bush and don't have that kind of power and don't commit those kind of crimes, think they have a personal relationship with god. A lot of preachers think they have a direct pipeline to god. Richard Pryor had this whole routine about the movie, *The Exorcist.* This is a movie about a young girl who supposedly was possessed by the devil—her head spun around and her bed jumped up and down, she puked bile out everywhere, and so on. Priests were called in, to exorcise the devil, and it was a long drawn out struggle. Well, Richard Pryor said, this movie would have been a lot shorter and simpler if it had been a Black preacher taking care of things. Because the Black preachers have a direct pipeline to god. And, as Pryor enacted it, a Black preacher would say:

> You know, God, there's a per-son here that's possessed. And I was wonderin'—I know you're busy, I *checked* your schedule—but the devil's just actin' a mother-fuckin' fool. And I was wonderin' if you could exorcise this motherfucker to Cleveland, someplace. [Laughter]

Well, I have to say that I laugh almost uncontrollably every time I hear that—it's one of my favorite Richard Pryor routines, But there is also a very serious side to this. Not too long ago, there was a story in the news about Christian fundamentalists in Detroit who killed this young boy who has autism, a mental disorder, because they believed that he was possessed by a demon: they sat on him and suffocated him, trying to get the demon out of him.

So, when people take this literally, and act on it, this is deadly serious. And it is an extremely serious and potentially fatal error to not recognize that many, many people *do* take all this literally and with deadly consequences, and that a potential force of mindless, fanatical storm troopers, numbering in the millions, is being led, conditioned and trained to see the world in this way and to be prepared to act accordingly—despite the ways in which all this stands in profound and sharp contradiction to what can be accepted by most people in modern society.

The book *The Republican Noise Machine*, by David Brock—who used to be part of this whole right-wing propaganda machinery but broke with it and has now become a liberal—discusses (particularly in Chapter 7, "Ministers of Propaganda") some of the things that Christian fundamentalist ministers who are part of this whole right-wing movement advocate and the ways in which they argue that all these horrific things that I've been referring to *should* be upheld and applied as guiding principles and laws in society. Brock also quotes Pat Robertson, making statements that are at one and the same time chilling and sobering, in light of the fact that they are typical and representative of the Christian Fascist mindset and objectives, and that Robertson has for many years been a powerful figure within the Republican Party, and more generally he, and many others with the same views, are powerfully connected at the highest levels of the ruling circles in the U.S. Here are Robertson's comments, as cited by Brock:

> We have enough votes to run the country. And when people say, "We've had enough," we are going to take over....It's going to be a spiritual battle. There will be Satanic forces....We are not going to be coming up just against human beings, to beat them in elections. We're going to be coming up against spiritual warfare....
>
> There will never be world peace until God's house and God's people are given their rightful place of leadership at the top of the world. How can there be peace when drunkards, drug dealers, communists, atheists, New Age worshippers of Satan, secular humanists, oppressive dictators, greedy money changers, revolutionary assassins, adulterers, and homosexuals are on top? (Cited in Brock, *The Republican Noise Machine, Right-Wing Media and How it Corrupts Democracy*, p. 189. Brock's note relating to these statements by Robertson (note #11 on p. 391) cites an article by Chip Berlet, "The Right Rides High; Dogmatism and Religious Fundamentalism in U.S. Republican Party," *The Progressive*, October 1994, 22. For the original source, see Pat Robertson, *The New World Order*, Word Publishing, 1991, p. 227.)

Unfortunately, many people who should know better don't want to face up to what is going on with this, and its implications, and they dismiss it as just the rantings of lone lunatics. Well, these **lunatics** include, among others, George W. Bush, a significant number of powerful Senators and Congressmen, and members of the Supreme Court. So, yes, we are talking about lunatics, but lunatics who have their hands on the levers of power.

Religion and Oppressive Ruling Classes

Napoleon Bonaparte, who a couple of centuries ago became the ruler of France, spoke very clearly to why the ruling classes, which exploit and oppress masses of people, need religion—and specifically why they need to promote it among the masses of people. He said, very simply: Society is impossible without inequality. Inequality cannot be sustained without a morality to justify it. And morality in turn cannot be sustained without religion.

There is also a very instructive scene from the movie *Spartacus*, where a couple of members of the ruling Senate in Rome are talking about this question of the populous and how to keep it under control, and the role of religion in this. One of these Roman senators says to the other: Don't you actually believe in the gods? The second senator replies: "Privately I believe in none of them; publicly I believe in them all." That is another way of making the same point that Napoleon was emphasizing.

In this context, we can understand more fully the role of someone like Ronald Reagan. Reagan, who himself has been raised to the level of iconic status by the ruling class in the U.S., played a major role in promoting religion, and in particular Christian fundamentalism. Now, it is true that, before Reagan, Jimmy Carter introduced the question of religion into his campaign for President in 1976, making a point of identifying himself as a "born again Christian." But Carter never has advocated, and in his own way has opposed, the kind of religious fundamentalism that is characteristic of the Christian Fascists; nor did Carter generally seek to use his position as head of state to officially propagate religion. But, in significant ways, Ronald Reagan did all of this. As part of his overall role in aggressively pursuing American imperialist interests in the world and championing the program of a certain section of the American ruling class—which aimed at discrediting and dismantling many of the social programs and government regulations that stood in the way of unbridled capitalist exploitation, undisguised dominance by big capital, and unapologetic white supremacy and patriarchy—

Reagan, to a significant degree, revived the use of religious imagery in his political pronouncements, and in political discourse more generally, using this to sanctify the notion of a special place and a special and glorious role in the world for what is in reality white Christian America and American imperialism.

Today, Reagan has been repackaged as a kindly avuncular figure, even as a leader who advanced the cause of peace in the world. But the reality is that this is a man who took the world to the brink of nuclear war with the Soviet Union. As a small but significant indication of the mentality which characterized Reagan, and which he promoted, it is worth recalling that, on one occasion, when he was going to make a radio address, before he started officially broadcasting but while he was being recorded, he made a "joke": "We begin bombing in five minutes. Ha, ha, ha." Now, think about what kind of person and what kind of ruling class thinks that's funny—joking about the start of a nuclear war. And not only did Reagan take the world to the brink of such a war, he was clearly willing to push things over the brink, in the effort to make sure that the U.S., and not the Soviet Union, came out as the dominant imperialist power in the world.

Or look what this "kindly uncle" Reagan did in Central America: brutal military dictatorships were imposed on people there, with use of widespread and wanton terror by governments, and death-squads linked with governments—all of which was firmly backed by the U.S. In the book *Democracy. Can't We Do Better Than That?*,[7] I talked about how in Guatemala, for example, one after another of these military dictatorships would send the army out to commit mass murder, and other atrocities, in the countryside. One of the brutal butchers who, as head of the Guatemalan government, ordered these murderous acts, was a born-again Christian, Rios Montt. While Reagan gave backing to Rios Montt, the likes of Jerry Falwell and Pat Robertson openly prayed for God to give support

---

7. *Democracy: Can't We Do Better Than That?*, Bob Avakian, Banner Press, 1989.

and help to Montt. And what did the armed forces of Guatemala do under Rios Montt and these other dictators? Repeatedly, when they went into villages which they believed were harboring or supporting rebel guerrillas, the government armed forces would round up all the people, slaughter all the males that they considered to be of fighting age, rape all the women, and then take the little babies down by the river, or somewhere away from the village, and smash their heads in, so that they couldn't grow up to oppose the government. I am not exaggerating any of this. This went on time and time again. Perhaps Rios Montt, that born-again butcher, was inspired by the many places in the Bible where it calls for bashing in the heads of babies (as, for example, in the book of Isaiah, or in Psalm 137).

Now, more recently, we hear about the terrible killing that has been taking place in Africa—what went on in Rwanda a number of years ago, or today what is going on in the Darfur region of Sudan. All these imperialist politicians are wringing their hands, exclaiming: "Why haven't we done anything to stop slaughter like this?" But this is the sheerest hypocrisy, especially in light of the whole history of imperialist colonial conquest and, yes, mass slaughter in Africa (as well as in other parts of the world), and in light of the fact that it is the system of imperialism itself which has created, and continually recreates and reinforces, the fundamental conditions that give rise to the conflicts in Africa, and elsewhere; and it is often the case that imperialist financial agencies, along with imperialist political institutions and political operatives, are *directly* involved in and promoting such conflicts, with their terrible toll in human suffering.

Here, too, Ronald Reagan is a model, in a perverse sense. During the 1980s, in Africa, just as in Guatemala and elsewhere in Latin America, the U.S. supported, financed and helped to organize the most bloodthirsty death-squads (and governments that spawned these death-squads), which carried out unspeakable atrocities. For example, in Mozambique, when a government came to power which the U.S. identified as standing in the way of its interests and tending in the direction of alignment with the Soviet Union and its camp, the Reagan government supported and aided an opposition group called RENAMO, which, over a period of years, systematically carried out the most grotesque brutality and mass murder. RENAMO forces would kill and maim people, then they would go into the hospitals where people were being treated and they would kill and maim still more. All this was organized and funded by the CIA and the U.S. government under the "kindly" Ronald Reagan.

And there is another incident which, on the scale of what was going on in the world may have seemed like a small thing but nonetheless spoke very loudly to what Ronald Reagan, and the "morality" he promoted, was all about. Again, keep in mind that this is a man who, as President, actively promoted religion and fundamentalist Christian morality (even though it seems that, like that Roman Senator in the *Spartacus* movie, privately Ronald Reagan was an agnostic—and we know Nancy Reagan believed in and practiced things like astrology—publicly, as President, Ronald Reagan promoted religion on a big scale). And, especially in light of the relentless attempt of the Christian fundamentalists to impose their morality on the world, and even to identify morality in general with their specific notion of it, it is important to talk about *what was* the morality of this man, Ronald Reagan, and what he actually did in the world. This seemingly small incident, which however tells a big story, happened during the 1970s when Reagan was governor of California. A small underground group calling itself the Symbionese Liberation Army kidnapped Patty Hearst, who was heir to the big Hearst family fortune. (The Symbionese Liberation Army, or SLA, was not a genuine revolutionary force, and their overall outlook and strategic orientation, and the tactics that went along with that, did not and could not make a positive contribution to a real, liberating, revolutionary struggle. But, of course, that did not prevent them from being ruthlessly and murderously hunted down and suppressed by the powers-that-be.) One of the demands raised by the SLA, while they were holding Patty Hearst, was that free food be given out to poor people in California. The Hearst family agreed to pay for and distribute this food—they set up distribution points in different areas around the state. In the midst of this, and specifically in reference to this distribution of free food to poor people, Ronald Reagan declared that he hoped there would be an outbreak of botulism (deadly food poisoning)!

Now, by what conceivable standard could you wish deadly food poisoning on thousands of poor people receiving food that they can't afford to pay for? Whatever you want to think about the Symbionese Liberation Army, on what possible basis could a decent person wish an outbreak of botulism on poor people? And if someone wants to say that this comment by Reagan was a joke, what kind of person could think that's funny?

Stepping back from Ronald Reagan in particular, to the larger process and the larger dynamics into which he fits, and looking at the present situation in the world, let's recall Napoleon's statement about the role of religion and how it helps to justify and enforce oppressive relations. Given the stakes involved with what is going on in the world today, and what's been unleashed by the "juggernaut" (the rolling monster of war and repression) driven forward by the Bush regime—which has brought us the invasion and occupation of Iraq and everything that has set loose, along with continuing war in Afghanistan; the looming threat of war with Iran; Guantanamo, Abu Ghraib, and openly justified torture on a large scale; the Patriot Act and the Military Commissions Act and the gutting of basic rights, such as habeas corpus and the right to trial; Supreme Court decisions and other means through which there have been continuing attacks on abortion and the aggressive assertion of patriarchy and male supremacy, as well as the reversal of gains made in the struggle against white supremacy and racism; officially-promoted attacks on science and rational thought and on the separation of church and state—given all that, and more, think about what it means that religion in general, and fundamentalist Christian Fascism in particular, is playing such a powerful role within major institutions of U.S. society—including not only all the branches of the "civilian" government but also the armed forces—and in influencing the course of events as well as in setting the standard for what is right and moral.

Evolution, the Scientific Method— and Religious Obscurantism

One of the main ways in which religion serves its "Napoleonic" role for ruling classes which exploit and oppress masses of people is in maintaining a unifying mythology which serves these ruling classes while at the same time obscuring—and obstructing people from learning about—the actual causes and reasons for things in nature and society, and the basis and possibility for radical change. Today, in the U.S. in particular, one of the sharpest expressions of this is in relation to the scientific fact of evolution. Many people in this country—and, among other things, this is a profound indictment of its educational system—do not know, or accept, that evolution *is* a scientific fact. And especially among the poor and oppressed, most don't even know what evolution is. Instead of being taught this, increasingly they are indoctrinated with the fables and fairy tales of creation as told in the Bible, and a false view of natural history as well as the history of human society.[8]

---

8. Recently, *The Science of Evolution and the Myth of Creationism—Knowing What's Real And Why It Matters*, by Ardea Skybreak, which originally appeared as a series of articles in our Party's newspaper, has been published as a book. This book is rare in that it provides a thorough explanation of what evolution is and how it works, as well as providing a living refutation of Creationism, in its various forms (including the most recent mutation, "Intelligent Design"), *and* it does this in a manner that is consciously aimed at being accessible to people who are ordinarily denied access to and understanding of scientific questions and the scientific method, as well as speaking to those who are more familiar with this. At the same time, while popularizing the scientific method, as it relates to natural phenomena, this book also shows how this scientific method—and in particular the most comprehensive and systematic scientific outlook and method, communism—can and must be applied to social as well as natural phenomena and processes and the interconnection between the natural realm and the realm of human beings and their societies. For all these reasons, this is an extremely important book.

The truth is that in scientific circles—among the overwhelming majority of people who are professionals in science, people whose life's work is in science—evolution has for some time been a settled question and is not at all a disputed or controversial issue; and this is especially true for scientists in the field of biology. Moreover, in today's world evolution is foundational for science as a whole—without it there could be no science. But most people don't even know this—they are kept in ignorance of this and preyed on in this way: their ignorance is used to get them to act against their own interests, to keep them from really understanding the world and thereby being able to change it—from understanding why they're in the conditions that they're in and what can be done about this.

To the degree that there is a controversy in society about evolution, and ignorance broadly about evolution, this is controversy and ignorance that has been deliberately created, fostered, and promoted by religious fundamentalists, with backing from powerful forces within the ruling class. While, in the field of biology and science in general, evolution is a well-established fact, one of the most solidly established facts in all of science, George W. Bush has insisted that "the jury is still out on how God created life" and he has undermined the teaching of evolution by promoting the notion that "Intelligent Design" should also be taught in science classes, even though "Intelligent Design" has no scientific basis whatsoever. Now, in fact, the jury may still be out on whether George Bush is capable of rational thought [Laughter]; but that is not what is at the heart of his deliberate promotion of ignorance and superstitious nonsense. Beyond the fact that a number of Christian Fascists may actually believe in a kind of irrational anti-Enlightenment, Biblical absolutism, and that Bush himself may be among that number, more fundamentally at play is the fact that powerful sections of the ruling class are convinced that such a worldview provides a powerful cohering ideological force, which they believe is necessary in these times especially, given everything that is at stake and everything that has already been set loose by—and the potential for far greater chaos and upheaval to result from—the drive to establish an unchallenged, and unchallengeable, U.S. empire, and radical changes within the U.S. itself accompanying that drive for world domination.

This is why there is a relentless and many-sided campaign to promote not only religion in general but more specifically Christian Fascist fundamentalism. This is why this kind of Christian fundamentalism has not only been allowed but encouraged within the military of the U.S., and particularly among the ranks of the officers. It is why, for example, someone like General Jerry Boykin can not only proclaim, but can be promoted after proclaiming, that the war in Iraq is justified and righteous because his God is a real God and the god of Islam is a fake god, and that in 2000 George Bush didn't win the popular vote but he's in the White House because: "He was appointed by God." Among other things, Boykin has also declared: "The battle that we're in is a spiritual battle. Satan wants to destroy this nation, he wants to destroy us as a nation, and he wants to destroy us as a Christian Army." (Cited in *Revolution* newspaper, issue no. 98, August 13, 2007. See also "The Pentagon Unleashes a Holy Warrior," by William M. Arkin in the *Los Angeles Times*, October 16, 2003.)

The reality is that an insistence on a literal and absolutist interpretation of the Bible—or the Qur'an, or the scriptures and traditions of any of the world's major religions—can only lead to upholding and enforcing oppression and torment of the most horrendous kind. Someone, after having read some of my writings on religion, sent me a bumper sticker, which I really like   it says, "When religion ruled the world, they called it the Dark Ages." And this is what these people represent. They embody and seek to enforce an outlook and values characteristic of the "Dark Ages," but they do so in the service of an oh-so-modern form of exploitation, domination and plunder—capitalism-imperialism—and with the most up-to-date arsenal of modern military weapons.

If Gods Do Not Exist, Why Do People Believe in Them?

In looking for a way to get into this particular subject, I thought maybe I could just boil the whole thing about "god" down to a really great line from a not really great movie which came out a couple of years ago. The movie is called *The Big Bounce*. Overall it is a not remarkable movie—it is a rather typical "crime caper" movie, with these various con men and women all trying to outsmart each other and get over—but at one point, one of the characters, who is played by Owen Wilson, is talking to this other character, a corrupt judge, played by Morgan Freeman, and as they are discussing how to run a con, Owen Wilson's character says: "Yeah, but what about all these problems we're going to run into? How are we gonna deal with that?" And Morgan Freeman replies: "Well, we just have to have faith." Owen Wilson says, "You mean like in God?" And Morgan Freeman's character comes back with the great line: "God is just an imaginary friend for grown-ups." [Laughter]

Well, I thought maybe I could just begin and end with that, but of course it is more complicated than that—and more serious—so it is necessary to dig into this more fully and deeply.

So, let's step back and get a broader picture from history. Throughout the world, people in ancient societies and people without a scientific approach to studying, to engaging, and to changing reality—people who have not yet developed or who have been denied access to such a scientific approach, or people who have resisted and rejected such a scientific approach—these people have brought forth and rallied around various myths in the attempt to develop a meaningful story of how they came to be, of the reality they experienced, of the larger reality they perceived outside themselves, and of how they wished reality to be. They have treated these myths as the defining element of reality.

For example, the story of creation, as it's called in Genesis in the Bible, is nothing but the origin myth of the ancient Jewish people. It doesn't correspond to reality, it is not borne out by what science has taught us about how the earth and the "heavens"—the stars, the galaxies—have actually developed. The earth is not the center of all this, and the stars and everything else were not put there for the benefit of man on the earth. In fact, many of these stars have existed long before the earth came into being. Some of them existed and then went out of existence in the period before the earth actually came into being and before humans (billions of years after the formation of the earth) came into being. And there are many things that are historically inaccurate, besides things proven to be wrong by science, in this creation story in Genesis. This is not unique. Peoples throughout the world have myths that represent their attempts to explain things like where they came from and how they relate to the rest of reality.

In the book *The Science of Evolution and The Myth Of Creationism—Knowing What's Real And Why It Matters*, there is a graphic illustration of different creation myths from around the world, including the early Jewish origin myth that's in the Bible. Some people believed that they were formed in the earth and then rose up to the surface of the earth. Some people believed they were formed in the sky and then fell down to earth. Some people believed the whole existence that we know is just the back of a giant turtle. Now when we hear these things, we're tempted to laugh at *everybody else's* creation myths—because we're taught that *ours* is the one that's true—but if you step back from it, whatever myth we were taught to believe in is no less silly than all the others. [Laughter] And no less disproved by the reality of what's actually happened in the history of humanity and the history of the natural world.

So what we learn from this is that in actuality these stories were not and are not a true description of nature, of the development of human beings and of particular peoples and their relation to the rest of humanity and to the natural universe. They were not, and are not, timeless and enduring truths handed down or inspired by some supernatural beings (gods) or by one all-knowing, all-powerful supreme being—God, the Almighty—who surpasses all human existence and knowledge while ruling the entire universe in some mysterious way that none of us can understand. Religious stories and scriptures were and are precisely rooted in myths: fanciful products of the human imagination; attempts to explain things which people could not accurately, rationally and scientifically understand and explain at the time.

In this connection it is worth thinking about a very interesting fact: with regard to scientists—people who practice science as their profession—the majority of them who have ever lived are alive now. What this reflects is the fact that, for the great, great part of human history, there was very little scientific knowledge and very few people who were investigating reality from anything like a scientific standpoint. Doing that is a very recent thing, and the reasons why that is so are bound up with why all these myths grew up and became so much fastened to people's minds.

But that is not all. The explanations that religion attempts to provide for seemingly mysterious aspects of reality, and for the larger and defining principles of reality—these explanations are not just wrong in some neutral sense. They are not harmless. They do a great deal of harm and cause a great deal of anguish and suffering.

Let's look again at some examples from Christianity and the "Judeo-Christian tradition." As referred to earlier, today we know, as a result of scientific advancement, that epilepsy—which causes seizures that for most of human history were very mysterious and frightening to people, not just the one suffering the seizure but others as well—is actually owing to material factors and processes having to do with the functioning of the brain and the nervous system. But for most of the existence of humanity, people thought things like epilepsy were a sign of something terrible—for example, those suffering from epilepsy and related seizures were possessed by the devil or demons—and people suffered terribly as a result of this ignorance. Well, as we have seen, this ignorance is put forward right in the Bible, including in the way that the Bible tells us that Jesus cured epilepsy by casting out demons.

Or look at the story of the creation in Genesis. There we find the fanciful notion of Adam and Eve in the Garden of Eden, knowing no guilt or innocence, no sin, having no knowledge of good and evil because it was just all good; but somehow Eve got tempted by a serpent, ate the one fruit they were forbidden to eat—the apple—and then seduced Adam into eating it...and it all went downhill from there. So we have the fall of man, which is the reason why we have to have Jesus come and assume human form, die and be resurrected, in order to provide a means to save mankind from its fallen condition. We can see that, through this mythology, humanity is cast in the position of being a damned and a failed species that could only cause tremendous havoc and harm on its own.

And within this—not surprisingly, given the kind of patriarchal, male-dominated societies that have existed for thousands of years—we see a special curse upon women. For example, in Genesis chapter 3, especially verses 14 to 16, we are told how, because of Eve's supposedly treacherous role in the Garden of Eden and bringing about the downfall of mankind, childbirth is to become a *curse* on all women thereafter. Every woman who suffers pain in childbirth, according to Christianity and the "Judeo-Christian tradition," suffers it because of the sin of Eve—not because of very real, material factors that we know a lot about nowadays, but supposedly because of the treachery and seductive nature of Eve. Listen to this—I brought my Bible [Laughter]—listen to Genesis 3:16, this is the curse put upon women, and it is God whose words are being recounted:

> To the woman he said, "I will greatly increase your pangs in childbearing; in pain you shall bring forth children, yet your desire shall be for your husband, and he shall rule over you."

All because of Eve's supposed misconduct in the Garden of Eden.

These myths and stories are not harmless. They do a great deal of harm, and have done great harm down through centuries. This curse upon women, including in childbirth, is not just something of the Old Testament—it is also upheld in the New Testament by Paul. For example, if you look at 1 Timothy chapter 2, verses 8 to 15, you will find Paul repeating this curse upon women.

Or let's take the story of Noah's Ark. Well, I have sad news for those who have believed this story—it never happened. [Laughter] There is absolutely no historical evidence—from anthropology, from archeology, from any kind of historical investigation—to suggest that a flood like this covered the whole earth for 40 days and 40 nights. Sure, there were local floods in the area of Mesopotamia (in and around what is now Iraq), because there are major rivers there (the Tigris and the Euphrates) and they flood from time to time, just like the Mississippi or other rivers do in the U.S. But there never has been any evidence for a flood that covered the whole earth, as is described in the Bible—and never any account, outside of the Bible, of Noah's Ark being the basis on which humanity (and species needed by humanity) escaped extinction and were able to start anew after the world-wide flood which God sent because God was displeased with what mankind had done. If such a flood had occurred, it surely would have affected civilizations that existed at that time all over the world. It surely would have left its mark, both in terms of the actual physical structures of those societies, and in terms of disrupting the whole nature of those civilizations. Yet you can look through historical records and archeological records from one part of the world to another, and there is absolutely no evidence of this kind of a flood ever having occurred—leaving aside the total unreality of the story of Noah's Ark, with two of every species that has existed since that time crowded into the Ark along with Noah and his family!

Once again, this is not reality, it is mythology. And it's one thing when people make up mythology, especially when they don't have a basis to know any better—but upholding this *now*, and especially insisting that it is *literally true*, is to uphold and promote superstition and ignorance of how the world really is and how it has developed and changed throughout its *real* history. It is to promote all the suffering that goes along with and is reinforced by this superstition and ignorance. **It is not harmless**—it does a great deal of harm. It keeps people mentally enslaved, unable to face reality and to change reality on the basis of understanding how reality actually is and how it has come to be the way it is.

These myths, and other fanciful stories in the Bible, were an essential part of what came to be crystallized and set down in writing as the ancient Jewish scriptures, or the Old Testament of the Christian Bible. But these scriptures were not just the embodiment of different myths and attempts to explain reality in the abstract or without any social content or impact on society; they were, and are, the reflection of the human societies in which these myths arose. They are a reflection of the relations in those societies between different groups of people, as well as the relations between those societies and other societies, and a reflection of all the ideas that go along with and reinforce those relations. (I will keep coming back to and illustrating this point as we go along.) But, beyond that—and this is a crucial point—once relations of exploitation and oppression arose—relations embodying the domination of the means to live and to create wealth, and the domination of political power and intellectual life, by a small group or class of people—once this arose in human society, religion has been used by the ruling classes to enforce and extend these relations of exploitation and oppression.

As a leaflet put out by our Party on the movie *The Passion of the Christ* summarizes it:

> Not only is the Bible not literally true—not only is it a book full of what can charitably be described as a hodge-podge of remarkably violent legends, tall tales and tribal history, interspersed with a little lyric poetry, a lot of revenge-filled fantastical rants and some origin myths—but these were all told and then set down in writing to reinforce first, a patriarchal desert agriculture society several thousand years ago, then a slave empire in Rome, and then an oppressive feudal society

in Europe. It is filled with codes of behavior that are either hypocritical or openly oppressive. Now this same ancient stuff is being adapted to reinforce the capitalist oppression of today, in a 25-million-dollar, cleverly-promoted, Hollywood film.

Why Do People Believe in *Different* Gods?

To help shine a light on the question of why people in different times and places have believed in different gods, and why people today do not all worship the same god, let me recount a story told by someone in our Party who went with his deeply-religious mother to a museum where there was an exhibit about Mexico in ancient and modern times. The first part of the exhibit focused on the ancient peoples who lived in Mexico, the Olmecs and others, and then you came to the period of the Aztecs several hundred years ago—there were examples of artifacts from the Aztec civilization, including things that were used in their religious ceremonies. But then, at a certain point there was a huge cross in the middle of the exhibit. This cross signified the time when the Spanish conquistadores came and conquered Mexico, defeating and decimating the Aztecs and devastating their civilization. Along with that, the Spanish imposed the Christian religion on the people there, and brutally repressed and killed people who tried to continue the old religious ways. Well, the comrade was going through this exhibit with his mother (who grew up in Mexico but moved to the U.S. when she was young and was a very devout Catholic); and after they went through the Aztec exhibit and got to the big cross and then everything after that, as far as religion was concerned, was a representation of Christianity, he said to her: "See, Ma"—pointing to the Aztec side—"if *those* people had won, instead of these other people"—the Spanish—"you'd be worshipping *those* gods instead of the one you worship now."

This gets to something very deep: Why do people believe in the god or gods they do? Why do they practice religion the way they do? Does it really have to do with supernatural things that have been handed down to people, or does it have to do with very earthly things—like the invasion and conquest of Mexico by the Spanish who then forced the people there to take up this new religion of Christianity? And now, someone like this comrade's mother—generations and centuries later—doesn't know that *this is why* she worships the Christian god, because that's all in the past, hidden from her, and she's just come to accept this as true because the Bible, and a whole religious tradition built around the Bible, tells her it is so.

Let's look at this from a different angle. Why is it that the cross associated with Jesus, and the crucifixion of Jesus which that cross symbolizes, is a central icon and major point of reference (and reverence) in this society, but the cross on which Spartacus was crucified does *not* play that role? In fact, many people don't know whom I'm referring to when I talk about Spartacus. Spartacus was a slave who, less than a century before the time of Jesus, led a rebellion of slaves in the Roman Empire that threatened that Empire to its foundations before that rebellion was finally drowned in blood. And, as a result of being finally defeated, Spartacus and thousands of his followers were crucified on crosses, lining the main road from Rome out toward the provinces, for miles and miles and miles. Why is *that* cross and that crucifixion not a big symbol in our society, and why is it not in other societies in the world today? The answer is simple and basic: because what is represented by Spartacus, even in his defeat—that is, the slaves rising up—is not something the ruling classes in the societies we live in, and the ruling classes down through the ages, have wanted to promote. Yes, a movie got made about Spartacus, but that's nothing compared to the continual barrage of propaganda about Jesus, the life of Jesus, and the crucifixion and supposed resurrection of Jesus. Because, again, the people who rule over us don't want us to have symbols that call to mind slaves rising up in rebellion. They want us to believe that such rebellions are pointless and that we are bound to, and have to, live the way we live because that's the way God wants it to be, that's the way God made the world and all you can do is accept God's will.

Or let's look at another example. There is a sect of the Jewish religion centered in New York called the Lubavitchers. They're fundamentalist Jews. The head of their sect until 1994 was a man named Rabbi Menachem Schneerson. As you know, Jews do not accept that Jesus was the Messiah, but the followers of Rabbi Schneerson, or many of them, started believing that *he* was the Messiah that was prophesied in the old Jewish scriptures (the Old Testament of the Bible). And their promotion of this idea actually went to very humorous and ridiculous lengths—a kind of perverse illustration of the combination of very modern technology with very backward, Dark Ages ideas. They were all getting their cell phones and their pagers out as Schneerson was approaching his death, waiting to find out if "the Rabbi" was going to finally announce that he was, after all, the Messiah. So here you had this really ridiculous and strange scene where all these people were practicing this medieval religion, while carrying around this modern technology in order to get the word in "real time": is the Rabbi going to tell us he's the Messiah after all? Then he died without ever giving the word.

But what if, for a combination of reasons—having to do with geopolitical factors, including developments in the Middle East, and the interrelation of that with what was happening with the U.S., and among its ruling circles in particular—what if, out of all that, what is represented by the likes of Rabbi Schneerson came to predominate within Israel, and specifically among the elite in Israel, and that in turn came to be supported by well-placed groups within the power structure of the U.S.? Then, perhaps, instead of being just a relatively small sect, those who proclaimed Schneerson as the Messiah might come to hold a much more powerful position and exert a much more extensive influence, not only within Israel but on the world stage. It is true that, at this time, this seems highly improbable. But it is worth thinking about how probable it would have seemed, 2000 years ago, that a small sect within Judaism—whose leader, Jesus, had just been executed—would, within a few hundred years, become a major religious force in the world, known as Christianity—and indeed that this Christianity would be adopted, and enforced, as the official religion of the powerful Roman Empire. So, changes within the ruling structures and corresponding changes in the official (or semi-official) ideology of major empires can bring about major changes in the role and influence of various religious currents—and in fact this has already happened a number of times in the history of humanity.

Or let's look at the Rastafarians, in Jamaica and other places, who believe that Africa will become for Black people a heaven on earth, and that Haile Selassie (also known as Ras [Prince] Tafari), head of state of Ethiopia for a number of decades in the last century, was actually the returning and conquering Messiah. A few years ago, I saw a movie about Bob Marley, where a woman in Jamaica was talking about the time when Haile Selassie came to Jamaica, and she believed that she actually saw the stigmata—the wounds from the nails driven into Jesus's body—she actually saw them, she believed, in Haile Selassie's hands. Well, in reality they weren't there. But this delusion about the stigmata flowed from the belief that this person, Haile Selassie—who was actually a brutal oppressor of the people of Ethiopia and a pawn and instrument of imperialist rule in Africa—was somehow the savior and Messiah.

In "Redemption Song" by Bob Marley, who was a Rastafarian, there are these compelling lines [Singing·] "Emancipate yourself from mental slavery, none but ourselves can free our minds." Yet the irony is that Rastafarianism is just another form of mental slavery. But what if, somehow, the world turned and, a century or so from now, Africa emerged as the continent where the most developed imperialist powers were centered and, along with that, those African imperialists held up Haile Selassie as the real Messiah. Then people all over the world who were conquered by them would be worshiping Haile Selassie as the Messiah, and many of them would believe that the stigmata had been there in Haile Selassie's hands.

Or take the Mormons. The Mormons believe—if you read *The Book of Mormon*, you will see this—that hundreds of years before Jesus, an offshoot of the Jewish people left their homeland and somehow got across the seas over to America. In the Mormon doctrine there is a whole history of peoples in America battling each other—some of them were on the side of god, and then not on the side of god, and back and forth they went—and then at some point in this ancient "history," Jesus supposedly appeared to the Latter Day Saints of the Mormon religion in America and told them all the things that he would do when he rose. This is all in *The Book of Mormon*—which was supposedly revealed to the founder of this religion, Joseph Smith, about 200 years ago, when an angel allegedly appeared to Smith and guided him to a set of plates on which all this history was written (and the angel also revealed to Smith how to translate these plates from a previously unknown language). Well, obviously this is in very sharp conflict with traditional Christianity—and, in fact, is in greater conflict with reality, because there were no such tribes of people in the Americas: there were Native Americans, but not the peoples that are talked about in *The Book of Mormon*. There is absolutely no evidence that these people ever existed or did anything here. Now you have Mormon so-called archaeologists desperately digging around all over the place trying to find evidence for this Mormon mythology, but they can't find any that ever stands up. All this "history," and the theology that it was meant to support, was the product of the mind of Joseph Smith.

But one thing that's interesting about the Mormons—and this may well have something to do with why they are no longer persecuted in the U.S., as they were in the beginnings of their religion—is that there are a lot of Mormons in government institutions like the FBI. The Mormon religion is a very conservative, straight-laced, obedient-to-authority kind of religion, and this lends itself very well to being in the FBI or the CIA. Today, Mormonism is not only not a persecuted religion but it is not a marginalized religion. In fact, it is one of the fastest growing religions in the world. Part of the reason for this is that, from the beginning, its doctrine and practice have included a very aggressive proselytizing. All Mormons are required, upon becoming adults, to serve two years as missionaries. Well, let us suppose that at some point powerful enough sections of the ruling class decided that it would be good to have Mormons running the whole state apparatus in the U.S. Then it could well be the case that (just as in the state of Utah now, where the Mormon Church is centered and exercises a very great influence) throughout the U.S. the Mormon religion would be something that was widely promoted by the government. And then many more people would believe the fantastic tales that are in *The Book of Mormon,* instead of the fantastic religious myths that they now believe; and children growing up would think that was just as natural as they now think it is natural to believe in the story of Jesus in the Bible, and all the other myths that are in the Bible.

We could go on and on like this. And this illustrates a very profound and important point—that people believe these things and assume they are true because powerful institutions in society have indoctrinated them with these ideas, it has been ingrained into their mind; and when you grow up within a tradition that is so deeply ingrained in this way, and promoted throughout society, it is very easy to just assume that this is the way the world is, and often difficult to recognize that reality is actually a very different way. At the same time, if you are in another part of the world, where Islam is the dominant religion, then for the same kinds of reasons you very likely don't believe that Jesus is the Messiah, you believe he's a prophet and that Muhammad was the last prophet and Islam is the true religion. And if you live somewhere else—if you are among the billions of people in China and India, for example—then you believe things that are very different—but for essentially the same reason: because the institutions and traditions of society have, from a very early age, conditioned you to believe those things.

Of course, those who long for—and those who, beyond that, are actively working for—a radically different world, without relations of domination, exploitation and oppression, and without the corresponding ideas, have every reason to hope, and a basis in the real world to recognize the actual possibility, that, long before thousands, or even hundreds, of years have passed, humanity will be far along in the struggle to achieve such a new and radically different world—and, as a key part of that, will be in the process of finally casting aside the institutionalized and enforced ignorance and superstition that is represented by religion and belief in the supernatural in general.

As a kind of summation, then, of the basic points I have been coming at from various angles:

The notion of a god, or gods, was created by humanity, in its infancy, out of ignorance. This has been perpetuated by ruling classes, for thousands of years since then, to serve their interests in exploiting and dominating the majority of people and keeping them enslaved to ignorance and irrationality.

Bringing about a new, and far better, world and future for humanity means overthrowing such exploiting classes and breaking free of and leaving behind forever such enslaving ignorance and irrationality.

Part Two:

CHRISTIANITY, JUDAISM, AND ISLAM— ROOTED IN THE PAST, STANDING IN THE WAY OF THE FUTURE

The Historical Development and Role of Christianity: Doctrines and Power Politics

Bart D. Ehrman, Chairman of the Religious Studies Department at the University of North Carolina at Chapel Hill, notes in his book, *Misquoting Jesus, The Story Behind Who Changed the Bible and Why*: "Many Christians today may think that the canon of the New Testament simply appeared on the scene one day, soon after the death of Jesus, but nothing could be farther from the truth." (Ehrman, *Misquoting Jesus*, p. 36) Through the course of this book, Ehrman goes on to analyze how the canon that now is in the Bible, and in particular the New Testament, came about—how it came to be "The New Testament of our Lord and Savior Jesus Christ," as the Christian Bible puts it. More specifically, Ehrman goes into the fact that, first of all, if you're going to believe that these scriptures represent the "inerrant word of God", you have a problem: the original manuscripts of these scriptures don't exist. Even the first or second copies of the original manuscripts don't exist.

A slight detour here, but something that is an important and relevant story, is Ehrman's account of the development of his own thinking and approach to the Bible and Biblical studies. As a youth he went to the Moody Bible Institute in Chicago—at that time he was an evangelical fundamentalist himself. Then he went on to Wheaton College, near Chicago, which is a fundamentalist Christian college (as Ehrman indicates, Wheaton "is only for evangelical Christians and is the alma mater of Billy Graham, for example"). Ehrman's experience in going to Wheaton is very revealing. When he left for Wheaton from Moody, he was, as he puts it, "warned that I might have trouble finding real Christians at Wheaton—which shows how fundamentalist Moody was." So, although Ehrman himself, at the time he first went to Wheaton, was a strict fundamentalist, at a certain point, he recounts, he became "intent on pursuing my quest for truth wherever it might take me....my study of English literature, philosophy, and history—not to mention Greek—had widened my horizons significantly, and my passion was now for knowledge, knowledge of all kinds, sacred and secular....I resisted any temptation to change my views....But my studies started catching up with me." (*Misquoting Jesus*, pp. 6, 8)

So, he developed an orientation toward and a facility for critical thinking. And one of the things that struck him pretty early on, was that, if God had "an inerrant word" that he wanted everybody to know about, and insisted that everybody follow, then why wouldn't God provide this word in the original form so that everybody could be very clear on what it was? Or, if somehow the original manuscripts got lost, why wouldn't God find some other means to make clear what his word was, as set forth originally? Questions like this further propelled Ehrman on a course of critical study of the scriptures and of Christianity and religion more broadly—going into all different fields, learning different languages so he could read scriptures in the originals, and so on. On the basis of his studies, Ehrman shows how there are conflicting versions of many different parts of these scriptures—speaking specifically about the New Testament, although this is also true of the Old Testament. He points out that there were basic errors in copying scriptures, in addition to political decisions that went into deliberately changing the scriptures at different points. And in relation to all this, it is important to remember that, for many centuries when these scriptures were being reproduced, this was not the age of the Internet—it wasn't even the age of the printing press—these scriptures were being copied by hand, often by people in different places who were in contact with each other only very infrequently, if at all.

For example, Paul—or one of Paul's followers in Paul's name—

would write a letter to a Christian community somewhere in the Mediterranean area, and at first they would have the only copy of that letter, and then they would copy it and pass it on to others in another early Christian community somewhere else—and they would copy it, and so on. And as these letters got copied, frequently there were errors, just simple transcribing errors. One of the ways this would happen is that somebody would write a note in the margin while copying the text—maybe it would say something simple like "this doesn't sound right" or "it must have happened that way"—and, at a certain point that marginal note would get incorporated into the actual body of the text by someone copying it later on. Scriptural scholarship has revealed all kinds of things like this, just in terms of incidental changes from one manuscript to another.

And then, as Ehrman points out, there were also conscious and deliberate changes made for theological and political reasons. There were political decisions made about the canon—the scriptures that actually went into the Bible as it is now, essentially. Particularly in the fourth century, a Roman general Constantine was facing a major battle against a rival Roman general, Maxentius—a battle whose outcome would decide who would rule the Roman empire—and, according to the story that Constantine and his mother, Helena Augusta (who was his confederate in this) propagated afterward, as Constantine was spending the night before this major battle, he saw the sign of the cross in the sky and the words, "By this sign you shall conquer." Constantine conveyed this to his troops and used it as his symbol in battle; and, having won the battle and become Emperor, he adopted Christianity as his religion. Soon after that Christianity was adopted as the official religion of the Roman Empire and, at the point of a sword, it was forced on everyone conquered by the Roman Empire.

So Constantine's role is pivotal in the history of Christianity. Not only because he rose to the position of Emperor and took Christianity on as his religion, but because he was determined to structure and shape the religion and its scriptures according to his interests and his designs. So he called conferences of religious scholars and had them, under his ultimate direction, develop a unified doctrine and resolve key disputes of doctrine—such as the Trinity, which *nobody* understands and which has been the focus of bitter and violent disputes. There is God, the Father; but then there is Jesus, the Son of God. Did Jesus *emanate from* the father at a certain point, which would in effect make Jesus a lesser essence? Or was Jesus there from the beginning, part of the same essence as, and co-equal with, God, the Father—and then at some point Jesus took human form? And then there's the whole matter of the holy spirit. Holy shit, nobody knows anything about what that means. [Laughter]

There have been many different interpretations of the Holy Trinity. And, in addition to the way in which Christian authorities have over centuries persecuted non-believers and "heretics," early Christians, on opposite sides of the disputes about the Holy Trinity, fought with each other, often in the most bloody ways, slaughtering each other in the thousands and committing all manner of atrocities in the process. As referred to earlier, if you read Edward Gibbon's *The Decline and Fall of the Roman Empire*, you will find all this chronicled there. And, because unifying Christianity and its doctrines and institutions became very important to Constantine as a part of unifying the Roman empire under his rule, Constantine in effect enforced the resolution of much of this doctrinal dispute and factional fighting.

Political decisions were made about what got into the Bible, which versions of which scriptures, all under Constantine's direction. And then further political decisions about doctrine were hammered out and fought out in the following centuries as the Christian Church became a powerful institution.[9]

---

9. You can learn about much of this in the book by James Carroll *Constantine's Sword, The Church and the Jews: A History.* Carroll is a believing Catholic, but he does reveal a lot of this history because he is very much opposed to what Cornel West has characterized as Constantinian Christianity—Christianity that is a weapon and ideological arm of empire (see Cornel West, *Democracy Matters, Winning the Fight Against Imperialism*, The Penguin Press, 2004, especially chapter 5, "The Crisis of Christian Identity in America"). In *Constantine's Sword*

Returning to the scholarship of Bart Ehrman, he discusses the fact that there are many discrepancies between different versions of the same scripture in different manuscripts, and discrepancies between what is said about the same subject in one part of the scripture and another part. For example, in *Misquoting Jesus*, Ehrman reveals how the Gospel of Mark has Jesus utter a mistaken version of earlier scripture. Mark is considered by almost all Biblical scholars to be the original gospel which other gospels, in particular Matthew and Luke, borrowed from and added to. Ehrman examines how Mark (in chapter 2) tells of Jesus having a hostile encounter with the Pharisees (religious authorities among the Jewish people). They confront Jesus because he and his disciples are walking through a grain field, eating the grain as they go, on the Sabbath, which is a violation of Mosaic law about the Sabbath. And, according to Mark, in answering the Pharisees, Jesus refers to David as a precedent and justification for what he and his disciples are doing. Now, keep in mind how important David is; David establishes the Messianic lineage, he is the great king from which the Messiah will come. Remember what David did, says Jesus, how David and his men went into the temple when they were hungry in the days when Abiathar was the high priest. But as Ehrman points out, the problem is that in the passage that Jesus is referring to, from the Old Testament (1 Samuel 21:1–6), it indicates that when David did what Jesus is referring to, it was *not Abiathar, but his father, Ahemilech*, who was the high priest. (See *Misquoting Jesus*, p. 9, and compare Mark 2:26 with 1 Samuel 21:1–6.)

Now what happened here? How could Jesus—the inerrant co-equal divine substance from the beginning of time—make this mistake? You would think that Jesus would not have any trouble getting his own scriptures right, especially since he's all-knowing and they're inerrant. Once again, the reality that's revealed here is that

Carroll does a lot of exposure of the role of Constantine and of his mother, Helena Augusta, in shaping Christian doctrine. And the point to emphasize here is that what is shown by this, and indeed by the entire history of Christianity, is once again that Christian scripture is hardly the "inerrant word of God" that was spoken one day and then immediately appeared in printed version.

this can hardly be the "inerrant word of God" since, among other things, it contradicts itself from one place to another (in this case from 1 Samuel to Mark).

Or let's take another example from Ehrman's *Misquoting Jesus*— a famous story in the Bible, of the woman taken in adultery, which, says Ehrman, "is arguably the best-known story about Jesus in the Bible; it certainly has always been a favorite in Hollywood versions of his life. It even makes it into Mel Gibson's *The Passion of the Christ*."

This is the story of a woman found in the act of committing adultery, which is a sin punishable by death. She is about to be stoned to death. But Jesus intervenes, uttering the now famous warning (at least to all those familiar with Christianity): let he who is without sin cast the first stone. This prevents the killing, according to the Bible. This story is found in the Book of John in the New Testament, from Chapter 7 into Chapter 8.

The problem once more, as Ehrman points out, is that there are real difficulties and discrepancies here with this whole passage in the Bible. As Ehrman notes, this raises serious questions concerning Jesus's view of the law of Moses, since according to the law of Moses this woman *should* have been stoned to death. But there is the even more significant fact that, as Ehrman puts it:

> Despite the brilliance of the story, its captivating quality, and its inherent intrigue, there is one other enormous problem that it poses. As it turns out, it was not originally in the Gospel of John. In fact, it was not originally part of any of the Gospels. It was added by later scribes. (*Misquoting Jesus*, pp. 63–64)

Ehrman goes on to discuss some instances in the scriptures where there are different ways to interpret what happened and it is not entirely clear whether there is a discrepancy in fact—or, if there is a discrepancy, what it arose from. But with regard to this story about the woman taken in adultery, Ehrman indicates that "scholars who work on the manuscript tradition have no doubts about this particular case." And he points to

> a few basic facts that have proved convincing to nearly
> all scholars of every persuasion: the story is not found in
> our oldest and best manuscripts of the Gospel of John;
> its writing style is very different from what we find in
> the rest of John (including the stories immediately be-
> fore and after); and it includes a large number of words
> and phrases that are otherwise alien to the Gospel.

"The conclusion," says Ehrman, "is unavoidable: this passage was not originally part of the Gospel." (*Misquoting Jesus*, pp. 64–65)

So, yet again, we see that what we're dealing with, in reading the Bible that people have today, is not the "inerrant word of God" (not even "the original word of God").

In another work by a Biblical scholar—one that in my opinion is more controversial but nonetheless very interesting—a book called *The Jesus Dynasty, The Hidden History of Jesus, His Royal Family, and the Birth of Christianity,* by James D. Tabor (who is the Chair of the Religious Studies Department at the University of North Carolina at Charlotte), some very intriguing themes are discussed. Now, as I've alluded to, there are some problems with this book. For example, Tabor engages in certain speculations and then more or less takes his specu-lations as facts a little later on in the book. This applies particularly when he's discussing the genealogy of Jesus: Tabor's interpretation of how to understand what is said in Luke and in Matthew about the lineage of Jesus is somewhat strained, in my opinion (this is a subject I will return to later). But there are important parts of this book, par-ticularly where it analyzes something that is crucial to understand in regard to Christianity and its whole historical development, namely, the dominance of Paul in Christianity. *The Jesus Dynasty* puts forward an analysis of not only how this dominant role of Paul is reflected in the Bible, but also how this came about. Tabor points out:

> Jesus was a Jew, not a Christian. This single historical
> fact opens the door to understanding Jesus as he really
> was in his own time and place; it's a door that many
> have never thought to enter. (*The Jesus Dynasty*, p. 109)

And the reason why "many have never thought to enter" this door is not difficult to discern. This analysis does not really fit with the Christian religious tradition, the tradition of the Christian church, which essentially presents Jesus as preaching and practicing a new religion, Christianity, and portrays the Jews as the killers of Christ. Tabor goes on:

> To understand Jesus in his own time and place we have to understand his deep commitment to the ancestral faith of his fathers. He saw himself as doing nothing other than fulfilling the words of Moses and the Prophets, and the messianic hope that guided his life, and led him to his death, was the central core of his innermost being. (*The Jesus Dynasty*, p. 109)

Now, here, as elsewhere in Tabor's book, important aspects of his arguments are controversial and open to dispute. For example, many have argued that Jesus saw his mission and message as transcending—and in some ways going against, even negating—the law and commandments of Moses in the Old Testament. But, as pointed out earlier, there is no doubt that the Bible as we have it today (and as it has existed for centuries) portrays Jesus and the claim that he is the Messiah as based in the Jewish religious tradition and scriptures. And there is also no doubt that under the influence of Paul, more than anyone else, Christianity increasingly moved away from its Jewish religious roots and character, even while it did not and could not eliminate its foundation in Judaism. Paul, it should be noted, claimed to have seen Jesus in a vision after Jesus had died and ascended to heaven, but in real life Paul never met Jesus. Nevertheless, there is a very sound basis to view Paul as the dominant influence in Christianity as it developed historically and as it exists today, including in its rupture with and its eventual antagonism with Judaism.

It is also undeniably and irrefutably true that over the centuries, after the time of Jesus, as Christianity fully ruptured with Judaism, as it became an established religion itself—and especially after it was adopted as the official religion of the Roman Empire as a result in large part of the influence and role of Emperor Constantine—Christianity became one of the main forces contributing to and carrying out the relentless persecution of people of other religions, with a particularly venomous hatred directed toward the Jews, who were cast increasingly in the role not only of rejecting Jesus as the Messiah but also as responsible for his excruciating death on the cross—the "Jews as the Christ killers" narrative, that has been propagated down through centuries with terrible consequences.

Today, in a country like the U.S., there is a real and perverse irony in the fact that, as far as persecution and Christianity is concerned, what is mostly portrayed, and incessantly insisted upon by fundamentalist Christian Fascists, is the image of Christians themselves being persecuted. There is, on the part of these Christian Fascists, a conscious effort to invoke—sometimes directly and explicitly, and sometimes more by implication—the specter of the persecuted Christians in the Roman Empire: These Christian Fascists in the U.S. today like to act as if they are in a perilous position similar to that of the early Christians in the Roman coliseum about to be devoured by the lions. They repeatedly denounce "unelected judges" as "anti-Christian," insisting that instead of interpreting the laws, as they are supposed to do, these "unelected judges" are making laws to discriminate against and persecute Christians. In reality, Christianity is the all-but-official religion of the world's most powerful and aggressive empire, the world's only imperialist superpower, the USA; this religion is being used as an ideological instrument to reinforce domination and exploitation of the most cruel and barbarous kind throughout large parts of the world; and yet, because, in the U.S. itself, these Christian Fascists have—so far—encountered some limitations and constraints in their drive to use the machinery of the state as official backing to ram their absolutist version of Christianity down everyone's throat, and to promote it through public institutions, such as schools, they howl that "Christians are being persecuted."

If you live in this kind of society and you grew up within the Christian tradition, you are very likely to have the sense that, from the time of Jesus and for centuries, Christians were consistently, ruthlessly and relentlessly persecuted by the Roman authorities. In fact, that is not a true portrayal of the experience of Christians in the Roman empire. Persecution of the early Christians did occur, and at times was quite severe, but it was periodic; it became pronounced when it served the interests of a particular Emperor, like Nero for example, in deflecting anger toward a particular group, or when in some way what the Christians represented came into significant conflict with the interests of the ruling classes and in particular the Emperor of Rome.

One of the things that Bart Ehrman explains—and this is important to understand—is that the pagan religion in Rome was a polytheistic religion, it had many gods. So when the Christians came along and said they had another god, a lot of people said, in effect, "Yeah, okay, that's cool, why not? There's plenty of room for another one." The Romans believed in Apollo the Sun God, Diana the Moon Goddess—all kinds of different gods, many of which referred to different aspects or manifestations of nature. The reason the Christians ran into trouble was because at the same time as you worshiped these pagan gods, you had to not only swear allegiance to the Emperor, but you had to recognize the divinity of the Emperor. But the Christians refused, and that refusal especially landed them in a lot of trouble. Still, the image of Christians every day being thrown into the coliseum with the lions is not an accurate picture of what went on, most of the time, in the early days of Christianity before it rose to the position of the official religion of Rome.

And, again, religious persecution in the Roman Empire changed dramatically once Christianity was adopted, and enforced, as the official Roman religion, and in the eyes of the Christians the last became first and the first became last: then the persecution—of *non-Christians*, and of people alleged to be "heretics"—became systematic and ruthless, on a continuing basis. Once more, Edward Gibbon's *The Decline and Fall of the Roman Empire* vividly illustrates the lengths to which Christianity, once triumphant in the Roman

Empire, went in persecuting those it identified as its enemies. And, although I believe he overstates the extent and aim of the persecution of Christianity in its first centuries within the Roman empire, the following statement by F.E. Peters, in his book *The Harvest of Hellenism*, does capture and concentrate the dramatic reversal that took place once Christianity was decisively adopted as the religion of the Roman empire: "As the resources of the Roman state were once directed toward the extirpation of Christianity, so they were now turned against heretics and pagans."

And, Peters points out:

> Very few of the incredible variety of cults and beliefs followed in the Empire possessed much vitality in the fourth or fifth century, but the difference between a dying religion and a dead religion is considerable, and to achieve this latter, a constant ideal from the time of Theodosius (A.D. 379-395), increasingly stringent measures had to be taken. The ideal was, of course, the Church's, but it was shared and executed by the state. (*The Harvest of Hellenism, A History of the Near East from Alexander the Great to the Triumph of Christianity*, "Epilogue: The End of Paganism," p. 713)

James Carroll speaks to the same phenomenon in broader and even more graphic terms:

> It was only after Julian, through the successive reigns of the emperors Valentinian and Theodosius, that the empire came to be formally proclaimed Christian; only then that Christian heresy was pronounced a capital crime; only then that pagan worship was officially banned; only then that the authority of the Jewish patriarchate was abolished forever. And it was then that the question of what to do about the Jews who refused either to yield or to disappear surfaced in the official discourse of secular and religious authorities. From one side, it seemed simple. Once church and state had agreed that

> it was righteous and legal to execute those Christians—
> Docetists, Donatists, Nestorians, Arians—who dissent-
> ed from defined dogma on relatively arcane matters of
> theology, why in the world should stiff-necked persons
> who openly rejected the entire Christian proclamation
> be permitted to live? (*Constantine's Sword*, p. 206)

From that time on, in the "Christian world," life has been hell for all those who have refused to practice Christianity, or who were declared to be enemies of Christianity: those who were attacked in the course of the Crusades, including not only Muslims but Jews and various sects and denominations of Christians declared hereti-cal by the official Church; the people who were victimized by the Inquisitions carried out over centuries by the Christian Church, in which religious and government authorities tortured and slaugh-tered millions of people who refused to convert to Christianity or to renounce beliefs that were damned as heretical; or others who ran afoul of Church authorities in some way. Down to the present age, wherever Christianity has been the official (or the all-but-official) religion, people who have attempted to practice other religions, or no religion, have been discriminated against where they have not been more viciously persecuted. (In this connection, besides the works that have been cited so far, see also Arno J. Mayer, *Why Did The Heavens Not Darken? The "Final Solution" In History*, Pantheon Books, 1990.)

Christianity as a New Religion: The Pivotal Role and Influence of Paul

But let us go back before all this, before Christianity became a state religion in the Roman empire, and return to the question: how did Christianity grow and become a significant force? As I have already touched on, in the days right after the death of Jesus, this was mainly owing to Paul. Paul was a very aggressive organizer and proselytizer for his version of the Christian religion. And I emphasize *his* version. The reason for this emphasis is that in fact there were a number of different versions and different organized groups within Christianity in its early days.

To get a clearer sense of this, let's go back to the time right after the crucifixion of Jesus. Here the leader of this sect is dead. This is a devastating blow. The Christians were scattered around in small clusters, trying to figure out how to regroup. What are they going to do and say about the fact that their leader has been executed, not long after one of the other key figures associated with Jesus, John the Baptist (or John the Baptizer), has also been executed? Imagine, you have a movement, and all of a sudden the top leaders are wiped out. So then you have to figure out what to do in the face of this devastating loss. If this is a kind of apocalyptic religious group, based on prophecies of the end of days, or in any case the notion that monumental changes, mandated by god, are approaching—and this sect of Judaism which became Christianity was such an apocalyptic movement—well, then, it's not too surprising that among those who carried on there arose the mythology that the leader was not dead after all, but had risen and overcome death.

These kinds of ideas are not at all uncommon among people who have been part of a movement led by a charismatic leader. For example, about a century ago, many peasants in Mexico, after the rebel leader Emiliano Zapata was killed, used to repeat stories about how Zapata wasn't really dead, after all—he was still out there in the mountains. Well, Zapata was about as alive as Jesus was, after he was crucified. But often, when people in situations like this feel a need not to be devastated and demoralized, they come up with a way to not only console themselves but to keep the movement going. It's either that or give up the whole thing. So, while some followers of Jesus undoubtedly gave up, others regrouped. But they didn't regroup all in one Christian congregation, with all the, now familiar, dark-robed figures going around spreading darkness everywhere, throwing incense this way and that way, and mumbling incoherently.

That took some centuries to develop and institutionalize. [Laughter] Instead, you had different factions. One was more or less grouped around Peter, who was one of the main followers, or disciples, of Jesus. Another was grouped around Jesus's brother James, who is very little emphasized in the Bible. This is one of the points that Tabor emphasizes—that James is very little emphasized in the Bible, even though James is known and acknowledged to be the brother of Jesus. According to Tabor—and this is somewhat controversial— Jesus passed the mantle on to James as his successor. But, whatever the truth of that is, there's no question that James was the head of a Christian sect in and around Jerusalem. And—this might suggest something about what Jesus's beliefs were, although it is not definite proof—from what scholarship has shown, James was an advocate of strict Judaism and clearly regarded Christianity (or the "Jesus movement") as the true form of Judaism, which meant the insistence upon strict laws and commandments, in line with the tradition associated with Moses and the Jewish scriptures generally.

While I will return to, and go more fully into, essential aspects of the Christian message and doctrine a little later, first it is important to examine further the relation between the Christian religion and the Jewish religion (Judaism). That is, to discuss Christianity as it first developed within, and then as it separated itself from and increasingly came into hostile conflict with, Judaism; and from there the love/hate orientation and relationship that Christianity has had toward Judaism throughout the history of Christianity.

Shortly after Jesus was crucified, Paul began to emerge as a major leader. In fact, as alluded to before, Paul is actually the dominant figure in the New Testament of the Bible, even more so than Jesus: It is Paul who sets the terms to a large degree for the New Testament. But, in the very early days of "the Jesus movement" after Jesus, before Paul's influence became dominant within Christianity, a struggle developed among the different groupings of this movement. In this regard, it is important to keep in mind that insofar as people believed Jesus was the Messiah, they expected that he would be a *triumphant* Messiah. In the Jewish tradition, the Messiah was not supposed to be executed on the cross—he was supposed to be a conquering hero, right in this world and for the benefit of the Jewish people. That is no doubt a major reason why the great majority of the Jewish people rejected Jesus as the Messiah: What kind of Messiah is this? He's supposed to lead us out of bondage and conquer our enemies, and look what happened to him. [Laughter]

So the early Christian communities began to have struggle among themselves, over what to do in the face of the fact that Jesus had not conquered, but had been utterly defeated, crucified. They had to start inventing stories and myths to take this apparent defeat and turn it into a victory. Here again is the basis for the story of the resurrection—for which, of course, there is no evidence anywhere outside the Bible. But as these struggles developed within the early Christian communities over what direction to take with this religious movement that had been fractured because of the death of its leader, Jesus, they came up against some really tough questions and they had different positions—or, as we communists say, different "lines"—on what to do about this. For example, given his devotion to traditional Judaism, the position of Jesus's brother James was to insist that they had to stay strictly within the Jewish tradition and recruit only among Jews. Peter had sort of a middle position: we should still be based mainly among Jews, but we shouldn't exclude other peoples. But Paul increasingly took the stand: If we're going to really spread this religion, we have to go out among the gentiles (non-Jews) in a big way, because the Jews are rejecting this and we're going to die off if we don't get some new recruits.

In reading Paul's letters (or the letters attributed to Paul) in the Bible, it is very clear that he is placing emphasis on the need to go to the gentiles. He carries on polemics with other people in the Christian leadership at that time. This struggle took place around a number of issues but a particular focus was the commandments and requirements of the Old Testament. For example, there are a lot of very strict dietary requirements in the Old Testament, and in the

Jewish religious tradition. And the early Christians were having a lot of difficulty getting people to join their movement because, among the gentiles, people hadn't grown up with all those dietary restrictions and they didn't want to adopt them. Paul's position was: You don't have to actually uphold the law to the letter; you just have to uphold the spirit of it.

But beyond this—and this was heightened by the fact that theirs was a religion dominated by men, and their efforts focused on recruiting men—the biggest problem they faced was circumcision. Now, Jewish children were circumcised early. But let's say that you're a gentile, and Paul (or another member of the "Jesus movement") comes to you and calls on you to convert to this religious movement. Well, there wasn't any anesthesia, and they didn't have the kind of medical technology that exists today. Getting circumcised as an adult was a big deal. And this was really holding back their recruitment. [Laughter] So, if you read the Bible, you find Paul arguing: You don't have to be circumcised in the flesh—you can be circumcised in the spirit. Well, that helped them a lot. [Laughter] And this is one of the reasons why Paul became the dominant figure within the Christian movement—he had his finger on the pulse of things more, if you'll pardon the expression. [Laughter]

Now, there are humorous aspects to this, but all this also has a very serious and deadly side. As discussed earlier, as Christianity continued to develop in this way, over the next generations, largely as a result of Paul's influence (even after Paul himself was executed), it not only increasingly separated itself from but took on an antagonistic stance toward Judaism. And, along with this, the whole story of "the passion of Jesus" developed, in which Jewish authorities and the Jewish people in general came to be blamed, and condemned, for the crucifixion of Jesus. In this story, at the trial of Jesus the Roman official Pontius Pilate says that he can find no criminal activity on Jesus's part, but the Jewish mob and the Jewish authorities who are present cry out for Jesus to be punished. So Pilate washes his hands of this, saying "I am innocent of this man's blood," and Jesus is condemned to be crucified (see Matthew chapter 27, especially verse 24). This continues to be promoted and promulgated even today—Mel Gibson's movie *The Passion of the Christ* is a striking example of this. But, once again, it is rather clear from the work of Biblical scholars that this whole story of how the Jews were the ones responsible for Jesus being crucified is very improbable; that it is very unlikely that the Roman authorities, when faced with a person who is accused of being a rebel and a trouble-maker, would allow the Jewish mob to decide what to do about him. But, unlikely as it is, this is a story that, as scholarship has shown, was worked into the Christian tradition about a century after the death of Jesus.[10]

---

10. As a result of protests, Mel Gibson took out of *The Passion of the Christ* the part where the Jewish people call out about Jesus, "His blood be on us and on our children!" (Matthew 27:25) But Gibson left in more indirect references to this.

It is important to recognize, however, that something like the movie *The Passion of the Christ* was not just a particular personal passion or project of Mel Gibson. This was supported—openly and aggressively, or more subtly and quietly, or even indirectly—by Protestant Christian fundamentalists like Jerry Falwell and Pat Robertson, and others with connections right up to the highest levels of the American government, as well as the Catholic Church and its Pope at the time, John Paul II. But in today's world, given the determination of the U.S. imperialists to further reshape the Middle East in a way even more favorable to their designs for domination not only in that strategic region but in the world as a whole, and given the particular and special role of the state of Israel in relation to that, reactionary Christian fundamentalists, and in particular those at the highest levels of the U.S. government, including the President, at the same time as they promote a religious tradition which has mercilessly targeted the Jews as "Christ killers," they must provide and insist upon the most uncritical and unflinching support for the state of Israel, a Jewish state. The U.S. continues to massively finance, arm and assist Israel in all the many ways in which Israel has not only robbed the Palestinian people of their homeland and continues to viciously oppress them, but also the ways in which Israel serves as a military outpost and instrument of U.S. imperialism in the world, not just in the strategic region of the Middle East, but even in far-flung parts of the globe, such as Latin America and East Asia, where Israel does dirty work for U.S. Imperialism. (Important exposure and analysis of different aspects of this role of Israel, as well as the history of Israel's founding, and its relation to U.S. imperialism overall, is found in *Revolution* newspaper [on the Web at revcom.us], including my talk "Bringing Forward Another Way." Much of value in this regard is also found in works by Norman Finkelstein, including *The Holocaust Industry* and *Beyond*

Now, to be clear, Paul is not responsible, in some direct sense, for this level of antagonism toward Jews on the part of Christianity, and the awful consequences of this, down through the centuries, especially after Christianity was adopted and enforced as the official religion of the Roman Empire, and has been the official, or

---

Chutzpah, On the Misuse of Anti-Semitism and the Abuse of History.)

The imperialist rulers of the U.S. face a rather acute contradiction in relation to all this. And here is the way in which they are dealing with that contradiction: they promote an interpretation of the Bible, and in particular the book of Revelation, which insists that the Second Coming and the triumphant return of Jesus cannot happen unless the State of Israel exists—and if the state of Israel ceases to exist, that will delay the Second Coming, the triumph of Jesus will be greatly set back and the forces of the anti-Christ will greatly benefit. Therefore, it is crucial to support Israel. Of course, it is also important to keep in mind that, in the worldview of the Christian fundamentalists, when the Second Coming actually comes about, the choice for the Jews will be to convert to Christianity or be condemned to eternal damnation. This is yet a further contradiction built into all this—which a number of Jews, including even some die-hard supporters of Israel, are aware of, with many having very ambivalent feelings, or even serious misgivings, about it. For now, in the main these contradictory impulses among the Christian fundamentalists are being held together in a way that serves U.S. imperialist interests, including in regard to Israel and its special role in relation to those interests. This has been possible to a large degree precisely because, in essence and by definition, fundamentalist movements of this type are made up of and appeal to people who are searching for simple and absolute answers to the complexities and volatility of the world today, and who therefore, as long as they cling to this mentality, are inclined to blindly follow people who strongly assert this kind of fundamentalist, absolutist authority.

Unfortunately, while the expressions of this Christian fundamentalism can take on ludicrous dimensions, it represents a very dangerous reactionary, fascist-minded force—and a lot of oppressed people are, at this point, caught up in this. At the same time, there is the phenomenon that, however much imperialist rulers and reactionary religious authorities may try to distort it, reality does exist independently of them and does exert itself, as has been seen sharply, for example, in Iraq over the nearly 5 years since the U.S. invasion and occupation of that country.

A fuller analysis of this contradiction, bound up with the fact that the Christian Fascists in the U.S. have been conditioned to see Jews as "Christ Killers" and at the same time to be fanatical supporters of the state of Israel—and some discussion of the larger context and political implications of this—is contained in the Question and Answer section of the DVD of my talk *Revolution: Why It's Necessary; Why It's Possible; What It's All About*, Three Q Productions, Chicago IL.

semi-official, religion of oppressive empires since then, right up to today. In Paul's time, and largely through his influence, Christianity became set on a course which would lead to its separation from Judaism; that separation, in turn, would lead to growing hostility on the part of Christians toward Jews who rejected—and, in so rejecting, objectively undermined—the claim that Jesus was the Messiah; and, once Christianity became a powerful force and then an official state religion, that hostility found expression in brutal persecution and bloody massacre, sanctioned and enforced by the state.

Looking at this with historical perspective, it is important to recognize that the course that Christianity took after the death of Jesus involved a definite element of accident and contingency. The struggle between the different groupings among the early "Jesus movement" could have turned out differently. For example, Paul could have been killed earlier than he was—he was eventually executed by the Roman authorities, but not until he had spent several decades organizing the Christian movement and spreading it around the Mediterranean area. Or, it could have been the case that, for a combination of reasons, Paul was not so effective, and so successful, in propagating and organizing people around his version of Christianity. But, as things actually turned out, he was very effective, and by the time he was killed, several decades after the crucifixion of Jesus, there were established Christian communities in a number of areas. Now, they, in turn, could have been wiped out. But, as it turned out, they weren't, and instead they began to grow and spread and become a feature of the Roman Empire.

And, once again through a combination of causality and accident (or contingency), a couple of centuries later Constantine found that adopting Christianity served his larger purposes, and so did Emperors after him (and the rulers of the Roman Empire in general), in part at least because Christianity was a single-god (monotheistic) religion, which came to serve the unification of the diverse peoples of the Roman Empire under one rule. As new territory would be conquered, it had to be integrated into an empire in which Rome ruled; and after a certain point having a single religion was an important unifying factor in this process. For that, and no doubt for other reasons, Christianity came to be adopted, and enforced, by the ruling class of that Roman Empire.

Down through centuries after that, this religion has been spread and imposed by force, as well as by preaching and proselytizing, in large parts of the world. So, today, hundreds and hundreds of millions of people practice this religion, most of whom believe that the scriptures they're familiar with (whether they read them, or only have them presented by others) were, in fact, handed down by god directly and have been the same ever since. In fact, as we can see, even from what I've been able to briefly recount and review here, all this was the product of very earthly factors, including political struggles as well as ideological-theological struggles, over doctrine and the practical implications of following one doctrine or another.

If, for whatever combination of reasons, the outlook and program (what we could call the "line") of James had prevailed in the very early days of Christianity, that would have placed very serious restrictions on the spread of that religion. But because the doctrine identified with Paul was brought forward and fought for by the person of Paul; and because, for whatever combination of reasons, Paul was effective in attracting, winning over, organizing and providing direction to followers—giving them a doctrine which they could act on and which could be a unifying and cohering factor—this movement grew.

Here we come back to James D. Tabor, who argues that Jesus and his closest followers during his lifetime, including in particular James, the brother of Jesus, came to see Jesus as a Messiah of the Jewish people who would bring a new kingdom based on God's word to the Jewish people—then and there in this world. Tabor flatly states: "There is no evidence that James worshipped his brother or considered him divine." (*The Jesus Dynasty*, p. 282) Now, some of Tabor's assertions are certainly open to dispute, and some of the things he cites in support of those claims are open to different interpretations;

but one important thing that he argues is clearly in line with what is known—that it was Paul who shaped Christianity more than anyone else, even more than Jesus. As one indication of this, there are many more words of Paul in the New Testament than there are words of Jesus. Tabor also argues that it was Paul who introduced into Christianity the whole idea of the divinity of Jesus, the notion that he was not only crucified but rose from the dead, and in so doing provided salvation, or the means of salvation, for a fallen and sinful mankind.

Well, without here attempting to resolve arguments that are bound to go on for some time in relation to this, among Biblical scholars and others, it can definitely be said that it is the case that Paul played the pivotal role in bringing about a major shift in Christianity: a shift away from the Old Testament—and from the notion of works, based on carrying out the laws of the Old Testament, as the means to salvation—and toward an essentially exclusive emphasis on faith. Along with this, Paul brought a shift away from concern with *this world* toward preoccupation with the supposed next world, and what would be brought about through the Second Coming of Jesus. At the heart of this, as the most essential and defining element of Christian doctrine, is the story of Jesus's crucifixion and his resurrection, with its promise of redemption from sin, and an everlasting life with Jesus and the Father in heaven, for all of mankind who believed in this, who accepted this through faith.

Demystifying Jesus and Christianity

Why have I gone into this to such an extent? What is the importance of this? Well, first of all, on an obvious level, the story of Jesus and the Christian religion organized around this story—or, more accurately, Paul's version of it—has exerted a widespread and powerful influence and played a key part in the history of the world in the 2000 years since the time of Jesus. And, again, this has been especially so after Christianity was adopted as the official religion of the Roman Empire and spread throughout large parts of the world, and has been taken up as the state religion by many powerful ruling classes through the centuries down to the present time—or has been promoted as the favored religion in effect, if not officially the state religion, as is the case with the U.S., the most powerful imperialist state in the world today. And now there is a move by powerful forces within the U.S. toward installing Christianity as not simply the favored religion, but the *official state religion* of America—and, as with Constantine in the Roman Empire, to make this religion the banner under which the imperial armed forces of America carry out their crusade throughout the world. For these reasons, understanding the actual nature and history of this religion is important; and, more specifically, the particular aspects of this religion and its historical development that I have focused on here are important in understanding how Christianity came to have the character it does and to play the role it does: how this is owing *not* to the existence of god and to the role of Jesus as his son who sacrificed his life on the cross in order to be the savior of a sinning mankind, and not to the "inerrant word of God" embodied in the Bible, *but rather to very earthly factors, including ideological, political and military struggles among human beings and human societies.*

In other words, this is important, first of all and most fundamentally, as a matter of basic outlook and methodology, which is crucial in understanding important aspects of social and historical reality, and reality in general, and in transforming this reality in a way that is actually in the interests of and will lead to the emancipation of the masses of oppressed people and ultimately all of humanity. As a part of that—and this has very particular and great importance now—it is necessary to *demystify* Christianity (and all religion), to remove it from the realm of superstitious awe for some mythical but non-existent god and for the scriptures which are presented as the perfect and inerrant word of this god; to reveal the very human mainsprings and dynamics of the development of this religion as well as its doctrine and its role in the world; to help make more clear the need to rupture with, and rupture beyond, this and all similar modes of thinking that are chains on the minds of people—mental shackles holding down masses of people and restraining those masses and ultimately humanity as a whole from achieving emancipation from a society and a world rooted in ruthless exploitation and oppression, reinforced with ignorance, superstition and, in fact, errant ways of approaching reality.

As for Jesus in particular and his teachings, despite words and sayings of his that can be cited about love and peace and concern for the poor and the marginalized in society;[11] and despite what certain people try to say by way of presenting Jesus as a model and a means for achieving a more just world among human beings; if, somehow, Jesus were transported from his time to ours and we were to encounter him, the fact is that we would not, and we *should not*, like this Jesus very much. The Jesus who comes through in the Bible, and in what Biblical scholarship has shown about him, is an apocalyptic figure, steeped in the superstitions and ignorance of his time and place, who was religiously fanatical, and who insisted, in his fanaticism, that only by following *him* and his teachings could people find the way to a righteous redemption and, if they did not follow his way, they would be damned to eternal torment and torture. What comes through of Jesus and the whole religious tradition of which he was a part at the time—and the influence that the religion associated with him has continued to exert to this day   all this belongs to the past.

---

11. Such words and sayings, it should be noted, can also be found in scriptures that make up the Old Testament of the Bible, including in books such as Isaiah, where, along with pronouncements about justice and lyrical descriptions of the day when peace shall reign, we also find the advocacy of and the insistence on the most horrendous atrocities, such as the mass raping of women and the bashing in of the heads of babies, all as part of wantonly slaughtering and destroying whole peoples. And it should be noted, again, that the book of Isaiah was said to be the favorite book of Jesus in the Jewish scriptures, and one that he frequently refers to.

This belongs to the past, not just in some general or abstract sense, but to a past marked by cruel oppression and brutality that humanity not only must but can move beyond in order to have a future worth living. What is celebrated and advocated in this religious tradition has not led, and cannot lead, to the liberation and the elevation of humanity. That tradition and its scriptures, especially as this is taken literally, has led and can only lead to the perpetration and perpetuation of horrors. Only by breaking with that, and with all religious doctrine, ways of thinking and traditions, will it be possible for humanity to finally and fully put an end to all such horrors.

Islam Is No Better (and No Worse) Than Christianity

Up to this point I have been focusing on Christianity and the Bible. While of course there are significant differences, theologically and in terms of religious practice, between Islam and Christianity (and Judaism), the world outlook that each expresses and the social content each embodies—what they say about how human society is and ought to be—are not only similar in many ways but are fundamentally in the service of the same kinds of systems of exploitation and enslavement. In the holy book of Islam, the Qur'an, no less than in the Christian Bible (and the whole "Judeo-Christian tradition"), all kinds of oppressive relations are upheld and even celebrated.[12]

---

12. In this work I have focused on the world's three major monotheistic religions—Islam, Judaism, and Christianity—and I have not attempted to deal directly, or in any depth, with other religious and "spiritual" belief systems that revolve around, or at least posit the existence of, entities that are supposedly different from and beyond the realm of the material universe—whether gods, other supernatural forces, "one universal life force," etc. Nor have I delved into the various trends within each of these three monotheistic religions, because even though there are differences, even some significant differences, between these trends as regards religious doctrine and practice, that is secondary to the basic worldview and tenets of the religion of which they are a part. And, I am firmly convinced, the fundamental and essential criticisms that are made here with regard to Christianity, Judaism, and Islam apply as well to all such belief systems.

The historical origins of Islam provide a context for, and further insight into, the content and role of Islam, as a religion and as a geopolitical force in the world, historically and down to today. The pivotal, and seminal, figure in Islam is, of course, its founder, Muhammad, who was born about 1500 years ago in Mecca and spent his early years there. Muhammad (Muhammad bin Abdullah) was from a relatively minor subgroup within the dominant tribe in the area of Mecca, the Quraysh. His status became somewhat more elevated when he married a wealthy widow, Khadijah; but, although more or less financially secure, he was still not a prominent figure among the Quraysh in Mecca. At that time, Mecca was becoming an increasingly important trade site and center of commerce. Along with this, it was a significant religious center; and the shrine in the city, the Ka'ba, was a holy site for the many tribes, with their differing local religions, who travelled to, and traded in, Mecca. This too was a source of wealth for the Quraysh. But, at the same time, this role of Mecca as a growing commercial center was in some significant ways undermining the traditional tribal way of life and the *superstructure*—the politics and political structures, the ideology and the culture expressed to a large degree in religious terms—that more or less corresponded to that traditional mode of life.

It was in these circumstances that Muhammad began to spend long periods alone in the desert and the mountainous areas around Mecca. And it was during these solitary periods, when he would often fast for several days, that, according to Muhammad, he began to hear revelations from God (Allah), as spoken to Muhammad by the angel Gabriel, which Muhammad memorized and recited. These recitations would continue throughout the rest of Muhammad's life and would come to constitute the foundation of the Islamic religion, set down in the Qur'an and other holy works of Islam.

Now, of course, it is impossible for me (or, really, for anyone at this point) to say whether (or to what degree) Muhammad actually believed that he was receiving revelations from Allah, or whether (or to what degree) he was conscious that he, himself, was the source of these supposed revelations. There are some places in the surahs (chapters) of the Qur'an (such as Surah LXVI, "Banning," where instructions from Allah are relayed by Muhammad to his wives, telling them not to be jealous, to be more obedient and cause less trouble for Muhammad, and warning them that otherwise Allah may appoint better wives for the Prophet—see verse 5 in particular) which are, to say the least, rather convenient for Muhammad and seem more likely to have been consciously contrived by him. But it is quite probable that, for the most part and in essence, Muhammad was himself convinced that he was receiving, and conveying, the word of the one true God, Allah. And it would not be surprising if, in the course of spending days in the desert or the mountains while fasting, and probably with very little water, Muhammad would hear voices and would come to believe that he was hearing the voice of the angel Gabriel in particular, relaying revelations from Allah. What is clear is that Muhammad became familiar with at least some of the doctrines and beliefs of Christians and of Jews, and this is reflected in the Qur'an—both in what Muhammad seems to have adopted from these religions and in what he came to reject and even denounce. And what is also clear is that, out of these various influences and experiences, Muhammad created, over the course of several decades, what became the Qur'an and the new religion of Islam.

Now, of course, it was not predetermined that Muhammad's recitations would come to be invested with the aura of divine revelation—they could have been ignored or dismissed as the ramblings of a lunatic. In fact, this is how the elders and powerful forces in the Quraysh tribe in Mecca treated this, for some time. When Muhammad persisted and, moreover began to challenge the established rulers and religious beliefs and practices, and to denounce them as corrupt, he was forced to retreat to Yithrab (which was to become known as Medina). There, Muhammad found more favorable circumstances and, over a period of time, was able to establish himself as both a religious and political authority.

Not only was Muhammad a skillful politician—in Medina he

helped to settle disputes among the population there, including a number of Jews who lived in the area, although these Jews ultimately rejected Muhammad and his new religion of Islam—but he also proved to be a skillful military leader. From Medina, once having consolidated his rule, he began to lead his forces in raids against the trading caravans headed for Mecca, which caused significant losses for and put a lot of pressure on the Quraysh in Mecca. Finally, after a series of battles in which Muhammad was able to inflict damage on his Meccan enemies and to avoid death or capture himself, Muhammad was able to march triumphantly back to Mecca and, combining military presence with adroit diplomacy—promising to spare the lives and the property of his adversaries—he was able to achieve the capitulation of the leaders of the Quraysh. Mecca became the center of the new religion of Islam, and the Ka'ba became a holy shrine of that religion.

In all this, once again, we can see the role of accident (or contingency) as well as causality, and the interplay between the two. Had certain events turned out differently, at a number of points, this new religion might never have been brought fully into being, or in any case would never have became a major force in the world. Muhammad could have died much earlier than he did—and in particular he could have been killed during the years when he was in Medina and engaged in warfare with powerful enemies then centered in Mecca. But this was not all a matter of accident. The new religious doctrine and the new religious and political institutions that Muhammad forged and developed over several decades, including during his reign in Medina, had an attractive power not only because of the military force that Muhammad was able to marshal on behalf of this, but because this religion provided a cohering set of beliefs and practices for the growing and diverse groups of people drawn to Mecca, which could unify them beyond more narrow tribal interests and customs. Not simply in some linear and mechanical sense, but in a larger and more overall way, Islam conformed to the new conditions that had been brought into being as a result of the growth of Mecca as a commercial center, drawing together people from many different areas and tribes.

Here we see the dynamic—or, in Marxist terms, the dialectical—relation between the economic mode of life and the superstructure of politics and ideology (including religion), a relation in which changes in the economy (in this case the development of Mecca as a commercial center and accompanying transformations) give life to new modes of thinking, and in turn these new ways of thinking become formulated in doctrines and programs around which people are organized and for which they fight, in opposition to those forces (in this case, the Quraysh rulers in Mecca) seeking to uphold and enforce the old way of life, even in the face of major changes. Of course, as emphasized here, this relationship is not one where changes in the superstructure follow directly and automatically from changes in the economic mode of life, nor are the forces representing a new superstructure, conforming more or less to those changes in the economic mode of life, bound to prevail, in some predetermined sense, or in the short run. As has been discussed, there is the role of accident in all this, but it is not all accident, there is causality as well—there are real material factors, in particular changes in the economic mode of life and relations among people, which are providing an impetus toward and a more favorable basis for corresponding changes in the superstructure of ideology and politics—and there is the continual interplay between changes in the economic base and developments, and struggles, in the superstructure. All this is illustrated in the way in which Muhammad and the new religion of Islam was not bound to but did in fact develop and eventually triumph in the new circumstances that were coming into being as a result of changes in Mecca (which were themselves, in turn, related to changes in the larger world, beyond Mecca and beyond Arabia, which gave further impetus to the development of Mecca as a commercial center).

The same basic principles and dynamics apply to the spread of Islam after the time of Muhammad. Through a combination of military conquest and often skillful diplomatic and political-administrative means, Islam and institutions of Islamic rule were spread over a very large area in the centuries after Muhammad. And, even where an Islamic caliphate as such no longer is the form of state (as well as in places, such as Iran, where an Islamic Republic now exists), Islam and its religious-political institutions have continued, down to the present time, to exert powerful influence among large numbers of people in the Middle East and other parts of the world.

In all this, we can also see a fundamental similarity with the development and spread of Christianity, from its origins among small sects in one geographic area to its emergence as a major force exerting its power and influence in large parts of the world and among huge numbers of people. In both cases we see the crucial role of certain key individuals—such as Jesus himself, but also Paul and Constantine in the history of Christianity, and Muhammad and the early caliphs in the history of Islam—and we see how this is situated, in an overall sense, in the larger dynamics (the living, dialectical interplay) between accident and causality and between the economic base and the superstructure of ideology and politics (including military struggle). It is as a result of *all this*—and not because of the existence and will of one or another god, or incarnation of god, (whether Yahweh, the god of the ancient Israelites; or Allah; or the Christian Trinity; or any other supernatural being or force)—it is because of *material and earthly factors* that people today still believe in and worship a god (or gods), or other supernatural beings or forces, but do *not* all believe in *the same* god or gods, and in fact often denounce the gods and religions of *others* as false and even blasphemous.

Returning specifically to Islam, a reading of not only historical accounts of the life and teachings of Muhammad, but of the Qur'an in particular, makes clear that Muhammad's views—what he understood and what he was ignorant of, what he upheld and praised, as well as what he opposed and condemned—all this reflected the society and world in which he lived, and involved many unequal, cruel and oppressive relations, and the corresponding values, views and customs which Muhammad regarded as necessary, legitimate and just. This includes: slavery; the notion of children, as well as women, as essentially the property of men; the subordination of women to men; the right and indeed the duty of the believers to make war on unbelievers and to carry off plunder, including women, as prizes of war; and overall relations in which some are raised above and exploit and oppress others—all in the name and under the banner of the merciful and beneficent god, Allah.

The following are just a few selections from the Qur'an that clearly—and in many cases graphically—illustrate all this. In looking at these passages from the Qur'an, keep in mind that according to the Qur'an, it is Allah who is speaking to Muhammad, usually through the medium of the angel Gabriel.

> They question thee (O Muhammad) concerning menstruation. Say: It is an illness, so let women alone at such times and go not in unto them till they are cleansed. And when they have purified themselves, then go in unto them as Allah hath enjoined upon you....Your women are a tilth [tillage] for you (to cultivate) so go to your tilth as ye will, and send (good deeds) before you for your souls, and fear Allah, and know that ye will (one day) meet Him. (From Surah II, "The Cow," verses 222–23, *The Glorious Qur'an, Text and Explanatory Translation by Mohammad M. Pickthall*, 10th Revised Edition, 1994, Library of Islam. All citations from the Qur'an are from this edition; unless otherwise indicated, all words and phrases in parentheses are in the original. The word in brackets [tillage] has been added here.)

In this, there is a striking similarity to the Bible, and the laws and commandments in the Old Testament in particular, which portray women who are menstruating as something unclean which must be avoided by men. In both cases, this is part of a tradition which treats women in general as a source of contamination and as inferior and unworthy in relation to men.

So we read in the Qur'an:

> If two men be not (at hand), then a man and two women
> of such as ye may approve as witnesses [may testify] so
> that if the one erreth (through forgetfulness) the other
> will remember. ("The Cow," v. 282—the phrase within
> brackets ["may testify"] has been added here.)

Here we see that the testimony of women is considered to be
only half as reliable and valuable as that of a man in legal proceed-
ings: it takes two women to substitute for or replace one man in
such a proceeding.

This view of women is also illustrated in the following from the
Qur'an:

> Beautiful for mankind is love of the joys (that come)
> from women and offspring, and stored-up heaps of
> gold and silver, and horses branded (with their mark),
> and cattle and land. That is the comfort of the life of
> the world. Allah! With Him is a more excellent abode.
> (Surah III, "The Family of Imran," v. 14)

Here the point is being made that worldly things, while they
may have their value, cannot compare to the glory of Allah and a
life of service and submission to Allah—which is what Islam means:
submission. But the view here of what is beautiful for mankind
reflects social relations in which women, as well as children, along
with horses that are branded and cattle and land, are, in effect or literally, possessions of men. Again we notice a striking similarity with
the Bible—for example, the Ten Commandments, and the tenth in
particular, where women are listed, along with slaves, houses and
farm animals, as things of "thy neighbor's" which "thou shalt not
covet."

Another passage from the Qur'an presents this view of women
even more graphically: "And all married women (are) forbidden unto
you save those (captives) whom your right hands possess."

Here women as captured slaves or concubines of the faithful

(men) is upheld and celebrated. (See Surah IV, "Women," v. 24.)

And there is the following:

> Men are in charge of women, because Allah has made
> the one of them to excel the other, and because they
> spend of their property (for the support of women). So
> good women are the obedient, guarding in secret that
> which Allah hath guarded. As for those from whom ye
> fear rebellion, admonish them and banish them to beds
> apart, and scourge [whip] them. Then, if they obey you,
> seek not a way against them. Lo! Allah is ever High Ex-
> alted, Great. (Surah IV, "Women," v. 34—the explanatory
> word "whip" was added here, in brackets.)

The meaning of this—and the unequal and oppressive social relations this embodies and promotes between men and women—are all too familiar.

"As for the thief," the Qur'an instructs, "both male and female, cut off their hands. It is the reward of their own deeds, an exemplary punishment from Allah. Allah is Mighty, Wise. But whoso repenteth after his wrongdoing and amendeth, lo! Allah will relent toward him. Lo! Allah is Forgiving, Merciful." (Surah V, "The Table Spread," v. 38–39.)

Women thieves as well as men will have their hands cut off—here we see women finally receiving equal treatment. [Laughter]

Another passage from the Qur'an:

> They ask thee (O Muhammad) of the spoils of war. Say:
> The spoils of war belong to Allah and the messenger, so
> keep your duty to Allah, and adjust the matter of your
> difference, and obey Allah and His messenger, if ye are
> (true) believers. (Surah VIII, "The Spoils of War," v. 1)

The emphasis here is on regulating the distribution of the spoils of war, and on the priority that must be given in this distribution to Muhammad, the messenger of Allah, and to the developing state that Muhammad headed, in which he ruled as the representative of Allah. And, it should be kept in mind, the spoils of war to be distributed among the faithful (men), include women who are captured and carried off (see above in relation to the surah "Women," v. 24).

And in the following passages from the Qur'an, the owning of slaves, as well as treating wives as the possessions of their husbands—and spoils of war—is upheld, and extolled as well:

> Successful indeed are the believers/Who are humble in their prayers,/And who shun vain conversation,/And who are payers of the poor-due/And who guard their modesty—/Save from their wives or the (slaves) that their right hands possess, for then they are not blameworthy. (Surah XXIII, "The Believers," v. 1–6)
>
> And marry such of you as are solitary and the pious of your slaves and maidservants. If they be poor, Allah will enrich them of His bounty. Allah is of ample means, Aware. (Surah XXIV, "Light," v. 32)
>
> O Prophet! Lo! We have made lawful unto thee thy wives unto whom thou hast paid their dowries, and those whom thy right hand possesseth of those whom Allah has given thee as spoils of war. (See Surah XXXIII, "The Clans," v. 50)

Elsewhere in the Qur'an, Allah, speaking through Muhammad, says:

> Each do We supply, both these and those, from the bounty of thy Lord. And the bounty of thy Lord can never be walled up. See how We prefer one above another, and verily the Hereafter will be greater in degrees and greater in preferment. (Surah XVII, "The Children of Israel," v. 20–21)

So here we see that, along with slavery, and the plundering of women, the exalting of some over others is the way and the will of Allah.

Or, again:

> We have apportioned among them their livelihood in
> the life of the world, and raised some of them above
> others in rank, that some of them may take labour from
> others; and the mercy of thy Lord is better than (the
> wealth) that they amass. (Surah XLIII, "Ornaments of
> Gold," v. 32)

Worldly worth is considered a value in one context but as nothing compared to the glory and the largesse of Allah. According to
the Qur'an, Muhammad is relaying the words of Allah here, who is
angry at the ingratitude of some who doubt the word of Allah as told
to his messenger, Muhammad. But there is also expressed here, on
the part of Muhammad, and in the name of Allah, a clear approval
and advocacy of worldly divisions in which some are elevated above
and exploit others.

The same outlook and view of what the relations are, and ought
to be, between different groups of people (men and women, masters
and slaves, and so on), which I have cited so far from the Qur'an
(and these are only a few representative examples) is projected by
Muhammad from this life into the promised afterlife:

> Lo! the doom of thy Lord will surely come to pass;/There
> is none that can ward it off....Then woe that day unto
> the deniers/Who play in talk of grave matters;/The day
> when they are thrust with a (disdainful) thrust, into
> the fire of hell....Lo! those who kept their duty dwell in
> gardens and delight,/Happy because of what their Lord
> hath given them, and (because) their Lord hath warded
> off from them the torment of hell-fire....Reclining on
> ranged couches. And We wed them unto fair ones with
> wide, lovely eyes....And there go round, waiting on them
> menservants of their own, as they were hidden pearls.
> (Surah LII, "The Mount," v. 7–8, 11–13, 17–18, 20, 24)

And shortly after that, the Qur'an further elaborates on and embellishes this vision of paradise, including the following:

> Therein are those [women] of modest gaze, whom nei-
> ther man nor jinni [spirits capable of assuming human
> form] will have touched before them. (Surah LV, "The Be-
> neficent," v. 56—"women" and "spirits capable of assum-
> ing human form" have been added here, in brackets.)

Here are the much talked about virgins who are rewards in
paradise for the faithful—men. And then this vision is repeated, and
further elaborated on:

> Fair ones, close-guarded in pavilions—/Which is it, of
> the favours of your Lord, that ye deny?—/Whom nei-
> ther man nor jinni will have touched before them—/
> Which is it, of the favours of your Lord, that ye deny?—/
> Reclining on green cushions and fair carpets. ("The
> Beneficent," v. 72–76)

And again in another surah:

> There wait on them immortal youths....And (there
> are) fair ones with wide, lovely eyes,/Like unto hidden
> pearls/Reward for what they used to do. (Surah LVI,
> "The Event," v. 17, 22–24)

In light of all this, the questions are very sharply posed: Are the
words and commandments and the vision of Islam anything that
people should submit to and carry out? Is the Allah of Islam any
different, in any meaningful way, from "God The Original Fascist"
of the "Judeo-Christian" religious tradition? Is it not the case that,
like the Bible and the religion(s) based on it, Islam and the Qur'an
embody and advocate horrors that humanity no longer can afford
to, or needs to, endure—and, instead, can and must move forward
to cast off and finally bury in the past?

Religious Fundamentalism, Imperialism and the "War on Terror"

Here it is important to answer the argument that is not infrequently made—including by people whose stance is to oppose religion in general—that while all religious fundamentalism is bad and harmful, there is something particularly evil and dangerous about Islamic fundamentalism. This, for example, is the position of Sam Harris, author of *The End of Faith, Religion, Terror, and the Future of Reason* and *Letter to a Christian Nation*; and it is the stand rather obviously and quite aggressively insisted on by Christopher Hitchens, whose recent book, and in a concentrated way its title, *God Is Not Great, How Religion Poisons Everything*, encapsulates the contradiction I am speaking to here. On the one hand, as expressed in the secondary part of the title, Hitchens' book is a broadside against religion in general; but the first, and main, part of the title involves—and is no doubt meant to involve—a very definite salvo directed against Islam in particular: it is a "negative echo," so to speak, of the common Islamic invocation: God is Great. It is not hard to see how this position dovetails rather neatly with that of the Bush regime and the U.S. imperialists in general, with their "war on terror" and its declared target of "Islamic extremists."

To begin with, from what has been shown so far, it should be very clear that, with regard to the scriptures and the religious tradition of Christianity there is no basis for arguing that it is, in any fundamental or essential sense, different from or better than Islam. Any attempt to take and apply this religious tradition and its scriptures—and still more to impose and enforce this—in a literalist sense, insisting that it is the inerrant word of God which must be followed to the letter, as the Christian fundamentalists do, can indeed only lead to horrors of the greatest magnitude. Once more, all this is something which humanity needs to move beyond and forever leave behind.

Perhaps in recognition of the reality that there is nothing to choose between Islamic fundamentalism and Christian fundamentalism, as such and on the level of the literal word, a common component of the position that somehow Islamic fundamentalism is worse than fundamentalist Christianity is the argument that, yes, the latter may be just as awful in its content, but particularly in a country like the U.S.—where it is increasingly hard to ignore or deny that Christian fundamentalism is a major phenomenon—the effect it can have and the danger it poses is restrained and mitigated by the fact that one of the pillars of Constitutional government in this country is the separation of church and state. Well, first of all, that separation, while real, has always been anything but absolute; and, moreover, it is a separation that is under concerted attack by the Christian fundamentalists and powerful forces in the ruling class representing, or allied with, these fundamentalists (while the sections of the ruling class that are not themselves advocates of this religious fundamentalism are at great pains to compromise and conciliate with it and to promote religion in public life—witness, as just one example, the repeated professions of profound religious faith on the part of every major candidate for the Democratic Party presidential nomination). The danger posed by theocratic Christian Fascists—and the lack of any real ruling class opposition to this—is very real. And this assault on the separation of church and state has not at all been rendered toothless, or strategically weakened, by the fact that Bush has become an extremely unpopular president.[13]

Generally speaking (although not uniformly so) it is true that in the parts of the world where Islam is the dominant religion, there

---

13. Besides what I, and our Party generally, have been doing to call attention to and build opposition to Christian Fascism, a number of others have also, from various points of view, been giving emphasis to the dangers posed by right-wing Christian fundamentalists. See, for example, *American Fascists, The Christian Right and the War on America*, by Chris Hedges; *The Baptizing of America: The Religious Right's Plans For the Rest of Us*, by Rabbi James Rudin; *The Theocons: Secular America Under Siege*, by Damon Linker; *Kingdom Coming: The Rise of Christian Nationalism*, by Michelle Goldberg; *With God On Their Side: How Christian Fundamentalists Trampled Science, Policy, and Democracy in George W. Bush's White House*, by Esther Kaplan; and *Contempt: How the Right is Wronging American Justice*, by Catherine Crier.

has not been the same phenomenon of a bourgeois-democratic transformation of society than has occurred in countries like the U.S., in which one of the main aspects of that transformation has been a (relative) separation of church and state. The prevailing, and institutionalized, doctrine and tenets of Islam reject a separation between religion, on the one hand, and politics and the law, on the other hand, as well as between religion and what is generally referred to as "civil society." But that has been true of Christianity, and the states where Christianity has been the dominant religion, for most of their history—and it is only a relatively recent period, historically speaking, that has seen a change in this, through the kind of bourgeois-democratic transformation to which I have referred. And it is important to recognize that, as a rule, it is those countries which have undergone such a bourgeois-democratic transformation, as part of the emergence and triumph of the capitalist system, which have developed into imperialist powers, and whose imperialist conquest and domination of countries throughout the Third World, including those where Islam is the dominant religion, has been a major factor in obstructing, in those countries, the kind of transformation that would involve the separation of church and state. The relative "backwardness" of those Third World countries has repeatedly been invoked as justification for colonialism and imperialist conquest. And, in turn, this imperialist conquest and exploitation, with all the consequences it has led to, including the installing and backing of corrupt and tyrannical "local governments" and the devastation of much of the way of life and the living conditions of the large majority of the population, has actually *strengthened* tendencies which identify ideas associated with "the West"—such as the progressive aspects of the Enlightenment, with its spur to critical thinking, its challenging of religious dogma, and its contribution to the separation of politics from official religion—as alien and antagonistic to the needs of the people.

This speaks to the argument that is also frequently raised that, even if it is true that the ideas embodied in Christian fundamentalism are every bit as bad as those of Islamic fundamentalism, there is a great difference in that Christian fundamentalists do not go around blowing up people and buildings and generally engaging in terrorist activity, while such activity is common among Islamic fundamentalists. Besides the fact that Christian fundamentalists have indeed engaged in acts of terror, including within the U.S.— such as the bombing of clinics where abortions are performed and the murder of doctors who perform abortions—and that Christian fundamentalist forces are being "primed" to carry out reactionary violence on a much greater scale, should that be deemed necessary by those for whom they are in fact being readied as shock and storm troops—there is the reality that, up to this point, **violence which serves ends that are passionately supported by the Christian Fascist fundamentalists has been carried out on a massive scale** *by the imperialist ruling class of the U.S., utilizing the armed forces and police of the imperialist state*—with more of that violence currently being threatened (such as an attack on Iran, in addition to the wars presently being waged in Iraq and Afghanistan). And one of the distinguishing features of those armed forces in this period is precisely that they are being increasingly influenced by, and even indoctrinated with, a fundamentalist Christian Fascist outlook, from the top levels of the military on down.[14] Therefore, up until now at least, there has not been a need or compulsion among

---

14. Regarding the influence of Christian Fascism within the U.S. military (and in particular its higher ranks), in addition to the continuing exposure and analysis of this which is found in *Revolution* newspaper (available at revcom.us), see for example *Making the Corps*, by Thomas E. Ricks, Scribner, 1997, and *Black Hawk Down, A Story of Modern War*, by Mark Bowden, Atlantic Monthly Press, 1999—both of which were written before the advent of the Bush Presidency, which has been marked by an increasing growth of and support for Christian fundamentalism within the U.S. military. Also, a very relevant phenomenon in regard to all this is the emergence of "private" military organizations, such as Blackwater, which has played a very significant, and very brutal, role in the U.S. occupation of Iraq, as well as within the U.S. itself—for example, New Orleans in the aftermath of Hurricane Katrina. And it is worth noting that Blackwater itself is characterized by a fundamentalist Christian Fascist worldview and ethos.

Christian Fascist fundamentalists to engage in terrorist activity and reactionary violence on a large scale, separately from the "official" armed forces and police of the ruling class—although, again, it has certainly been carried out by Christian Fascists on a smaller scale and there is definitely the potential for this to be carried out on a much wider scale.

All this, once again, is a reflection of the "lopsided" relations of a world which is dominated by a handful of imperialist countries, and one imperialist superpower in particular at this time, while the great majority of countries, and of people, in the world, and particularly in the Third World, endure extreme conditions of poverty, exploitation, massive dislocation and upheaval—all enforced on the basis of imperialist rule.

In today's world, a particular expression of these contradictions is the mutually reinforcing opposition between imperialist globalization and its effects, on the one hand, and Jihadist Islamic fundamentalism on the other hand. Utilizing a phrase (actually a book title) from Benjamin R. Barber, who refers to the phenomenon of "Jihad vs. McWorld," and expanding on this to include the element in which Christian Fascist fundamentalism is in fact a significant element within the prevailing program and ideology of the imperialist ruling class of the U.S., I have put it this way:

> What we see in contention here with Jihad on the one hand and McWorld/McCrusade on the other hand, are historically outmoded strata among colonized and oppressed humanity up against historically outmoded ruling strata of the imperialist system. These two reactionary poles *reinforce* each other, even while opposing each other. If you side with either of these "outmodeds," you end up strengthening both.

This speaks precisely to what is wrong with the position that somehow Islamic fundamentalism is worse than Christian fundamentalism and to how that position lends support to the "historically outmoded ruling strata of the imperialist system." And, as I have also emphasized in relation to these "two outmodeds":

> it is important to be clear about which has done and continues to do the greater damage, which has posed and does pose the greater threat to humanity. Clearly, and by far, it is "the ruling strata of the imperialist system."
>
> It is interesting, I recently heard about a comment that someone made relating to this, which I do think is correct and getting at something important. In relation to these "two historically outmodeds," they made the point: "You could say that the Islamic fundamentalist forces in the world would be largely dormant if it weren't for what the U.S. and its allies have done and are doing in the world—but you cannot say the opposite." There is profound truth captured in that statement.
>
> As a matter of general principle, and specifically sitting in this imperialist country, we have a particular responsibility to oppose U.S. imperialism, our "own" ruling class, and what it is doing in the world. But, at the same time, that doesn't make these Islamic fundamentalist forces not historically outmoded and not reactionary. It doesn't change the character of their opposition to imperialism and what it leads to and the dynamic that it's part of—the fact that these two "historically outmodeds" *do* reinforce each other, even while opposing each other. And it is very important to understand, and to struggle for others to understand, that if you end up supporting either one of these two "historically outmodeds," you contribute to strengthening both. It is crucial to break out of that dynamic—to bring forward another way. (See "Bringing Forward Another Way," at revcom.us.)

Why Is Religious Fundamentalism Growing in Today's World?

Among the most distinguishing features of today's situation are the leaps that are occurring in globalization, linked to an accelerating process of capitalist accumulation in a world dominated by the capitalist-imperialist system. This has led to significant, and often dramatic, changes in the lives of huge numbers of people, often undermining traditional relations and customs. Here I will focus on the effects of this in the Third World—the countries of Africa, Latin America, Asia and the Middle East—and the ways in which this has contributed to the current growth of religious fundamentalism there.

Throughout the Third World people are being driven in the millions each year away from the farmlands, where they have lived and tried to eke out an existence under very oppressive conditions but now can no longer do even that: they are being thrown into the urban areas, most often into the sprawling shantytowns, ring after ring of slums, that surround the core of the cities. For the first time in history, it is now the case that half of the world's population lives in urban areas, including these massive and ever-growing shantytowns.

Being uprooted from their traditional conditions—and the traditional forms in which they have been exploited and oppressed—masses of people are being hurled into a very insecure and unstable existence, unable to be integrated, in any kind of "articulated way," into the economic and social fabric and functioning of society. In many of these Third World countries, a majority of the people in the urban areas work in the *informal* economy—for example, as small-scale peddlers or traders, of various kinds, or in underground and illegal activity. To a significant degree because of this, many people are turning to religious fundamentalism to try to give them an anchor, in the midst of all this dislocation and upheaval.

An additional factor in all this is that, in the Third World, these massive and rapid changes and dislocations are occurring in the context of domination and exploitation by foreign imperialists—and this is associated with "local" ruling classes which are economically and politically dependent on and subordinate to imperialism, and are broadly seen as the corrupt agents of an alien power, who also promote the "decadent culture of the West." This, in the short run, can strengthen the hand of fundamentalist religious forces and leaders who frame opposition to the "corruption" and "Western decadence" of the local ruling classes, and the imperialists to which they are beholden, in terms of returning to, and enforcing with a vengeance, traditional relations, customs, ideas and values which themselves are rooted in the past and embody extreme forms of exploitation and oppression.

Where Islam is the dominant religion—in the Middle East but also countries such as Indonesia—this is manifested in the growth of Islamic fundamentalism. In much of Latin America, where Christianity, particularly in the form of Catholicism, has been the dominant religion, the growth of fundamentalism is marked by a situation where significant numbers of people, in particular poor people, who have come to feel that the Catholic Church has failed them, are being drawn into various forms of protestant fundamentalism, such as Pentecostalism, which combines forms of religious fanaticism with a rhetoric that claims to speak in the name of the poor and oppressed. In parts of Africa as well, particularly among masses crowded into the shantytown slums, Christian fundamentalism, including Pentecostalism, has been a growing phenomenon, at the same time as Islamic fundamentalism has been growing in other parts of Africa.[15]

---

15. For many of the same reasons that have been touched on here, religious fundamentalism has also been strengthened in recent decades among sections of the poor, oppressed and marginalized within the U.S. This includes the fact that there is a conscious strategy, on the part of powerful sections of the ruling class in the U.S., aimed at promoting religious fundamentalism among masses of people whose conditions of life cry out for radical change, and ensnaring them in the reactionary ideology and political program of which this religious

But the rise of fundamentalism is also owing to major political changes, and conscious policy and actions on the part of the imperialists in the political arena, which have had a profound impact on the situation in many countries in the Third World, including in the Middle East. As one key dimension of this, it is very important not to overlook or to underestimate the impact of the developments in China since the death of Mao Tsetung and the complete change in that country, from one that was advancing on the road of socialism to one where in fact capitalism has been restored and the orientation of promoting and supporting revolution, in China and throughout the world, has been replaced by one of seeking to establish for China a stronger position within the framework of world power politics dominated by imperialism. This has had a profound effect—negatively—in undermining, in the shorter term, the sense among many oppressed people, throughout the world, that socialist revolution offered the way out of their misery and in creating more

---

fundamentalism is a concentrated expression.

The growth of fundamentalism among significant numbers of people within the broad category of the "middle class" in the U.S. is largely due to other factors, including: a heightened sense of anxiety owing to an economy and a culture which promotes and provides seemingly ceaseless consumption on the basis of expansive credit and debt; a sense of volatility and insecurity in the economy and in society overall; a feeling of losing control even over their children in the face of technological changes (cable and satellite TV, the Internet, etc.); a sense of loss of "place" and community in a society and culture which produce atomization and promote extreme individualism. But what is very important to understand is that, especially among the "middle class" in the U.S., this phenomenon of growing fundamentalism is also a product of the parasitism of imperialism—of the fact that U.S. imperialism in particular is the world's dominant power, which lives off, and could not do without, the super-exploitation of masses of people throughout the Third World, and that people in the U.S., particularly within the "middle class," are "high up on the food chain" among the world's peoples. And, it is important to note, what is involved in the religious fundamentalism that finds adherents particularly in the suburbs and exurbs of America is a deep-seated sense of the role of America as "God's chosen nation," accompanied by an aggressive assertion of American chauvinism, as well as of traditional relations and values which embody white supremacy and male supremacy.

The phenomenon of fundamentalism, and in particular Christian Fascist fundamentalism, in the U.S. will be returned to in a later section of this book.

ground for those, and in particular religious fundamentalists, who seek to rally people behind something which in certain ways is opposing the dominant oppressive power in the world but which itself represents a reactionary worldview and program.

This phenomenon is reflected in the comments of a "terrorism expert" who observed about some people recently accused of terrorist acts in England that, a generation ago, these people would have been Maoists. Now, despite the fact that the aims and strategy, and the tactics, of genuine Maoists—people guided by communist ideology—are radically different from those of religious fundamentalists and that communists reject, in principle, terrorism as a method and approach, there is something real and important in this "terrorism expert's" comments: a generation ago many of the same youths and others who are, for the time being, drawn toward Islamic and other religious fundamentalisms, would instead have been drawn toward the radically different, revolutionary pole of communism. And this phenomenon has been further strengthened by the demise of the Soviet Union and the "socialist camp" that it headed. In reality, the Soviet Union had ceased to be socialist since the time, in the mid-1950s, when revisionists (communists in name but capitalists in fact) seized the reins of power and began running the country in accordance with capitalist principles (but in the form of *state* capitalism and with a continuing "socialist" camouflage). But by the 1990s, the leaders of the Soviet Union began to *openly* discard socialism, and then the Soviet Union itself was abolished and Russia and the other countries that had been part of the Soviet "camp" abandoned any pretense of "socialism."

All this—and, in relation to it, a relentless ideological offensive by the imperialists and their intellectual camp followers—has led to the notion, widely propagated and propagandized, of the defeat and demise of communism and, for the time being, the discrediting of communism among broad sections of people, including among those restlessly searching for a way to fight back against imperialist domination, oppression and degradation.[16]

But it is not only communism that the imperialists have worked to defeat and discredit. They have also targeted other secular forces and governments which, to one degree or another, have opposed, or objectively constituted obstacles to, the interests and aims of the imperialists, particularly in parts of the world that they have regarded as of strategic importance. For example, going back to the 1950s, the U.S. engineered a coup that overthrew the nationalist government of Mohammad Mossadegh in Iran, because that government's policies were viewed as a threat to the control of Iran's oil by the U.S. (and secondarily the British) and to U.S. domination of the region more broadly. This has had repercussions and consequences for decades since then. Among other things, it has contributed to the growth of Islamic fundamentalism and the eventual establishment of an Islamic Republic in Iran, when Islamic fundamentalists seized power in the context of a mass upheaval of the Iranian people in the late 1970s, which led to the overthrow of the highly repressive government of the Shah of Iran, who had been backed and in fact maintained in power by the U.S. since the ouster of Mossadegh.[17]

In other parts of the Middle East, and elsewhere, over the past several decades the imperialists have also consciously set out to defeat and decimate even nationalist secular opposition; and, in fact, they have at times consciously fed the growth of religious fundamentalist forces. Palestine is a sharp example of this: Islamic fundamentalist forces there were actually aided by Israel—and the U.S. imperialists,

---

16. In addition to what is contained in a number of writings and talks of mine that speak to this subject, an analysis of important aspects of the actual experience of socialism in the Soviet Union and in China—including very real mistakes and shortcomings as well as historically unprecedented achievements—and answers to the slanders and distortions of this experience, is provided by the project Set the Record Straight. This can be accessed, and more information about this provided, online at thisiscommunism.org.

17. An important source of information and analysis in regard to these events in Iran and their consequences is *All The Shah's Men: An American Coup and the Roots of Middle East Terror*, by Stephen Kinzer, John Wiley & Sons, Inc., Publisher, 2003.

for whom Israel acts as an armed garrison—in order to undermine the more secular Palestine Liberation Organization. In Afghanistan, particularly during the Soviet occupation of that country in the 1980s, the U.S. backed and provided arms to the Islamic fundamentalist Mujahadeen, because it was recognized that they would be fanatical fighters against the Soviets. Other forces, including not only more secular nationalists but Maoists, opposed the Soviet occupation and the puppet governments it installed in Afghanistan, but of course the Maoists in particular were not supported by the U.S., and in fact many of them were killed by the "Jihadist" Islamic fundamentalists that the U.S. was aiding and arming.

In Egypt, going back to the 1950s, there was the whole phenomenon of the popular nationalist leader Gamal Abdel Nasser, and of "Nasserism," a form of Arab nationalism which wasn't limited to Egypt but whose influence was very widespread after Nasser came to power in Egypt. In 1956 a crisis developed when Nasser acted to assert more control over the Suez Canal; and Israel, along with France and England—still not fully resigned to the loss of their large colonial empires—moved together in opposition to Nasser. Now, as an illustration of the complexity of things, in that "Suez crisis," the U.S. opposed Israel, France and Britain. The U.S. motive was not to support Arab nationalism or Nasser in particular, but to further supplant the European imperialists who had previously colonized these parts of the world. To look briefly at the background of this, in the aftermath of World War 1, with the defeat of the old Ottoman Empire, centered in Turkey, France and England basically divided up the Middle East between them—some of it was allotted to the French sphere of influence, as essentially French colonies, and other parts were under British control. But then after World War 2—through which Japan as well as Germany and Italy were thoroughly defeated, and countries like France and Britain were weakened, while the U.S. was greatly strengthened—the U.S. moved to create a new order in the world and, as part of that, to impose in the Third World, in place of the old-line colonialism, a new form of colonialism (neocolonialism) through which the U.S. would maintain effective control of countries and their political structures and economic life, even where they became formally independent. And, as part of this, Israel was made to find its place in relation to the now more fully realized and aggressively asserted American domination in the Middle East.

But, out of his stand in what became the "Suez crisis," and as a result of other nationalist moves, Nasser and "Nasserism" developed a widespread following in the Arab countries in particular. In this situation, the U.S., while not seeking overtly to overthrow Nasser, worked to undermine Nasserism and generally more secular forces—including, obviously, communist forces—that were opposed to, or stood in the way of, U.S. imperialism. And, especially after the 1967 war, in which Israel defeated surrounding Arab states and seized additional Palestinian territory (now generally referred to as the "occupied territories," outside of the state of Israel which itself rests on land stolen from the Palestinians), Israel has been firmly backed by and has acted as a force on behalf of U.S. imperialism.

Defeat at the hands of Israel in the 1967 war contributed significantly to a decline in the stature and influence of Nasser and Nasserism—and similar, more or less secular, leaders and trends—among the people in the Middle East; and by the time of his death in 1970, Nasser had already begun to lose a significant amount of his luster in the eyes of the Arab masses.

Here again we can see another dimension to the complexity of things. The practical defeats and failure of Nasser had the effect of undermining, in the eyes of increasing numbers of people, the legitimacy, or viability, of what Nasser represented ideologically. Now, the fact is that "Nasserism" and similar ideological and political trends, do not represent, and cannot lead to, a thorough rupture with imperialist domination and all forms of the oppression and exploitation of the people. But that is something which has to be, and is in fact, established by a scientific analysis of what is represented by such ideologies and programs and what they aim to achieve, and are actually capable of achieving; it is not proven by the fact that, in certain particular instances or even over a certain limited period of time, the leaders personifying and seeking to implement such ideologies and programs suffer setbacks and defeats. In the ways in which masses of people in the Arab countries (and more broadly) responded to such setbacks and defeats, on the part of Nasser and those more or less representing the same ideology and program, there was a definite element of pragmatism—the notion that, even in the short run, what prevails is true and good, and what suffers losses is flawed and bankrupt. And, of course, a spontaneous tendency toward such pragmatism, among the masses of people, has been reinforced by the verdicts pronounced by the imperialists and other reactionaries—not only, of course, in relation to secular forces such as Nasser but, even more so, in relation to communists and communism, which represent a much more fundamental opposition to imperialism and reaction.

In all this it is important to keep in mind that over a number of decades, and at least until very recently, the U.S. and Israel have worked to undermine secular forces among the opposition to them in the Middle East (and elsewhere) and have at least objectively favored, where they have not deliberately fostered, the growth of Islamic fundamentalist forces. During the "Cold War," this was, to a significant degree, out of a calculation that these Islamic fundamentalists would be much less likely to align themselves with the Soviet camp. And, to no small degree, this favoring of religious fundamentalists over more secular forces has been motivated by the recognition of the inherently conservative, indeed reactionary, essence of this religious fundamentalism, and the fact that, to a significant degree, it can act as a useful foil for the imperialists (and Israel) in presenting themselves as an enlightened, democratic force for progress.

Now, one of the ironies of this whole experience is that Nasser, and other Arab nationalist heads of state, viciously and murderously suppressed not only Islamic fundamentalist opposition (such as the Muslim Brotherhood in Egypt) but also communists. But, with what has taken place on the world stage, so to speak, in recent decades—including what has happened in China and the Soviet Union (as discussed above) and the widely propagated verdict that this represents the "defeat" of communism; the seizure of power in Iran by Islamic fundamentalists, with the fall of the Shah of Iran in the late 1970s; the resistance to the Soviet occupation in Afghanistan, which by the late 1980s forced a Soviet withdrawal and contributed significantly to the downfall of the Soviet Union itself; and the setbacks and defeats for more or less secular rulers like Nasser (and more recently someone like Saddam Hussein) in the Middle East and elsewhere—it has, in the short term, been the Islamic fundamentalists, much more than revolutionaries and communists, who have been able to regroup, and to experience a significant growth in influence and organized strength.

Another example of this whole trajectory, from the 1950s to the present time—which illustrates, in very stark and graphic terms, the points being made above—is the country of Indonesia. During the 1950s and 1960s Indonesia had the third largest communist party in the world (only in the Soviet Union and China were the communist parties larger). The Indonesian Communist Party had a massive following among the poor in the urban areas (whose slums, in the city of Jakarta and elsewhere, were already legendary, in the negative sense) as well as among the peasants in the countryside and sections of the intellectuals and even some more nationalist bourgeois strata. Unfortunately, the Indonesian Communist Party also had a very eclectic line—a mixed bag of communism and revisionism, of seeking revolutionary change but also trying to work through parliamentary means within the established government structures.

The government at that time was headed by the nationalist leader Achmed Sukarno. Now, an important insight into this was provided as part of a visit I made to China in the 1970s, during which some members of the Chinese Communist Party talked about the experience of the Indonesian Communist Party, and they specifically recounted: We used to struggle with comrade Aidit (the head of the Indonesian Communist Party during the period of Sukarno's government); we warned him about what could happen as a result of trying to have one foot in communism and revolution and one foot in reformism and revisionism. But the Indonesian Communist Party persisted on the same path, with its eclectic approach; and in 1965 the U.S., through the CIA, working with the Indonesian military and a leading general, Suharto, carried out a bloody coup, in which hundreds of thousands of Indonesian communists, and others, were massacred, the Communist Party of Indonesia was thoroughly decimated, and at the same time Sukarno was ousted as the head of government and replaced by Suharto.

In the course of this coup, the rivers around Jakarta became clogged with the bodies of the victims: the reactionaries would kill people, alleged or actual communists, and throw their bodies, in massive numbers, into the rivers. And, in a phenomenon that is all too familiar, once this coup—which the CIA led, organized and engineered—was unleashed and carried out, all kinds of people who were involved in personal or family disputes and feuds would start accusing other people of being communists and turning them into the authorities, with the result that a lot of people who weren't even communists got slaughtered, along with many who were. Once the imperialists and reactionaries unleashed this blood-letting, this encouraged and gave impetus to, and swept many people up in, a kind of bloodlust of revenge. The CIA openly brags about how they not only organized and orchestrated this coup but also specifically targeted several thousand of the leading communists and got rid of them directly, within this larger massacre of hundreds of thousands.

The fundamental problem with the strategy of the Indonesian Communist Party was that the nature of the state—and in particular the military—had not changed: the parliament was to a large degree made up of nationalists and communists, but the *state* was still in the hands of the reactionary classes; and because their control of the state had never been broken, and the old state apparatus in which they maintained control was never shattered and dismantled,

Suharto and other reactionary forces were able, working together with and under the direction of the CIA, to pull off this bloody coup, with its terrible consequences.

In this regard, another anecdote that was recounted by members of the Chinese Communist Party is very telling and poignant. They told a story about how Sukarno had a scepter that he used to carry around, and the Chinese officials who met with him asked him, "What is this scepter you carry around?" And Sukarno replied: "This scepter represents state power." Well, the Chinese comrades telling this story summed up, after the coup "Sukarno still had the scepter, they let him keep that, but he didn't have any state power."

The Indonesian Communist Party was all but totally wiped out, physically—its membership was virtually exterminated, with only a few remnants of it here and there—a devastating blow from which it has never recovered. And the decimation was not only in literal and physical terms but also was expressed in ideological and political defeat, disorientation and demoralization. Over the decades since then, what has happened in Indonesia? One of the most striking developments is the tremendous growth of Islamic fundamentalism in Indonesia. The communist alternative was wiped out. In its place—in part being consciously fostered by the imperialists and other reactionary forces, but partly growing on its own momentum in the context where a powerful secular and, at least in name, communist opposition had been destroyed—Islamic fundamentalism filled the vacuum that had been left by the lack of a real alternative to the highly oppressive rule of Suharto and his cronies that was installed and kept in power for decades by the U.S.[18]

All this—what has taken place in Indonesia, as well as in Egypt, Palestine and other parts of the Middle East—is a political dimension which has been combined with the economic and social factors

---

18. In addition to brutally oppressing the people of Indonesia itself, the regime of Suharto carried out a genocidal reign of terror in East Timor, massacring a huge section of the population there—and in this, too, it was backed and assisted by U.S. imperialism, through successive Administrations, including that of Bill Clinton.

mentioned above—the upheaval and volatility and rapid change imposed from the top and seemingly coming from unknown and/or alien and foreign sources and powers—to undermine and weaken secular, including genuinely revolutionary and communist, forces and to strengthen Islamic fundamentalism (in a way similar to how Christian fundamentalism has been gaining strength in Latin America and parts of Africa).

This is obviously a tremendously significant phenomenon. It is a major part of the objective reality that people throughout the world who are seeking to bring about change in a progressive direction—and still more those who are striving to achieve truly radical change guided by a revolutionary and communist outlook—have to confront and transform. And in order to do that, it is necessary, first of all, to seriously engage and understand this reality, rather than remaining dangerously ignorant of it, or adopting an orientation of stubbornly ignoring it. It is necessary, and indeed crucial, to dig down beneath the surface of this phenomenon and its various manifestations, to grasp more deeply what are the underlying and driving dynamics in all this—what are the fundamental contradictions and what are the particular expressions of fundamental and essential contradictions, on a world scale and within particular countries and regions in the world—that this religious fundamentalism is the expression of, and how, on the basis of that deeper understanding, a movement can be developed to win masses of people away from this and to something which can actually bring about a radically different and much better world.

Rejecting the "Smug Arrogance of the Enlightened"

There is a definite tendency among those who are "people of the Enlightenment," shall we say—including, it must be said, some communists—to fall into what amounts to a smugly arrogant attitude toward religious fundamentalism and religion in general. Because it seems so absurd, and difficult to comprehend, that people living in the 21st century can actually cling to religion and in fact adhere, in a fanatical and absolutist way, to dogmas and notions that are clearly without any foundation in reality, it is easy to dismiss this whole phenomenon and fail to recognize, or to correctly approach, the fact that this is indeed taken very seriously by masses of people. And this includes more than a few people among the lower, deeper sections of the proletariat and other oppressed people who need to be at the very base and bedrock of—and be a driving force within—the revolution that can actually lead to emancipation.

It is a form of contempt for the masses to fail to take seriously the deep belief that many of them have in religion, including religious fundamentalism of one kind or another, *just as* tailing after the fact that many believe in these things and refusing to struggle with them to give this up *is also in reality an expression of contempt for them*. The hold of religion on masses of people, including among the most oppressed, is a major shackle on them, and a major obstacle to mobilizing them to fight for their own emancipation and to be emancipators of all humanity—and it must be approached, and struggled against, with that understanding, even as, at any given time, it is necessary, possible, and crucial, in the fight against injustice and oppression, to unite as broadly as possible with people who continue to hold religious beliefs.

The Growth of Religion and Religious Fundamentalism: A Peculiar Expression of a Fundamental Contradiction

Another strange, or peculiar, expression of contradictions in the world today is that, on the one hand, there is all this highly developed technology and sophisticated technique in fields such as medicine and other spheres, including information technology (and, even taking account that large sections of the population in many parts of the world, and significant numbers even within the "technologically advanced" countries, still do not have access to this advanced technology, growing numbers of people actually do have access to the Internet and to the extensive amounts of information available through the Internet, and in other ways) and yet, at the same time, there is the tremendous growth of, let's call it what it is: *organized ignorance*, in the form of religion and religious fundamentalism in particular. This appears as not only a glaring but a strange contradiction: so much technology and knowledge on the one hand, and yet on the other hand so much widespread ignorance and belief in, and retreat into, obscurantist superstition.

Well, along with analyzing this in terms of the economic, social and political factors that have given rise to this (to which I have spoken above) another, and even more basic, way of understanding this is that it is ***an extremely acute expression in today's world of the fundamental contradiction of capitalism***: **the contradiction between highly socialized production and private (capitalist) appropriation of what is produced.**

Where does all this technology come from? On what basis has it been produced? And speaking specifically of the dissemination of information, and the basis for people to acquire knowledge—what is that founded on? All the technology that exists—and, for that matter, the wealth that has been created—has been produced in socialized forms by millions and millions of people through an international network of production and exchange; but all this takes place under the command of a relative handful of capitalists, who appropriate the wealth produced—and appropriate the knowledge produced as well—and bend it to their purposes.

What is this an illustration of? It is, for one thing, a refutation of the "theory of the productive forces," which argues that the more technology you have, the more enlightenment there will be, more or less directly in relation to that technology—and which, in its "Marxist" expression, argues that the greater the development of technology, the closer things will be to socialism or to communism. Well, look around the world. Why is this *not* the case? Because of a very fundamental fact: All this technology, all the forces of production, "go through," and have to "go through," certain definite *production relations*—they can be developed and utilized only by being incorporated into what the prevailing ensemble of production relations is at any given time. And, in turn, there are certain class and social relations that are themselves an expression of (or are in any case in general correspondence with) the prevailing production relations; and there is a superstructure of politics, ideology and culture whose essential character reflects and reinforces all those relations. So, it is not a matter of productive forces—including all the technology and knowledge—just existing in a social vacuum and being distributed and utilized in a way that is divorced from the production relations through which it is developed and employed (and the corresponding class and social relations and superstructure). This takes place, and can only take place, through one or another set of production, social and class relations, with the corresponding customs, cultures, ways of thinking, political institutions, and so on.

In the world today, dominated as it is by the capitalist-imperialist system, this technology and knowledge is "going through" the existing capitalist and imperialist relations and superstructure, and one of the main manifestations of this is the extremely grotesque disparity between what is appropriated by a tiny handful—and a lesser amount that is meted out to broader strata in some of the imperialist countries, in order to stabilize those countries and to mollify and pacify sections of the population who are not part of the ruling class there—while amongst the great majority of humanity there is unbelievable poverty and suffering and ignorance. And, along with this profound disparity, we are witnessing this peculiar contradiction between so much technology and so much knowledge, on the one hand, and yet such widespread belief in, and retreat into, obscurantist superstition, particularly in the form of religious fundamentalism—all of which is in fact an expression of the fundamental contradiction of capitalism.

This is an extremely important point to understand. If, instead of this understanding, one were to proceed with a more linear approach and method, it would be easy to fall into saying: "I don't get it, there is all this technology, all this knowledge, why are so many people so ignorant and so mired in superstition?" Once again, the answer—and it is an answer that touches on the most fundamental of relations in the world—is that it is because of the prevailing production, social and class relations, the political institutions, structures, and processes, and the rest of the superstructure—the prevailing culture, the ways of thinking, the customs, habits, and so on, which correspond to and reinforce the system of capitalist accumulation, as this finds expression in the era where capitalism has developed into a worldwide system of exploitation and oppression.

This is another important perspective from which to understand the phenomenon of religious fundamentalism. The more this disparity grows, the more there is a breeding ground for religious fundamentalism and related tendencies. At the same time, and in acute contradiction to this, there is also a potentially more powerful basis for revolutionary transformation. All of the profound disparities in the world—not only in terms of conditions of life but also with regard to access to knowledge—can be overcome only through the communist revolution, whose aim is to wrest control of society out the hands of the imperialists and other exploiters and to advance, through the increasingly conscious initiative of growing numbers of people, to achieve (in the formulation of Marx) the elimination of all class distinctions, all the production relations on which these class distinctions rest, all the social relations that correspond to those production relations, and the revolutionization of all the ideas that correspond to those social relations—in order to bring about, ultimately and fundamentally on a world scale, a society of freely associating human beings, who consciously and voluntarily cooperate for the common good, while also giving increasing scope to the initiative and creativity of the members of society as a whole.

Part Three:

RELIGION—
A HEAVY, HEAVY CHAIN

Religion, Patriarchy, Male Supremacy and Sexual Repression

One of the most important aspects of the role of religion as a shackle on humanity—and here again I am examining particularly the role of the world's three major monotheistic religions: Judaism, Christianity, and Islam—is the way in which this represents a concentrated expression, and reinforcement, of patriarchy and male supremacy. To put it simply, all of these religions are patriarchal religions. Each one of them pictures a god that is a powerful male authority figure: The Father, the Lord, Señor—in whatever language this is expressed. These are religions in which patriarchal relations, in the real world, are projected into an other-worldly realm—to then be, in turn, reimposed on *this* world—and in which patriarchy, and the reinforcement of patriarchy, is an integral and essential part of the belief system and of the behavior that this belief system is intended to enforce, as part of the broader network of oppressive and exploitative relations that characterize the societies in which these religions arose and the succeeding societies in which these religions have been perpetuated by the ruling classes.

The ways in which these religions promote a strong father figure, and absolute male authority, can be seen not only in how they portray the god which people are commanded to worship and obey—and this, of course, is all the more the case in the fundamentalist versions of these religions—but is found in the heart of the scriptures of all these religions. Christianity once again provides a clear illustration of this.

In a way you could say that the essential message of the Christian

religion is put forward in John 3:16. Now, some of you may be familiar with this—those of you who know the Bible, and/or others of you
who just watch sporting events, especially football games, where
often, when they kick the extra point after a touchdown, there is
some fool sitting behind the goalpost with a crazy wig on his head,
holding up a sign saying "John 3:16." [Laughter]

So let's talk about John 3:16: "For God so loved the world that
he gave his only Son, so that everyone who believes in him may not
perish but may have eternal life" (or in the classical English rendition:
"For God so loved the world, that he gave his only begotten son, so
that whosoever believeth in him shall not perish but shall have eternal
life"). Let's dig more deeply into this—what it is actually putting forward and what it is actually promoting. Let's go back to Genesis: once
again, the myth of the fall of mankind, the treacherous role of woman
in this, and the view of the nature and the fate of humanity that is put
forward in Genesis (see in particular chapters 2 and 3 of Genesis). It
would not have been necessary, according to the Bible, for God to
make this great sacrifice (of giving his "only begotten son") if it weren't
for the fact that human beings messed up in the Garden of Eden, and
in particular that Eve seduced man—Adam—into doing the wrong
thing and going against God's will. So, built into, or underlying, this
very verse (John 3:16) that tells us how loving God is to humanity, is
the notion that humanity is all screwed up—that it is the very nature
of humanity to do things wrong and to commit sin—that mankind
has a "fallen" nature, which, on its own, humanity can never change
or get away from. That's the first point to keep in mind here.

But, then, there is a second thing—think about it: "For God so
loved the world that he gave his only begotten Son." Why a *son*? And
anyway, the idea is absurd. [Laughter] If you believe in God, God
could have as many sons as he wanted. [Laughter] So what's the
point of "*only begotten* Son?" Well, for *human beings* who live in a
patriarchal society, giving up your son is one of the greatest sacrifices you can make, because in such a male-dominated society men
count for more than women. So, who cares about daughters? You

can give them up to be raped—and that's there in the Bible, too, for example in the story of how Lot offered up his daughters in this way (and remember that Lot is looked upon so favorably by God that Lot is spared when God destroys Sodom—see Genesis, chapter 19). But a *son*, that's a very different matter.

To bring out the point even more sharply, try thinking of the Bible saying: "For God so loved the world, that he gave up his only begotten daughter." It doesn't ring true, does it? [Laughter] It doesn't fit with the Bible—because the Bible was written by human beings living in a patriarchal society who are reflecting that society in what they write and projecting an imaginary god into the heavens who makes this great sacrifice of giving up his "only begotten son," which is the greatest sacrifice that these human beings can think of.

This takes us back to the role of women and the fall of man. This is not only a pivotal and seminal story in the Bible's history of mankind and mankind's relation with God, but it is picked up and carried forward by Paul in the New Testament. For example, in his first letter to Timothy, Paul repeats the notion of a curse on women, because of what Eve did in the Garden of Eden; but, says Paul, women can be saved by bearing children for their husbands and generally by having the "modest" qualities appropriate to women, including that they are obedient to their husbands and subordinate to men in general:

> Let a woman learn in silence with full submission. I permit no woman to teach or to have authority over a man; she is to keep silent. For Adam was formed first, then Eve; and Adam was not deceived, but the woman was deceived and became a transgressor. Yet she will be saved through childbearing, provided they continue in faith and love and holiness, with modesty. (1 Timothy 2:11–15)

So, right there, we see two things that are essential components of Christianity and the "Judeo-Christian tradition": women are to be submissive in relation to men, and women's essential role is to bear children. Think of the terrible influence of that, and all the oppression and pain it has contributed to, through the centuries and down to today.

Now let's return to the origin myth regarding Jesus and a point that was spoken to earlier in connection with this. When you read the Bible and you get to the first part of the New Testament, in Matthew, it starts off with something very few people can follow: the "begats." [Laughter] And so-and-so begat so-and-so, who begat so-and-so, who begat so-and-so...down through 14 generations; and then so-and-so begat so-and-so, who begat so-and-so, who begat so-and-so...down through another 14 generations; this passes through David and then on, through more generations, down to Joseph, Jesus's father. Now, if you actually look at history and compare the historical record with what is said here in the Bible, there are discrepancies: the schema that involves repeated reference to 14 generations doesn't correspond to what you can actually learn from history about the succession of patriarchs that is being referred to here.

But these "begats" are, once again, in the service of reinforcing male domination and patriarchy. The whole thing in Matthew is an attempt to trace Jesus's roots from Abraham—a patriarch of the ancient Jewish people, according to the Bible—through King David to Joseph, the father of Jesus, even though Joseph's "seed" had absolutely nothing to do with it. Think about this: A crucial part of the Christian mythology is that Jesus was born—of what? A virgin, Mary. So what the hell did Joseph have to do with it? [Laughter] The point is that *this is a history of patriarchs*—an attempt to put Jesus squarely within the tradition of patriarchs and patriarchal kings and rulers of the Jewish people in ancient times.[19]

Even though Mary is Jesus's blessed mother, her genealogy does not count. Why? Because she's a woman. Her role is to be the loving, long-suffering mother of Jesus (and, especially in the Roman Catholic version of Christianity, to be a kind of "intercessor" for people in

---

19. It is noteworthy that in Islam, Abraham is also greatly revered as a patriarch.

their supplications to God). But when it comes to tracing the lineage from the ancient patriarchs of the Jewish people down to Jesus, and to prove his right to be the Messiah, Mary doesn't figure into it at all. Joseph does figure in, even though, according to the Bible, he had no part, biologically, in all this.[20]

For many people who have lived in a society in which patriarchy and male domination and the consequent oppression of women is an integral and indispensable part—a part without which the society in that form could not exist—one of the attractions of these religions (Islam, Christianity, and Judaism) and of the fundamentalist versions of these religions in particular, in this period, is as *a forceful reassertion of that patriarchy*. Why is there a felt need for this? Because patriarchy is being undermined in various ways. Not eliminated. Not transformed in a qualitative sense. But being undermined in various ways by the very functioning of the society. Even in countries where there are still very open and powerful patriarchal traditions,

---

20. As pointed out above, in Luke, chapter 3, verses 23 to 38, there is a *different* version of this genealogy: the lineage, or family line, of Jesus and his ancestors is different than what is presented in Matthew, chapter 1, verses 1 through 17. In *The Jesus Dynasty*, James D. Tabor argues that in Luke the lineage of Jesus is, after a certain point, actually traced through Mary. But, frankly, Tabor's argument here seems somewhat tortured and contrived. Pivotal in his reasoning is that Luke says that Jesus had a grandfather named Heli; and, continues Tabor's argument, Matthew tells us that the father of Joseph—and the grandfather of Jesus on Joseph's side—was named Jacob; therefore, Tabor concludes, Heli must have been the father of *Mary*. But, first of all, there are many discrepancies, not just this one, between how Matthew presents the genealogy of Jesus and how this is done in Luke. Thus, when Tabor asks, "So who was Heli?" and then immediately answers, "The most obvious solution is that he was Mary's father," he is drawing a conclusion that is not at all obvious and making a leap that is not justified. (See *The Jesus Dynasty*, Chapter 2, "A Son of David?"—especially p. 52; and compare Matthew 1:1–17 with Luke 3:23–38.) Further, Tabor acknowledges that Mary is not mentioned in Luke's account of Jesus's genealogy because "Luke abides by convention and includes only males in his list." (p. 52) Thus, even if one were to allow for Tabor's conclusions regarding the role of Mary in Luke's account—which, again, is more than a little problematical—it is clear that in Luke, as much as in Matthew, it is a *patriarchal* version of that genealogy that comes through.

customs and conventions, the uprooting of people, and the changes that accompany this, tend to undermine aspects of the patriarchy. People are leaving—or being forced out of—the countryside in huge numbers and landing in the urban areas, often in the shantytown slums; families are moving from Pakistan to London, from Egypt or Turkey to Germany, from Algeria to France—and being confronted by a very different culture. The point is not to apologize for or to extol bourgeois society and *its* forms of the oppression of women; but, in some significant aspects, this is very different in these "modern" imperialist countries than it is in the countries where feudal relations and traditions, or remnants of them, continue to exert a significant influence, and where, along with that, patriarchal domination is more overt and more entrenched in a traditional form. That's important to emphasize: *in a traditional form.* So, in these new circumstances, fathers who have had absolute authority within the family, suddenly find that their daughters are harder to control. And supervising the behavior of daughters is one of the main roles of the father in these patriarchal family relations (although the father is generally assisted in this by his wife, or often his mother—the mother-in-law of his wife—will play a significant role as an enforcer of this).[21]

In some ways this is similar to what happens when people in rural areas in the imperialist countries get MTV and the Internet. All of a sudden the kids don't want to act any more in the ways that have been traditionally expected of them—or at least some of them don't—and this gives rise to a lot of clashes within the family, even in an "advanced modern country." Well, imagine people moving from Algeria to France—it's a whole different culture and very different forms of oppressive social relations. It is not that in these imperialist countries the social relations are not oppressive, but in significant ways they are in a very different form, one which envisions and embodies a different role for women and a different way in which they are oppressed and degraded.

---

21. Later in this discussion, I will return to the question of how this is codified in religious scriptures.

All this is very complex because, to a significant degree, the ways in which women are oppressed in a country like France, or the U.S., appears, especially to people coming from a traditionalist framework, to involve "an excess of freedom." Women are not regulated in all the same ways and not required to wear traditional clothing in the same way, nor to act in the same "modest" manner. In reality, this "freedom" for women is part of a different web of oppressive relations, which often assumes extreme expression in its own way. There is pornography, soft or hard core, everywhere you turn. Advertising, to a very great extent, is based on the use of the female body to sell commodities—and the female body itself is, in very extensive and very degrading ways, treated as a commodity.

So the opposite poles once again tend to reinforce each other. Even people who aren't steeped in traditional religious convention look at a lot of this exploitative decadence and justifiably say: "This is terrible. I don't want my kids exposed to this." And, especially if you are coming from a traditional patriarchal framework, you not only recoil at all this, you are inclined to all the more forcefully assert patriarchal authority.

Even if people in Third World countries don't leave their homelands altogether and emigrate to an imperialist country—even when, instead, they migrate to the urban areas within their own country—these urban areas in Third World countries are very different, in significant ways, from the countryside. The way of life in the shantytowns is very different, including in its volatility, from what the situation was in the rural villages. In these circumstances there can be a powerful attraction to a form of religion which forcefully asserts traditional patriarchal authority and reinforces that patriarchal authority with a seeming supernatural power behind it.

And then, more generally, in a world that appears to be full of uncertainty and the unexpected, and seems threatening in many ways—economically, but not just economically (all of a sudden, in the U.S., you have September 11th, for example)—there is a strong tendency for people, proceeding from within an established patriarchal framework to begin with, to feel the inclination to gravitate to a powerful father figure who will protect them. This is something that, in the U.S., George W. Bush and those around him consciously play on: "I'm a war time president," Bush continually repeats, with the implication: "I'm the big daddy, the big strong father figure who can keep you safe—if you just get in line with me." And, at the same time, a religious fundamentalist outlook is promoted to reinforce this.

So that is another way in which a form of patriarchy is asserted, amidst uncertainty, volatility and the feeling that there are constant, even if often vague, dangers. This feeling is not simply spontaneous—it is promoted and reinforced every time you turn around. If you turn on the news, anywhere in the U.S., what do you see? Crime, crime, crime. From this you would think that you are about to be jumped on by somebody every time you go out your front door—even though the probability of actually encountering crime, directly and personally, is very minimal if you are in the middle strata in a country like the U.S. But the constant barrage of "news" about crime, reinforced by "entertainment" which very extensively revolves around this same theme, adds to this general feeling of alarm. And, in a society which is steeped in a tradition, thousands of years old, of powerful patriarchal authority, what is a way to feel that you can get some security? Relying, once again, on a big powerful father figure, wielding big weapons, who will protect you—who is gonna get those "bad guys" out there before they can get you.

But just presenting such a powerful father figure in a *human* form is not enough for many people. So there is an aggressive assertion of an even more extreme and absolutist form of this father figure, in the image of an all-knowing, all-seeing, all-powerful God—for whom, lo and behold, the powerful head of state is a representative and for whom he speaks and acts.

Another major dimension of the way in which patriarchy is being threatened, and in which people feel it being threatened, is the whole gay question. In the U.S. right now this is rather acutely posed. It is not that something like gay marriage in itself is going to undermine and destroy patriarchy. So long as things remain within the confines of a system built on exploitation and oppression, patriarchal relations will assert themselves within gay marriage as well—and this is already the case in many gay relationships, even where they do not have the formal sanction of official marriage. But, at this juncture, the assertion of the right to marriage for gays and lesbians does, in some significant ways, pose a serious challenge to traditional patriarchy.

While Christian fundamentalists, from the U.S. President on down, repeatedly insist the Bible ordains that marriage must be only between a man and a woman, it is not at all the case that the Bible consistently presents things this way. In fact, Joseph Smith, the founder of Mormonism, and his successor Brigham Young, as well as Mormon fundamentalists today, have plenty of evidence for their claim that polygamy (a marriage in which one person has multiple spouses) and more specifically polygyny (where a man has more than one wife) is justified in many places in the Bible.

If you look at First and Second Chronicles, which discuss all the supposed great kings (as well as the bad kings) of Israel and Judah, you will see that the greatest king of all, David, had more than one wife, and besides that he had hundreds of concubines. Now, let's be clear: David is *not* condemned for this in the Bible. In fact, all this is presented as part of his majesty and glorious nature that is upheld and extolled in the Bible. And looking once more at the "begats" that I spoke of earlier (which in Matthew trace the genealogy of Jesus), these "begats" go from Abraham to David and from David down to Jesus—and once again the point of all these "begats" is to establish that the line of Jesus descends from David, which, according to the ancient Jewish scriptures (the Old Testament of the Christian Bible), was a necessary requirement for the Messiah. So David is hardly a negative figure in the Bible—on the contrary, he is highly exalted. Solomon, David's son and also an exalted figure in the Bible, had hundreds of wives and concubines as well. Abraham, too, had more than one wife—and, when Abraham's wife was apparently barren, he "went in to" his wife's servant in order to have a child. As we see in Genesis 29 and 30, another prominent Biblical patriarch, Jacob, also "went in to" his wife's servant in similar circumstances; and Jacob had more than one wife at the same time. In Deuteronomy 21, along with setting forth how, in war, if "you see among the captives a beautiful woman whom you desire and want to marry," you may do so, there is a whole discussion of what should happen "If a man has two wives, one of them loved and the other disliked, and if both the loved and the disliked have borne him sons." (See Deuteronomy 21:11–15 and 16–17.)

But, as we have seen, the Christian Fascist fundamentalists do not really strictly adhere to Biblical literalism—they, too, practice "salad bar Christianity" when it serves their purposes. And they misrepresent what is said in the Bible when that serves their purposes. Now, in their opposition to gay marriage and the ways in which they see it as a threat to patriarchy, they have fashioned this saying: "God created Adam and Eve, not Adam and Steve." Well, the fact is that God didn't create either Adam and Steve *or* Adam and Eve. [Laughter] Human beings came into existence as part of the overall process of natural evolution, stretching back over billions of years in the history of life on the planet earth. And in the history of human beings, they have had different kinds of societies, and many different sexual relations and practices, both exploitative and non-exploitative, depending ultimately on the basic character of the society. A study of human society throughout history reveals a very great diversity of sexual relations, both heterosexual and same-sex. In the ancient Greek society of Plato and Aristotle, which was definitely patriarchal, a man—a real "man's man"—had sexual relations with other men and boys all the time. My point is not to promote the notion of a "man's man," or any kind of "manhood," in the sense of male supremacy and domination. What we need is for people—female as well as male—to assert and give expression to their humanity, and moreover to become *emancipators of humanity*, struggling to finally abolish all relations of domination, oppression and exploitation. My point is precisely to emphasize that there is nothing about heterosexual or about same-sex relations, which, in and of itself, is either positive or negative, or in some way more or less "natural." And neither heterosexual nor same-sex relations, as such, constitute either an embodiment of, or a negation of, patriarchy. Rather, the essential question is what is the *content* of any intimate and sexual relation: does it embody and promote affection, mutual respect and equality between the partners—and contribute to the realization of equality between men and women—or does it constitute and further contribute to the degradation of people and the oppression of women in particular? But in a society in which patriarchy has been an essential and defining element, even breaking out of the more *traditional forms* of patriarchy—including by raising the demand for formal equality for same-sex relations—at particular junctures, such as the present one, can pose a serious challenge to traditional, oppressive relations, even while many of the individuals involved are simply trying to form traditional marriages. That's one of the ironies and complexities of this situation.

And the fact is that opposition to gay marriage is not simply an election gimmick to get more Republicans elected. Yes, some Republican Party functionaries have used this issue in that way. But what is involved is much more profound than that and has much bigger implications. The real objective of the Christian Fascists around the issue of gay marriage, and their condemnation of homosexuality in general, is to onforce "traditional morality" and all the relations of oppression embodied in and enforced by that traditional morality—including patriarchy and the oppression of women, the subordinate position of women in society, and their essential role, as the Bible presents it, as breeders of children within the confines of male-dominated marriage relations, sanctioned not only by the church, but also by the state.

This is all very deeply rooted, but in a real sense today it is being challenged at every turn. Not yet in a way that is going to lead to its abolition, but in a way that does undermine some of the forms in which it has traditionally existed. And the Christian Fascist offensive around this is a forceful and absolutist reassertion of these oppressive relations.

This has also found sharp expression in the contention around the raising of children: what should be the relationship in the family between children and parents? In this regard as well, there is a forceful reassertion of patriarchy. Among the religious fundamentalists in the U.S., there is a definite current that insists that one of the main reasons for (and one of main manifestations of) the fact that, in their view, the country is going to hell is that, for several decades now, parents have not been able to beat their children so freely. After all, what does the Bible advocate? There is that familiar saying from the Bible, "Spare the rod and spoil the child" (or, as it actually says in Proverbs 23:13–14: "Do not withhold discipline from your children; if you beat them with the rod, they will not die. If you beat them with the rod, you will save their lives from Sheol"—or, in the more classical English version: "Withhold not correction from the child, for if thou beatest him with the rod he shall not die. Thou shalt beat him with the rod and shalt deliver his soul from hell.") This is what a lot of these Christian fundamentalist leaders are actively promoting.

Here I have to say that, as much as I love Richard Pryor, I have never enjoyed his routines that seemed, in the final analysis, to uphold the beating of children to keep them in line. This was treated in a somewhat contradictory manner in the routines that he did where this was the subject, but it does seem that there was always a certain element of drawing the lesson that, "after all, when my grandmother beat me with a switch, this did have the effect of keeping me from getting completely out of line." In any case, sentiments like this are echoed even among people who are in many ways advanced politically and revolutionary-minded; even among such people, one will sometimes hear the complaint: "Things are all messed up now because you can't beat your kids anymore, can't get out that switch like grandma did and beat the kids back into line, so they do right." And it should be said that even though, as in the case of Richard Pryor, it sometimes might have been grandma who was wielding the switch, this was still done as part of an overall assertion of relations marked by patriarchal domination—relations in which a strong father figure would be the ultimate authority in disciplining the children and, with regard to daughters in particular, would ensure that they remained virgins so that their value as property, to be realized at the time of marriage, would not be diminished or spoiled. This is thoroughly embedded in the Christian tradition, every bit as much as the Islamic traditions which lead to the horror of "honor killings," where family members, and brothers in particular, are sent out to kill their sisters if it becomes known that they are no longer virgins before marriage—even if this occurs as a result of rape. While not, in itself, as extreme an expression of this, beating children ("sparing not the rod in order not to spoil the child") is part of the same overall package of oppressive patriarchal relations.

Let us be clear: female children, and children in general, should not be seen and treated as the property of their parents, and their father in particular. That is not the world we are aiming for, not a world worth living in. This is the way it has been for thousands of years, and this has been embodied in and promoted by religious scripture and tradition, but this is not how we want the world to be, and not how it needs to be. Yes, children need discipline. But they don't need to be beaten with a switch or a rod in order to be disciplined, and to have a sense of purpose. They need to be led—inspired, and yes, at times, taken firmly in hand—as part of an overall vision and goal of bringing into being a radically different and much better world. And, as they become older and more conscious of this objective, and capable of acting consciously to contribute to it, they can increasingly become a part of that process. But even before they are capable of being consciously a part of this, the principles that apply to bringing such a world into being should apply, in a fundamental sense, in relating to children—your own and others. Children are conscious human beings, even as their consciousness is in a process of development. They can be and need to be reasoned with—and yes, at times, they have to be told, "that's the way it is, and you just have to do it this way, because the ability to understand this, and why it has to be this way, is beyond you right now."

Now, at the same time, it is not hard to see why many people gravitate toward "spare the rod, spoil the child"—toward the logic that if you don't beat kids to keep them in line, they will turn out badly—because there are all kinds of things pulling kids in terrible directions. And, especially among sections of "the middle class," particularly in a country like the U.S., there is a whole approach of indulgence toward children—which may have less selfish motivations in some cases but in fact is often bound up with, and in the final analysis is another expression of, treating children as a commodity, who have to be pampered and indulged as part of giving them every opportunity and advantage in the race to achieve a privileged position in society, in the context of the overall parasitism that is part of living in a powerful imperialist country. Here I am talking about phenomena such as parents who start playing symphonies for a new-born child (or even for a fetus during pregnancy), especially if this is done with the idea that in this way the child, from an early age, will have a better chance to develop as a "talent," or a "genius"—will be able to go to the best music academy or the most prestigious university, and be launched into a lucrative career. Often permissiveness on the part of parents is bound up with—and seeks to be in the service of—that.[22]

Somewhat as a reaction to this kind of permissiveness—but more in response to the kind of madness that too many of the youth

---

22. While I disagree with him on a number of things these days, I do have a certain point of unity with George Carlin when he talks about excessive permissiveness toward children. He does a routine, which begins with this back-and-forth (all voiced by Carlin himself): "I want to say something about the way people are raising their kids." "He's not going to say something bad about *kids*, is he?" "*Yes*, he is." Now, some of this is tied up with a sort of narrow, "working class revengism" toward yuppies, which Carlin frequently gives voice to. But there are points that he is making that are valid about excessive permissiveness—which, again, is often wrapped up with views of commodity exchange as applied to relations involving children and their parents.

in the inner cities get caught up in—a lot of people in the oppressed communities look around and see the kids acting the fool and doing all kinds of crazy things, and they are drawn to the conclusion that something strong has got to be done to get these kids to act right. This becomes another factor reinforcing the role of the church and religion. What are two prominent alternatives that are available to the most oppressed in the U.S. right now? Well, there are the gangs on the one hand, with all the madness and mayhem that this involves; or the church, on the other hand, with its assertion of traditional, oppressive and, yes, patriarchal values, relations, codes and customs. For the youth in particular: when you get tired of the gangs, then go to the church; if you get sick of the church, then go back to the gangs. Neither of these offers a way forward for the masses of people, a way out of the oppressive conditions that are driving many to a lot of madness in the first place.

Here again, is another sharp manifestation of the need to "break through the middle." Just as, on another level, Jihad and McWorld/ McCrusade cannot be allowed to stand as the only two alternatives, here too there is an urgent need to bring forward a radically different alternative, on the basis of the communist world outlook and the communist program and objectives. It is necessary to be boldly saying to people: "We don't need the church, we don't need the switch, we don't need the rod and, no, we don't need the gangs and the drugs—**we need revolution.**"

Yes, this is a hard road. But what are people dying and killing each other over now? What is that serving? What is that reinforcing? Where is that leading people? What good is that doing for anyone—except those who rule over the masses of people and who couldn't be happier than to see them killing each other over nothing worthwhile? And what good does it do for the masses of people to go down on their knees to some oppressive and patriarchal authority, which is invested with the aura and awe of supposed supernatural power, and which acts as a shackle helping to reinforce conditions of enslavement and powerlessness?

The Bible Belt Is the *Lynching* Belt: Slavery, White Supremacy and Religion in America

For a number of years now, I have been thinking about—and pondering the implications of—the fact that what's called the "Bible Belt" in the U.S. is also the *Lynching* Belt. Those parts of the country where fundamentalist religion has been historically and most powerfully rooted, and is so even today, are also the places where historically the most brutal oppression has been carried out and has been justified, over and over again, in the name of Christianity. In America, with its whole history of oppression of Black people— beginning with slavery and continuing in various forms down to the present—upholding tradition and traditional morality, and insisting on unthinking obedience to authority, is bound to go hand in hand with white supremacy, as well as male supremacy.

The questions arise in this connection: Is this just an accidental association—between the Bible Belt and the Lynching Belt—or is this something more deeply rooted and causally connected? And, if the latter, what *are* the historical and material roots of this connection between the Bible Belt and the Lynching Belt, between Christian fundamentalism and white supremacy in the history of the U.S.?

One of the key events and turning points in relation to all this took place in the aftermath of the Civil War, with the reversal and betrayal of Reconstruction in the southern U.S. To briefly review this crucial period: For a decade after the Civil War, from 1867 to 1877, the federal troops that had conquered the South, remained in the South to enforce changes that were being brought about through amendments to the Constitution and government policy in general. And there was, for a very short-lived period of time, not equality but real advances for the masses of former slaves, and even for some poor people among the whites. This included what was then a decisive dimension: the acquiring of land. Not all the land that was promised to the former slaves who fought on the Union side in the Civil War (the famous 40 acres and a mule that you see referred to in Spike Lee movies), but some land was acquired by the former slaves, as well as some poor white farmers. And, although still under the domination of the bourgeoisie and within the structure of bourgeois relations, there were a number of important rights that were extended to the former slaves that obviously had not existed under slavery—including the right to vote. As a result of this, there were also a number of Black elected officials during this very brief period in the southern states.[23]

But then, the bourgeoisie centered in the North, having consolidated its control of the country, including the South, economically as well as politically, needed to expand further to the west, and it sent the army that had fought the Civil War (and had remained in the South for a decade after the Civil War) to the west, to carry out the final phases of the conquest and genocide against the native peoples, the theft of their land, and the driving of those who were left onto reservations, which were in effect concentration camps.[24] Pulling these federal army troops out of the South signaled the end of Reconstruction and returned the masses of Black people in particular to a situation of being viciously exploited and terrorized by old and new plantation owners and the Ku Klux Klan, which was started by former Confederate officers and soldiers seeking revenge for the defeat in the Civil War and a restoration of the "southern way of life."

---

23. The U.S. is a weird country—the oppressive relations in this country have taken some peculiar forms. I remember doing some research into this a number of years ago, and discovering that if you were determined to be $\frac{1}{16}$th African, you were counted as Black in some of these calculations in the South. And so, on the basis of this definition, there was one person (I still remember his name: P.B.S. Pinchback) who became Lieutenant Governor in a southern state during the period of Reconstruction; he held the highest political office in the South of any person of African origin (defined in this way), until quite recently. But even with certain peculiarities to this, it is a reflection of changes that were brought about as a result of the Civil War and the very brief period of Reconstruction.

24. These federal troops were also used against strikes carried out by what was then an overwhelmingly white labor movement.

Along with this came the development, among white southerners, of a certain strain of Christianity, and in particular Christian fundamentalism, that viewed the southern U.S.—and more specifically
the *whites* in the South—as a people who, like the ancient Israelites,
had been favored by their God but then had lost favor with and had
been chastised by Him. Their chastisement, in the eyes of these white
southerners, was *not because of slavery*, but rather because they had
not been strong enough in defense of their way of life—which in fact
was based on slavery. And now, in their view, there was going to be a
restoration of this people, as there was in past times when God had
returned his favor to the ancient people of Israel.

And what went along with this, not just in the South but in the
U.S. as a whole, was that increasingly the history of the Civil War was
rewritten, and the role of Black people in the Civil War was basically
washed out of historical accounts of this war (this is something that
David Brion Davis speaks to in his book, *Inhuman Bondage: The Rise
and Fall of Slavery in the New World*). Even the basic reality of what
the war was fought over was to a large degree blotted out, obscured,
and distorted. Though the Civil War involved a complex of factors
and motivations (people on the northern side were not fighting only
out of moral conviction, though there were many people motivated
to fight on a moral basis against slavery, and many who were inspired, for example, by the rebellion, even though unsuccessful, that
was led by John Brown against the slave system shortly before the
start of the Civil War), the essence and decisive point of the conflict
was—and it became increasingly clear that it was—the question of
slavery. On the side of the North, whose victory led to the abolition
of slavery, what was essentially involved was the fact that the interests of the rising bourgeoisie (centered in the North) were coming
into more profound and acute antagonism with the slave system
and the slaveowners in the South. This heightening antagonism between these two modes of production, these two different systems
of exploitation—capitalist and slaveowning—was at the root of
this conflict; and the reality, which became increasingly clear, was

that the bourgeoisie, and its mode of production, could not prevail without finally abolishing slavery. Still, notwithstanding the contradictory nature of the bourgeois side in this conflict (which, among other things, was manifested in the halting and partial way in which Lincoln approached the abolition of slavery), there is no doubt that the central and pivotal issue in the Civil War was slavery.

But, again, especially after the reversal of Reconstruction, there began to be a rewriting of this. "The War Between the States" was how it was increasingly referred to. And then you began to have re-enactments of key engagements in that war which were sanitized versions of what it was all about: people—overwhelmingly white people—would dress up in gray uniforms and blue uniforms (representing the South and the North) and re-enact key battles (this still goes on). This even found expression in the realm of sports. When I was a kid, and for some time after that, there was the annual Blue-Gray football game, an all-star contest pitting college seniors from the South against others from the North. The Civil War became ritualized, and reduced to almost a non-antagonistic conflict within the family, even while there was deeply harbored resentment among the un-reconstructed southern segregationists who looked back longingly to the "glory" of the Confederacy and slavery days. Actually, it was more among the people—that is, the *white* people—in the North that the sense of antagonism had largely faded.

This rewriting of history—and cultural expressions of this rewriting—were linked with a fundamentalist Christianity which had its roots in the South but was spread—and increasingly these days is being very actively spread—to other parts of the country, not only in rural areas but also within the suburbs and exurbs. And, in what is a terrible and outrageous irony, this same religious fundamentalism is being spread in the inner cities as well, promoted among Black people in particular by patriarchal-minded and reactionary preachers.

In the way that the Civil War has come to be presented as a national tragedy, there is great irony as well: In reality, the Civil War, on a far greater scale than the American War of Independence, had a genuinely liberating content, on the part of the North. Even though this was led by the bourgeoisie and was ultimately contained within the confines of bourgeois relations, the Civil War is the last war on the part of the U.S. capitalist class that can legitimately be considered just, and even glorious. And it's the only war that they are ashamed of. [Laughter] This is why we repeatedly hear of the terrible tragedy of "brother killing brother." Well, I don't believe it was seen that way by the slaves—I don't think the 200,000 former slaves who, once they were permitted to do so, fought heroically in the Union Army, thought that they were killing their "brothers" when they were fighting the Confederate Army. And I don't know if a lot of the white troops in the northern army who went to battle singing in praise of John Brown thought they were killing "brothers." I believe they thought they were carrying on a righteous fight to end a terrible evil.

But, as seen through the eyes of the ruling bourgeoisie today—and in the way it has molded, or sought to mold, public opinion—the Civil War was a terrible national tragedy. And the truth is that it *was* fought at terrible cost. The 600,000 who died in that war represent the equivalent of something like 6 million people, in relation to today's U.S. population. But, despite the very real cost, the people who fought it at the time—actually on both sides, but here I'm focusing on the people who were on the liberating side of the war, on the side opposed to slavery—they believed that they were fighting a righteous war, a just war. And that was profoundly true—but it has been rewritten.

In relation not only to the Civil War but to the larger phenomenon of religion and white supremacy in America—and why it is that the Bible Belt is also the Lynching Belt—there is important analysis in Kevin Phillips' book *American Theocracy: The Peril and Politics of Radical Religion, Oil, and Borrowed Money in the 21st Century*. In Chapter 4, "Radicalized Religion: As American as Apple Pie," Phillips makes this observation: "The South...long ago passed New England as the region most caught up in manifest destiny and covenanted relationship with God." (*American Theocracy*, p.125)

What Phillips is speaking to is the fact that, going back to the origins of the country, in New England there was a strong current among the settlers of seeing the establishment of their new home in America as expressive of a special relationship with God, and a carrying out of His will. But over the period since then, that has largely receded into the background in New England, while it has become much more powerfully felt and asserted on the part of southerners—that is to say, once again, *white* southerners (or a large number of them). And those southerners fervently believe that this applies both to the U.S. as a whole but also, more particularly and specially, to the southern U.S. Thus, referring with the term "American exceptionalism" to the notion that America occupies a special destiny and a special place in God's plan and is marked by a special goodness, Phillips continues: "It [the South] has become the banner region of American exceptionalism, with no small admixture of southern ...exceptionalism." (p. 125) In other words, in the eyes of religious fundamentalists who are rooted in the South and the traditions of the South, since America in general and the South in particular is characterized by this special exceptionalism, when the U.S. ventures into the world and does what might otherwise be regarded as evil, it is on the contrary good, because America has a special goodness inherent in it and what it does is, by definition...good—it is favored in a special way in the eyes of, and has the support of, God.

Phillips reviews how, in the aftermath of the Civil War, although the South was defeated and the slave system was abolished, after the reversal of Reconstruction the South "rose again" in terms of political power and influence within the country as a whole. In connection with all this, Phillips points out, a religious mythology arose, and took root widely among white people in the South, that the (white) South had a special covenant with God and was the object of a special design by God to restore it to its proper place, righting the terrible wrong that had been done through the Civil War. Phillips makes the very relevant and telling comparison between southern whites in the U.S. and white settlers (Afrikaners) in South Africa, as well as Protestants in Northern Ireland and the Zionists who founded and rule the state of Israel. When I read this, it immediately resonated with me, because I had been repeatedly struck by the fact that, in listening to a Northern Irish Protestant, an Afrikaner, or an Israeli spokesman (or Israeli settler in the West Bank), they all seemed, and in certain ways even sounded, remarkably similar, not only in terms of the kinds of arguments they would make, but in their whole posture and attitude. Phillips points out that all these groups, including fundamentalist southern whites, see themselves as people being restored to their rightful, and righteous, relation with God—re-establishing a broken covenant and exercising a special, divinely-established destiny.[25]

As Phillips sums up: "The reason for spotlighting history's relative handful of covenanting cultures is the biblical attitudes their people invariably share: religious intensity, insecure history, and willingness to sign up with an Old Testament god of war for protection." (*American Theocracy*, p. 128) This insightful observation on Phillips' part applies to the South of the U.S.—to southern whites in particular—and applies as well to those more broadly in the U.S. who are drawn to a literalist, fundamentalist Christian Fascism. And Phillips goes on to emphasize that the importance of this in today's world has "less to do with Ulster [Northern Ireland Protestants] and South Africa and more to do with the United States and particularly the South. Israelis and, to an extent, Scripture-reading Americans are on their ways to being the last peoples of the covenant." (p. 128) Phillips makes the chilling point that this outlook and the corresponding values are gaining currency and force among growing numbers of people all over the U.S.—and once more, in a bitter irony, this includes some among those who are most directly oppressed by white supremacy.

---

25. Here there is a notable irony, with regard to the Zionist rulers of Israel in particular: while many of them are actually secular, they nonetheless base their claim to the land of Palestine on religious-scriptural grounds. As a joke, which used to circulate in Israel itself, puts it: "Most Israelis don't believe in God—but they do know He promised them the state of Israel!"

As this worldview has increasingly spread beyond the traditional Bible Belt in the U.S., and as this gains increasing weight within the ruling class of the U.S., it poses the prospect of a move to impose, through force and violence, in the U.S. and on a world scale, all that is called to mind by the slave whip and the lynch rope. And today (employing again a formulation from Phillips) this is embodied as, and comes with, the destructive power of "the preemptive righteousness of a biblical nation become a high-technology, gospel-spreading superpower." (*American Theocracy*, p. 103)[26]

One of the things that David Brion Davis speaks to in *Inhuman Bondage* (and this is something I also pointed out in *Democracy: Can't We Do Better Than That?*) is that, along with arguments by Aristotle justifying slavery, one of the main things cited by the apologists and defenders of slavery in the southern U.S. was the Bible. More specifically, the story of how Noah's son Ham incurred the wrath of God—so that God cast Ham into Africa and put a curse on the descendants of Ham, beginning with his son, Canaan—was repeatedly invoked to give a religious sanctification to the massive enslavement of people of African origin in the American South.[27]

---

26. Along with the important analysis and insights in Kevin Phillips' book, *American Theocracy*, as well as in *Inhuman Bondage* by David Brion Davis, observations that are very relevant to this question are found in *The Baptizing of America*, by Rabbi James Rudin, as well as in a talk, in May, 2005, by African-American theologian Dr. Hubert Locke, "Reflections on the Pacific School of Religion's Response to the Religious Right."

27. In more recent times, once again we have seen arguments seeking to justify and reinforce white supremacy being treated very respectably in the bourgeois media and other "mainstream" institutions. This was the case with *The Bell Curve*, for example—a book that was published and was promoted very aggressively in the 1990s. In setting out to justify oppressive relations in general—and, more specifically, white supremacy—this book did not rely so much on religious scripture for justification, but based its arguments on pseudo-scientific rationalization for what it alleged were the innate inferiority and superiority of various groups. It explicitly argued that there is a genetically-based inferiority of people of African origin, particularly with regard to intellectual capacities. This was raised to oppose programs such as affirmative action, but also more generally to justify unequal and oppressive relations and to reinforce the ideology of white chauvinism (racism) that goes along with the way in which white supremacy is

For all the reasons that I've been speaking to (and which the statements I have cited from Kevin Phillips shine a light on), unavoidably bound up with religious fundamentalism in the U.S., given the whole history of this country, is a definite and pronounced component of white supremacy. And this is objectively true, even though not every individual caught up in this religious fundamentalism is conscious of this fact.

And, again, one of the bitter and acute ironies in all this is the spread of this religious fundamentalism—to a large degree with the battering ram of the forceful reassertion of absolutist patriarchal authority—among those who are most directly the victims of white supremacy. To the degree that this takes hold among them, it will have the effect of binding them more firmly into a whole process which will not only greatly intensify their oppression, but which has genocidal implications, particularly in a situation in which already huge numbers of inner city youth—a large percentage of Black youth and many Latino youth as well—are already in prison or ensnared in the "criminal justice system" in one form or another.

Before turning more directly to these genocidal implications, it is worthwhile looking at another dimension in which, in the history of this country, white supremacy has been mutually reinforcing with the promotion of religion. In the book *When Affirmative Action Was White: An Untold History of Racial Inequality in Twentieth-Century America*, in the course of analyzing the way in which the New Deal and the policies effected through the GI Bill, the Federal Housing Authority, the Veterans Administration, and so on, served to actually reinforce and promote white supremacy and a widening of the gap between whites and Blacks in the U.S.,[28] Ira Katznelson discusses

---

built into the whole history and foundation, and the dominant institutions and structures, of U.S. society. However, increasingly in these times in the U.S. we see religious fundamentalism being brought forward as a unifying ideological basis for the most openly reactionary viewpoints and political programs, including white supremacy as well as male supremacy.

28. An analysis of the role and effect of the New deal and related programs in reinforcing white supremacy and inequality is also found in *Working Toward*

specifically how this affected colleges and universities. He examines how government funds went in greater proportion to universities from which Black people were, in the early years after World War 2, still almost entirely excluded, and the disparity in government support, financially and otherwise, for Black universities compared to universities that largely, or entirely, excluded Black people. One thing he touches on, as part of this overall analysis, is the historically restricted curriculum of these traditionally Black colleges. With their limited resources and funding—but also partly under the influence of the whole tradition associated with Booker T. Washington—their curriculum was largely limited to, and emphasized, three things: trades, teaching, and theology. (See Ira Katznelson, *When Affirmative Action Was White*, W.W. Norton & Company, Inc., Publishers, 2005— Chapter 5, "White Veterans Only," especially part III, pp. 129–34.)

In other words, there was a much greater emphasis on religion in the traditionally Black colleges than there was in other universities, from which Blacks were largely excluded for many years continuing after World War 2. Katznelson's focus here is particularly on the period right after World War 2, but the differences he discusses cast a larger and longer shadow and have broader application and implications and effects, extending down to today. The promotion of theology in the traditionally Black colleges reinforced the role that historically had been played by the Black church, which was a highly and acutely contradictory role.

From the time of slavery, Christianity has been promoted among Black people in the U.S. by the powers-that-be. The various peoples in Africa from which the slaves were taken practiced a number of different religions, and along with forcing them to adopt a new culture and customs—down to the level of requiring them to take on new names (as dramatized, for example, in the televised special series *Roots*)—the slaveowners generally imposed Christianity in place of

---

Whiteness, How America's Immigrants Became White, The Strange Journey from Ellis Island to the Suburbs, by David R. Roediger, Basic Books, 2005.

the slaves' traditional religions.[29]

At the same time, as is not surprising among an oppressed people, beginning in slave times Black people have sought to take parts of this new religion, introduced to them under the yoke of the slave-master, and use it as a means of fighting back against oppression. So, for example, the Old Testament story of the Israelites enslaved in Egypt and of Moses leading the people out of bondage—the theme of "let my people go," expressed in gospel songs and in other ways—became a powerful part of the Black religious tradition and culture. But the role of the Black church has always involved a certain kind of dual role, and the role of Black clergy has always been a contradictory one, at times acutely so. It has involved negotiating with the slavemasters (and the white supremacist authorities who have exercised power after slavery was ended) to try to bring about some improvement in the conditions of the people—but always doing so on a basis that would keep things from getting out of hand in a way that would fundamentally threaten the interests of the oppressors; always waging the struggle, or seeking to confine struggle that breaks out, within a form that wouldn't fundamentally challenge the oppressive relations. Time and again, especially when tension would mount and the anger of the masses would threaten to boil over, the preachers would go to the oppressors and say, in effect: "If you don't give me something to go back to the people with, I won't have any way to keep things from exploding."

Martin Luther King played this role—and explicitly so. In the midst of the massive urban rebellions of the 1960s, King repeatedly took the stand: If you don't give me something, I'm not going to be able to contain the anger of the masses any more. And when it came down to it, when the anger of the masses did erupt out of the confines that were acceptable to the powers-that-be, King joined in the

29. Despite some definite limitations, some useful background in this regard is found in *Religions Of Africa: A Pilgrimage Into Traditional Religions*, by Noel Q. King, Harper & Row Publishers, 1970; and *The Religions Of The Oppressed: A Study of Modern Messianic Cults*, by Vittorio Lanternari [Translated from the Italian by Lisa Sergio], Alfred A. Knopf, 1963.

chorus calling for the government to send in the army to forcibly put down mass urban rebellion. This is the stand King took in the context of the extremely powerful urban rebellion in Detroit, in the summer of 1967; and it must be said that the when the army was sent into Detroit, violence did not then stop but was increasingly characterized by *violence on the part of the army* (together with the police and other agencies of the state) *directed against the masses of Black people*, many of whom were murdered in cold blood by the army and police. This is a matter of history.

Even if we allow that King did this because of sincere commitment to pacifism, a strategic opposition to violent struggle on the part of the oppressed and a feeling that Black people would only harm their own interests by engaging in violent uprisings, it must be said that this reasoning is fundamentally wrong and is objectively in line with the interests of the oppressors. In fact, King's role in relation to these rebellions, and overall, was consistent with his expressed view that equality and justice for Black people must, and could only, be achieved within the confines of the capitalist system, and on the terms of this system, when in reality this system has always embodied, in its very foundation, and continually reinforces, inequality and oppression, in the most murderous forms, for the masses of Black people, and only sweeping aside this system through revolution can put an end to this.[30]

This is the role that this whole stratum of Black preachers has

---

30. See *Cold Truth, Liberating Truth: How This System Has Always Oppressed Black People, and How All Oppression Can Finally Be Ended*, available at revcom. us/coldtruth, where the following statement by Martin Luther King is cited, which makes very clear his outlook and orientation and the unity between the objective he put forward of pursuing (the illusion of) achieving equality within this system and his insistence on what the character of the struggle must be:

"The American racial revolution has been a revolution to 'get in' rather than to overthrow. We want a share in the American economy, the housing market, the educational system and the social opportunities. This goal itself indicates that a social change in America must be nonviolent." (Martin Luther King Jr., *Where Do We Go From Here*, p. 130, cited in *Cold Truth, Liberating Truth*, Part 7, "Any Other Way Is Confusion and Illusion") played historically, even while they have been portrayed as the leaders of the struggle. In truth, their role has been much more contradictory—and often much more acutely contradictory—than that.[31]

In relation to all this, two things stand out very clearly today: One, it is necessary to be very clear that this ideology—the theology of Christianity, and of religion in general, and the overall worldview that it expresses—cannot lead the way to real and complete liberation, and on its own it will always end up seeking to confine things within the limits set by the existing system. To put it in basic terms, to the degree that they are willing to stand with the oppressed in the fight against oppression and injustice, religious clergy and others with this outlook can and must be united with, but the outlook and the political orientation that they represent cannot lead the

---

31. You can see these contradictions portrayed, for example, in a movie that came out in the '60s, *Nothing But a Man*. This movie was not widely distributed, but it is a very interesting and overall a very positive movie, even with its limitations, which are reflected to some degree in the title. It is the story of a Black railroad worker in the South who, because his job provides more mobility for him, and he has some experience with unions, doesn't want to put up with all the overt racist crap that Black people were subjected to in the South at that time. At one point he meets, falls in love with and marries the daughter of a preacher, and he comes into very sharp conflict with the preacher because of his whole attitude of refusing to put up with all this—and his contempt for Black people, including this preacher, who do put up with or compromise with the whole racist set-up. The movie very well portrays the kind of conciliating role of the preacher—negotiating to get a few concessions and at the same time struggling to keep the people in line, so that they don't anger the Man and upset the whole arrangement. This movie captures a lot of the acutely contradictory role, historically, of this stratum of Black preachers and the theology they have purveyed. Contrary to the mythology that's promoted by the ruling class, as well as by many of these preachers—that they've always been out in front, leading the struggle—the reality is once again much more contradictory: While some Black clergy have played a positive role and made real contributions to the struggle, there has also been a significant aspect in which many of them have sought to contain the struggle within limits that are more acceptable to the ruling class—particularly in circumstances when the struggle has powerfully strained against, and at times broken through, the limits they seek to impose on it in order to maintain this arrangement with the ruling class whereby the preachers can get certain concessions in return for keeping the masses in line and preventing them from getting all out of bounds.

struggle, or it will not go where it needs to go in order to bring about emancipation from oppression and exploitation. And secondly, there is at this time a whole stratum or section of Black preachers which is openly going along with and promoting the Christian fascist program, to a large degree on the basis of aggressively asserting patriarchy in particular. And that can only lead to disaster: it cannot be united with and has to be very vigorously exposed, called out for what it is, and relentlessly struggled against.[32]

---

32. As an aside here, dealing with a secondary but not insignificant part of the picture, it is worth thinking about why is there an unusually large representation of white people from the South not only in the U.S. military overall but more specifically in the officer corps. Now, as for the "grunts," that can be explained to a significant degree by the fact that there actually are a significant number of white people in the South whose options are limited. But there is also the whole macho and militaristic ethos that has historically gone along with the influence of religious fundamentalism and generally conservative culture and values—it is not accidental, or incidental, for example, that "patriot" and "patriarchy" are words with the same root. And, specifically with regard to the large numbers of white southerners in the officer corps of the U.S. armed forces, along with this macho and militaristic ethos, there is the whole history of the southern aristocracy, beginning with the slave system but then continuing after literal slavery was abolished (and replaced with a system of sharecropping and plantation exploitation, in what was essentially a feudal form, for a period of about 100 years after the Civil War). This whole aristocratic tradition in the South was consciously carried over and copied from Europe, and if you look at a country like England, with its aristocracy, there is the tradition where one son inherits the family's property, another joins the clergy, and yet another son goes into the military. And there are not only ideological but also practical factors that play into that. With a system where wealth is based on land ownership, to the degree that you are not able to more intensively exploit people on the land, then there is a limit to how much wealth you can accumulate; and if you keep dividing up the land, you will end up in a situation where the family wealth will actually begin to be used up. But, if you send one son into the clergy and another into the military, there will not be so many to divide the land among (and less basis for rivalry and antagonism among the sons). To a significant degree, this was historically part of the culture of the southern U.S.—that is, of the rich white land-owning aristocratic strata in the South—and this is quite possibly one of the factors that has contributed to there being so many white southerners not only in the U.S. military overall but specifically in its officer corps. And, in turn, given the historical particularities of the South, as spoken to above, this presence of a large number of white southerners is a factor contributing to a more favorable environment

Christian Fascism and Genocide

In this connection it is important to examine the genocidal implications that are part and parcel of the Christian Fascist outlook and program. This, again, is one of the great ironies and injuries of the promotion of this religious fundamentalism among the masses of oppressed people who are already the most direct victims of white supremacy. In "The Truth About Right-Wing Conspiracy...and Why Clinton and the Democrats Are No Answer," I pointed out that a leading Christian Fascist, Pat Robertson—and he is not alone in this—advocates a legal system based on the Old Testament of the Bible. And what does that call for? It calls for things like public floggings and the shaming of people who commit minor offenses, and with regard to people who commit more serious offenses, it insists upon the death penalty—not just for what are now considered capital crimes, such as murder, but also acts which, in the eyes of people like Robertson, would turn the society against God and destroy the fabric of society. As I pointed out in "The Truth About Right-Wing Conspiracy":

> it is necessary to place this in the context of American
> society today, in which, through conscious government
> policy as well as the "normal operation" of the laws of
> capitalist accumulation and competition, whole sec-
> tions of people are being consigned to the ranks of
> "unemployables," people for whom the only viable alter-
> native within this system may be participation in the
> underground economy. With this in mind, we cannot
> avoid recognizing that the logic of Robertson's call for
> applying "the biblical model" for crime and punish-
> ment involves an unmistakable suggestion of a "final
> solution" against the masses of people in the inner cit-
> ies as well as preparation for the use of extreme repres-
> sion, and even execution, to punish a broad array of

---

for the spread of religious fundamentalism—Christian Fascism—within the U.S. military, including its top ranks.

activities which today are treated as minor offenses or as no crime at all. ("The Truth About Right-Wing Conspiracy" was first published in the fall of 1998 in the *Revolutionary Worker* [now *Revolution*] and was reprinted in the October 17, 2004 issue [no. 1255]. It is available at revcom.us. For the arguments by Pat Robertson on applying "the biblical model for crime and punishment" that is referred to here, see Pat Robertson, *Answers to 200 of Life's Most Probing Questions*, Bantam Books, 1987 edition, pp. 198–99.)

As has been pointed out several times, among those things for which the Bible insists people must be put to death are homosexuality and adultery and—particularly for women—sex before marriage. And if you think of all the people who are currently caught up in the penal system in the U.S.—with over 2 million in prison at this time and many more on parole and probation—particularly youth from the inner cities, and then you add to that a certain logic that says, "why should we spend all this money housing these people in prisons," you can very easily see the genocidal implications of a Christian Fascist "Biblical" approach to crime and punishment.

This is not hyperbole. People like Robertson are very serious about what they're seeking to do. What did they say after 9-11? Jerry Falwell insisted that this was brought on by liberals, the ACLU, idol-worshippers and secularists, people upholding the right to abortion, homosexuals and others of like mind. This, Falwell claimed, brought down the wrath of God on America. And Pat Robertson jumped in, to express strong agreement with this.[33]

---

33. On September 13, 2001 Jerry Falwell appeared on *The 700 Club*, hosted by Pat Robertson, and here is a part of the exchange between Falwell and Robertson:

Jerry Falwell: The ACLU's got to take a lot of blame for this [terrorist attack].

Pat Robertson: Well, yes.

Jerry Falwell: And, I know that I'll hear from them for this. But, throwing God out successfully with the help of the federal court system, throwing God out of the public square, out of the schools. The abortionists have got to bear some

These people, and others like them, firmly and fanatically believe that the unadulterated assertion of their fundamentalist outlook, backed up by the force of law and the state, is essential in order to achieve and maintain their vision of what America is and should be, and what it needs to do as it goes out into the world to carry out the grand design of God and to realize the special destiny of an exceptional people whom God has chosen to rule the whole world—once they have gotten right with God.

Religion, Fundamentalism, and the Slave Mentality

At the same time, there is in religion, but more especially in literalist religious fundamentalism, the promotion of a mentality that sees people themselves as inherently sinful, that accepts the notion that the reason people who are suffering are in the situation they're in, is because they have come into disfavor with God, because they

---

burden for this because God will not be mocked. And when we destroy 40 million little innocent babies, we make God mad. I really believe that the pagans, and the abortionists, and the feminists, and the gays and the lesbians who are actively trying to make that an alternative lifestyle, the ACLU, People For the American Way, all of them who have tried to secularize America. I point the finger in their face and say "you helped this happen."

Pat Robertson: Well, I totally concur, and the problem is we have adopted that agenda at the highest levels of our government. And so we're responsible as a free society for what the top people do. And, the top people, of course, is the court system. (A press release from People for the American Way, dated September 17, 2001 provided a transcript of this discussion between Falwell and Robertson on *The 700 Club*, September 13, 2001, and this appeared on "Common Dreams progressive newswire," September 14, 2007.)

Coming under pressure from various quarters, Falwell issued an "apology" shortly after this. But this was the kind of "apology" in which someone "giveth with the left hand, while he taketh away with the right": In "apologizing" Falwell continued to make the same arguments about how America had become vulnerable to terrorist attack because God had been angered by the kinds of things Falwell spoke about in the statement for which he was supposedly "apologizing." (See CNN.com/U.S., September 14, 2001. Stories regarding this were also posted on the *New York Times* and the *Washington Post* websites [www.nytimes.com and www.washingtonpost.com], September 14, 2001.)

(or others close to them) have committed acts which have brought down the wrath of God on them; and if anything good happens to them, it is because, despite all this, God in his infinite greatness and mercy has shown compassion for them. Let's call this what it is—it is a *slave mentality*, with which people are being indoctrinated. All this "thank you Jesus!" is a slave mentality. It goes right along with "God works in mysterious ways," with all the horrors that involves.

Now, I know some people are highly offended when you say things like this. But, to paraphrase Malcolm X, I didn't come here to tell you what you want to hear, I came here to tell you the truth, whether you like it or not. Once again, it is a form of contempt for the masses of people to think that they can't be challenged with the truth and can't come to embrace the truth and wield it to emancipate themselves and to emancipate all humanity. When you say that people are being indoctrinated with, and are even taking up, a slavish mentality, you are not saying it is their fault, or that this is something they can't change. You are calling on them and challenging them to get rid of this, to cast it off—to rise to what they are actually capable of—and you are bringing to them an understanding of why they are *really* in the situation they are in today and *what is the way out* of this. But you can't do that without challenging this mentality. And you can't do it while being apologetic about challenging this mentality.

Now some people say, with regard to Black people in particular, "religion is an essential part of the Black experience." To this I say: What about slavery? Or segregation and Jim Crow? Sharecropping and the KKK? Or continuing discrimination today, along with massive imprisonment and brutality and murder at the hands of the police? Isn't *all that* "an essential part of the Black experience" too? The question is, if something is an essential or integral part of experience, *what role* has it played, and *what effect* does it have? Is it good or bad? Positive or negative? Where did this religion, where did the worship of Jesus in particular, come from?

I've talked about the contradictory character and effect of this historically. But in today's world—and where we stand in relation to the possibility of the emancipation of humanity from thousands of years of oppressive relations and tradition's chains—religion, and all the more so in its literalist fundamentalist form, is a direct obstacle, a shackle, a chain holding back the masses of people from being able to emancipate themselves and to leap beyond the situation where they feel drawn towards some kind of religion as consolation for oppression and suffering.

So, while it is right and necessary to build unity with many people who hold religious viewpoints, it is also crucial to be very clear on what can actually enable people to engage, to understand, and to transform reality in order to finally bring an end to all the truly horrific conditions to which masses of people are subjected—and, together with that, bring an end to the need to seek consolation for the suffering that accompanies these conditions.

To win real and complete emancipation means taking up a scientific, not a religious, approach to understanding and changing reality—changing it through revolution. And especially fundamentalist religion that insists on taking the Bible, or any other scripture, literally and as the absolute and inerrant truth—and which refuses to believe anything that contradicts a literal reading of the Bible or other religious scriptures—that kind of religious viewpoint and conviction is extremely harmful. It can only keep those caught up in it completely in the dark about what is really going on in the world and afraid of trying to change the world in the only way it can really be changed—through resistance and ultimately the revolutionary overthrow of this system that is oppressing millions and literally billions of people here and throughout the world. Fundamentalist religious fanaticism can only help to reinforce the oppression and enslavement of masses of people.

In this spirit and this light, it is crucial to grasp and to put forward, boldly and straight-up: **Oppressed people who are unable or unwilling to confront reality as it actually is, are condemned to remain enslaved and oppressed.**

Part Four:

GOD DOES NOT EXIST—
WE NEED LIBERATION
WITHOUT GODS

The "Left Hand of God"—
And the Right Way to Go About Winning Liberation

I want to turn now to a discussion of *The Left Hand of God: Taking Back Our Country from the Religious Right*, by Rabbi Michael Lerner. This is a book that seems to be having a fair amount of influence among a number of progressive people, and it represents a serious presentation of a position and a viewpoint which deserves to be engaged seriously.

I have spoken to many of the issues raised by Lerner, or closely related issues, in the second part of *Preaching From a Pulpit of Bones*, in commenting on Jim Wallis and his book *The Soul of Politics* (New Press, Orbis Books, 1994). But it is worthwhile speaking directly to Lerner's *The Left Hand of God*, which is written more recently, in the context of a situation marked by the growing power of what he calls the Christian right, which we identify as the Christian Fascists.

However, before getting further into a discussion of this book and some of the particular questions it addresses, I have to begin by first discussing this concept of the "left hand" and the "right hand" of god. As Lerner presents it, there are these two opposing worldviews (identified with two "hands" of God) within the religious tradition with which he identifies—the Jewish (or more broadly the "Judeo-Christian") tradition. The "left hand of god" is the one of compassion, of love, of concern for the poor, and for justice; and the "right hand of god" is the vengeful, wrathful aspect of god. But I don't think such a division can be regarded as valid.

To use a very relevant analogy, with people like Lerner, who accept a lot of the mischaracterization and distortions about communism—and the stories about horrors committed under Stalin, and even under Mao—I wonder how they would respond if, instead of examining what really happened in the Soviet Union and China when they were socialist, we were to argue instead: "Those things you're talking about, that's the *right hand* of Stalin, or the right hand of Mao. [Laughter] You're ignoring the *left hand*—that's the part we want to talk about—all the ways in which land was given to the peasantry and the people's needs were met. We're building our tradition on the 'left hand' of communism." Well, the fact is that, whether we're a talking about the actual historical experience of the communist movement and socialist countries where they have existed, and the actual content of communist theory, or about the scriptures of various religions and the traditions associated with those scriptures, these things have to be looked at overall, and not by applying yet another version of the "salad bar" approach: focusing on what we like and want to talk about, or what might seem more acceptable according the conventions of the times, while ignoring things that might be more controversial or things that we might not want to defend.

Now, having said that, I do want to emphasize that there are things to unite with in Lerner's position, and there are insights of his that we can and should learn from. So I want to begin by briefly characterizing some of this, and then examine more extensively some key aspects of what is put forward in this book.

Throughout *The Left Hand of God* Lerner emphasizes the need for—and in American society the crying lack of—larger meaning and purpose in people's lives, beyond narrow and selfish economic interests and what we would identify as an "economist" orientation—the whole approach of reducing everything to people's economic interests as the only real, or only legitimate, motivating factor in their lives. Lerner argues—and here I have basic agreement—that this is an impoverished vision of human beings and their capabilities. To put it another way, to use Biblical terms, Lerner is emphasizing that people cannot live by bread alone. As important as bread is to people—and he does not deny that it is important to them—this is not enough to make for meaningful and fulfilling human existence and human relations.

Along with this, Lerner makes a very sharp critique of consumerism and what we would call (and he does to some degree identify as) parasitism—which, among other things, is measured in the great amount of the world's resources that are consumed in the U.S., which is way out of proportion to the U.S. share of the world's population. Lerner emphasizes the need to struggle against this whole consumerist culture, and the idea that the worth of a person should be measured by what s/he is able to consume and that life should be organized around and given meaning through the pursuit and acquisition of consumer goods.

Lerner emphasizes repeatedly the need to change people's ways of thinking, and their motivation, in relation to this. He makes an extensive argument in this regard, which recognizes that if people were to strive for the kind of world that he envisions and argues for (which, as I'll get to, is ultimately unrealizable—although that doesn't mean there's nothing to unite with in his vision), then there would not be such a luxurious life for so many people in countries like the United States—but, he asks, what would be so terrible about that? What if people in the U.S. didn't consume so many things? What if they didn't use so much oil, what if the U.S. didn't control so much of the world's technology and use it for narrow and even destructive purposes? Wouldn't life, after all, be more meaningful—wouldn't that be a worthwhile tradeoff?

This is one of Lerner's main themes, and it is not without validity or value. There is real importance to struggling against the idea that Americans have some sort of inherent right to, and should pursue, a life which objectively and in significant ways amounts to being a parasite on the rest of the world. If you think about restructuring society on the basis of having had a revolution and no longer living off the backs of other people—no longer basing the economy on exploitation of people, in large numbers, within the country itself, and even more extreme exploitation of even greater numbers of people, including millions of children, all around the world—the ideological struggle over that question is going to be very sharp and very decisive; and in this regard, while there are certainly aspects of Lerner's views on this question that do not penetrate to the essence and foundations of the problem, still there is much to unite with in the emphasis he does give to this.

Similarly, there are important insights in his discussion of the corrosive effect of market relations, including how people are compelled to sell themselves in competition with others for jobs and advancement in the work place—the corrosive effect of this on relations generally in society, including personal and family relations, and the way that people are driven to see each other as obstacles to the realization of their desires and objectives. Lerner argues that this carries over from the realm of work, where it is the prevailing and defining principle, into all parts of people's relationships, including the most personal and intimate ones.

Besides these critiques in the realm of culture, there is, in the sphere of political struggle, much in Lerner's positions to unite with, including his opposition to the war in Iraq and much of the program of the Bush regime overall, as well as significant aspects of Lerner's opposition to "the Christian Right." And there is an additional dimension in which unity should be sought with people like Lerner, even while carrying out principled struggle over important and decisive ideological, as well as political, questions. The following from the conclusion of "The Truth About Right Wing Conspiracy...And Why Clinton and the Democrats Are No Answer," speaks to this, in emphasizing the need for building a united front culturally and in terms of values, as well as politically:

> we believe that, together with building this political unity in struggle, there is also a need and a basis to forge broad unity, among diverse forces, around values and cultural expressions that promote and celebrate equality, between men and women, and between peoples and nations; that stand against oppression and against violence which furthers and enforces such oppression;

that oppose imperial domination by one nation over others and military bludgeoning to impose that domination; that foster relations among people based on an appreciation for diversity but also for community; values and culture that prize cooperation among people in place of cut-throat competition, that put the needs of people above the drive to accumulate wealth, that actually promote the global interests of humanity as opposed to narrow national antagonisms and great-power domination.

The development of unity around such values and cultural expressions, like the furthering of political unity in struggle, will be an ongoing process. Building this unity is a challenge that must be taken up by all those who recognize the horror of what is represented by the fundamentalist reactionaries and the implications of this for the masses of people; who refuse to accept that the only "alternative" to this is one which shares essential things in common with it; who recognize the need to confront—and to offer a positive alternative to—the whole politics of poverty, punishment, and patriarchy and the ideological rationalizations for this politics. It is a challenge that must be boldly and urgently taken up.

At the same time, it must be said that there are some very real limitations and errors in analysis—and even, frankly, some very bad positions—in what is put forward by Lerner. Examining not only some of Lerner's political positions, but also his ideological and philosophical viewpoint, will help to bring some of this to light and to underline why, while unity can and must be sought with progressive religious people like Lerner, it is necessary, in the most fundamental sense, to bring to the fore a more radical critique of capitalist society and a corresponding program for revolutionary change, proceeding from a thoroughly and systematically scientific outlook and method, the outlook and method of communism.

While, as I have noted, Lerner speaks, in some ways penetratingly and insightfully, to effects of the capitalist market (and he does sometimes identify it as that—"the capitalist market") and how this carries over into all spheres of people's relations, including the most intimate and personal, what Lerner addresses are ultimately only the more outward and secondary expressions of a deeper and more essential problem. The problem is, in reality, rooted in the fundamental contradiction of capitalism itself, which involves the fact that exploitation is the driving means through which wealth is produced and accumulated under capitalism, *and* that this wealth is *produced socially* but *appropriated privately* by capital. In regard to the more outward expressions that Lerner speaks to, the deeper basis for this resides in the *production relations* of capitalism, as well as the social relations that correspond to these capitalist production relations.[34]

One of the things that is very important to stress in this regard is that production relations are not just—and not essentially—relations of *distribution*. But distribution is mainly what Lerner is dealing with when he focuses on the market. As Marx pointed out, in an overall sense the system of production determines the system of distribution. For a given system of production, there will be a corresponding system of distribution, and in an overall sense the system of distribution is derivative—it derives from and corresponds to the fundamental nature of the means and relations through which production is carried out and accumulation proceeds. The fact that,

---

34. In a talk I gave about a decade ago, *Great Objectives and Grand Strategy* (GO&GS), there is a discussion which overlaps to some degree with Lerner's observations about the cultural and ideological effects of the operation of the capitalist market. However, GO&GS puts this in the framework of a more fundamental critique of the capitalist-imperialist system, and in that framework speaks to how the functioning of the more unrestrained market and of capitalist relations generally in this period has in fact given rise to a certain spiritual malaise and how, in turn, this spiritual malaise has both impelled some people spontaneously toward religion, and religious fundamentalism in particular, but has also been consciously played on and utilized by powerful sections of the ruling class to strengthen the attraction of religious fundamentalism. (Excerpts from *Great Objectives and Grand Strategy* have been published in the *Revolutionary Worker* #1127–42 [November 18, 2001 through March 10, 2002] and are available online at revcom.us/avakian/avakian-works.html#gogs.)

under capitalism, things are distributed through capitalist market mechanisms flows from the ownership system, and from the production relations overall,[35] of capitalism, and from the fundamental contradiction of capitalism between *socialized production* and *private appropriation.*

Given the reality that the relations of production (and most decisively the ownership system) fundamentally determine the system and nature of distribution (and of distribution relations), if you merely try to change the market relations, without getting to the root of this and uprooting it, you will not be able to do so.

---

35. The production relations, in any economic system, consist, first of all, of the *system of ownership* of the means of production (land and raw materials, machinery and technology in general, and so on). Along with, and essentially corresponding to, this system of ownership, are the *relations among people in the process of production* (the "division of labor" in society overall) and the *system of distribution* of the wealth that is produced. To take the example of capitalist society: Ownership of the means of production is dominated by a small group, the capitalist class, while the majority of people own little or no means of production; the "division of labor" in society, the different roles that different groups of people play in the overall process of production, including the profound division between those who carry out intellectual work and those who carry out physical work (the mental/manual contradiction, for short), corresponds to these relations of ownership (and non-ownership) of the means of production; and the distribution of the wealth produced is also in correspondence with this, so that the wealth that is accumulated by capitalists is, in a basic sense, in accordance with the capital they have (the means of production they own or control) and their role as exploiters of the labor power (the ability to work) of others, who own no means of production; while those who are not big capitalists but may own a limited amount of means of production, and/or have accumulated more knowledge and skills, receive a share of the wealth in accordance with that; and those on the bottom of society find their small share in the distribution of social wealth to be determined by the fact that they own no means of production, and have not been able to acquire much beyond basic knowledge and skills. It should not be surprising that these—highly unequal—relations and divisions in society continue to be reproduced, and even tend to be accentuated, through the ongoing functioning of the capitalist system, the ongoing process of capitalist accumulation and the social relations, the politics, and the ideology and culture which are in essential correspondence with and which enforce, and reinforce, the basic nature and functioning of this system. And especially in today's world, this functioning of the capitalist system takes place not only within particular capitalist countries but above all on a world scale.

Along with this, it has to be noted that there is, on Lerner's part, more than a little romanticizing of feudalism, in contrast to capitalism; and this is accompanied by a prettifying of the role of religion and religious institutions in pre-capitalist society, and in the early stages of capitalism. In several places in *The Left Hand of God* Lerner argues that certain institutions have served to modify, or mitigate, exploitation in earlier periods of history. And, not surprisingly— given Lerner's position that there should be *more* of religion and god, or rather more of "the left hand of God," in American society, including in the public sphere—Lerner points especially to the church and religion as exercising this mitigating role. He asserts, and laments, that, with the further development and full triumph of capitalism, this mitigating role has been undermined, so that now exploitation is more naked and largely without this modifying influence. This view of Lerner's is seen, for example, in the following:

> Not that religious institutions hadn't long supported patriarchy and oppressive social relations. But they had also provided an important framework in which our human desire to care for one another could be legitimated and sustained. The medieval Church, for instance, imposed "fair wage" and "fair price" demands on those who employed workers or sold goods at market....Care for others was a major feature of what it meant to be a Christian, and a similar ethos has generally prevailed in religious communities around the world.
>
> When religious institutions declined, over the past three hundred years or so, however, it became easier for the marketplace to become a haven for manipulation and domination. With the weakening of the religious framework and the demand it made for mutual support and communal responsibility, the capitalist market was freed to reshape education and to create a media that would work in tandem to teach us that our primary responsibility in the contemporary world is to maximize our own advantage. (*The Left Hand of God*, pp. 59–60)

What Lerner argues here very much calls to mind what is polemicized against in the *Communist Manifesto*: certain critiques of capitalism which proceed in some respects from a romanticization of feudalism and put forward visions of a society in which feudal relations would be mixed in with—and sometimes presented as—what is alleged to be socialism. And, given what is known about not only the actual content of the Christian Bible but also the real role of Christianity and the Christian Church, especially since the time of Constantine—with the ruthless and relentless persecution and slaughter of heretics, Jewish "Christ killers" and others; the Holy Wars and Crusades; the Inquisitions and the savage suppression of knowledge and ideas that at any time challenged established Church doctrine—one is forced to ask what world it is that Lerner is talking about in which religion and the Church have played the kind of positive role he attributes to them? In reality, the Church and religion, for centuries and centuries, constituted a tremendous weight reinforcing and adding to the oppression and misery of the masses of people in feudal society—not a force mitigating and lessening the effect of this oppression. Besides the way in which religion has embodied organized ignorance and served to weigh the masses down with superstition, fear and guilt, the fact is—a fact which Lerner overlooks here—that the medieval Church was itself one of the largest feudal landowners and in that capacity ruthlessly exploited the serfs and other working people.

The following from "The Truth About Right-Wing Conspiracy... And Why Clinton and the Democrats Are No Answer" (written during the period when Clinton was impeached, though not removed from office) is very relevant in relation to what Lerner is raising—both in the aspect in which Lerner's arguments have some elements of truth and importance, and with regard to the limitations in his views and the ways in which his outlook also leads him in the wrong direction:

> in some important aspects, the "recovery" of the U.S. economy that has taken place during the Clinton

administration, and the more highly "globalized" and "flexible" production that has been a marked feature of this "recovery," has also contributed to "undermining the traditional family." And it has fostered the fluorescence of an outlook, particularly (though not exclusively) among more highly paid professionals, that involves no small amount of self-indulgence and, related to that, a weakening of some "traditional values," including old-style patriotism and the willingness to sacrifice for the officially defined and proclaimed "national interest."

In some significant ways, what was written 150 years ago in the *Communist Manifesto*, concerning the consequences of unfettered bourgeois commodity relations, is assuming a pronounced expression among sections of the U.S. population in the context of today's "post-Cold War" world capitalism. The following phrases from the *Manifesto* have a particular and powerful resonance: "The bourgeoisie, wherever it has gotten the upper hand...has left remaining no other nexus between man and man than naked self-interest, than callous 'cash payment.' It has drowned the most heavenly ecstacies of religious fervor, of chivalrous enthusiasm, of Philistine sentimentalism in the icy water of egotistical calculation. It has resolved personal worth into exchange value....In a word, for exploitation, veiled by religious and political illusions, it has substituted naked, shameless, direct, brutal exploitation." There is a great irony here: the very "triumph" and "triumphalism" of capitalism in today's circumstances has produced effects and sentiments which tend to undermine, among significant sections of the U.S. population, the willingness to make personal sacrifices for "god and country"—that is, for the interests and requirements of the imperial ruling class, within the U.S. itself and in the world arena. In reaction to this, the "conservatives," with the Christian Right playing a decisive role, are attempting to revive and impose precisely "the most heavenly

> ecstacies of religious fervor, of chivalrous enthusiasm,
> of Philistine sentimentalism"—to resurrect a situation
> where worldwide exploitation that is unsurpassed in
> its brutality is at the same time "veiled by religious and
> political illusions."

Here it is important to observe, among other things, that in these incisive passages in the *Communist Manifesto* (cited in "The Truth About Right-Wing Conspiracy") on the naked expressions of capitalist exploitation, and in their critique of capitalism in general, Marx and Engels were not looking *backward* to an idyllic, idealized and romanticized vision of feudalism—which in reality was characterized by endless horror for the masses of people—but, in contrast, were looking *forward*, to the overthrow and advance of humanity *beyond* capitalism, and **all systems of exploitation and oppression**, and any of their adornments, apologies and rationalizations.

Now, in this light, among other things we can see even more clearly the very severe shortcomings in Lerner's analysis of the Religious Right, even though the purpose of his book is, as reflected in the title, "Taking Back Our Country From The Religious Right." Lerner's approach to combatting—or, perhaps more accurately said, attracting people away from—the Religious Right is one that cannot succeed even on its own terms. His analysis of the problem in general and of the Religious Right in particular is marked, and marred, by a failure to grasp and fully confront the *fascist nature* of what is represented by this Religious Right, the depth of the danger it actually poses, and the kind of thoroughgoing and resolute struggle that must be waged to defeat it, while at the same time, yes, seeking to win as many people as possible away from it.

Even in this formulation ("Taking Back our Country from the Religious Right") the limitations of Lerner's outlook and objectives stand out. Why should the objective be characterized, and confined, in terms of "taking back" and "our country"? "Taking back" implies that there is something—the country—which once belonged to "us"—which presumably means the people of the U.S. But in a fundamental sense that has never been the case, since in reality the country has, from the beginning, "belonged to"—that is, it has been ruled by and the masses of people have been dominated, oppressed, and exploited by—the capitalist and slaveowning classes. The formulation "our country" not only suffers from the same shortcomings as "taking back" but also involves an aspect of national (American) chauvinism, even if unintentional, because it is not just "our country" that people should be concerned with—and that is all the more the case when the country in question is an *imperialist* country whose ruling class, through its state, not only oppresses masses of people at home but exploits, indeed super-exploits, and brutalizes people all over the world, most intensely in the Third World, and has time and again brought down horrible destruction and death on people in many other countries, whenever they have resisted domination by U.S. imperialism or become the target of U.S. attack for some other reason. And it is not, simply or essentially, the "Religious Right" from whom things must be "taken"—it is not the Religious Right alone but, more fundamentally, the imperialist ruling class as a whole, which holds power in the U.S. and uses that power for the exploitative and oppressive ends spoken to here.

Repeatedly in *The Left Hand of God* we find Lerner emphatically insisting that, while he strongly disagrees with and will strongly oppose the Religious Right, he refuses to say that those who make up the Religious Right are bad people. But that is not really the issue, or not the heart of the problem: bad people or good people. The issue is: what kind of program and ideology are these people being mobilized around, what does that represent, and how serious of a problem does that pose, if you're trying to get to a more just society, let alone get to communism?

In the "Introduction" to *The Left Hand of God* we find the following:

> It is perfectly legitimate to be alarmed at the growing power of those on the Right and the way they use it, to challenge their ideas forcefully, and to warn of the

> dangers should they succeed in their stated intentions. I will certainly do everything I can to prevent them from popularizing the notion that people have to be religious or believe in God to be moral and to challenge their particular understanding of what God wants of us.
>
> What I will not do, and what I urge my friends in liberal and progressive movements not to do, is attribute evil motives to those on the Religious Right or to view them as cynical manipulators solely interested in power and self-aggrandizement. The Religious Right certainly has its share of power mongers and hypocrites. But the vast majority of those involved are people who are driven by principles and who want what is best for the world. (pp. 8–9)

This, it must be said, is highly naive and seriously misses the mark. What matters, and is of great moment, is not whether these people are sincere, or even self-sacrificing, but rather around what viewpoint and toward what ends are they being organized and led; precisely what is the *content* of the "principles" these people are indeed "driven by"; and what would result if the vision of "what is best for the world" around which they are being galvanized were actually to be realized?

Lerner's limitations here are directly related to his own world outlook, to his proceeding from and through a religious standpoint and prism, including his notion that there is too little religion and spirituality in American life and society—too little! While the religion and spirituality that Lerner advocates and wants to see flourish and exert greater influence, as embodied in his conception of the "left hand of god," is in many significant ways very different from the religious fundamentalism of the Christian Fascists, Lerner does share the same religious traditions with them, in a broad sense, and his beliefs are, to a large degree, rooted in and flow from the same religious scriptures, even if Lerner may view and interpret parts of this scripture differently as well. Lerner's conviction and insistence that a religious and spiritual worldview and approach to reality needs to exert *more* of an influence in society promotes a way of thinking and of acting in the world that is, in fact, in essential conflict with reality, and therefore in conflict with the means for changing reality in accordance with the real and fundamental interests of the great majority of humanity, and ultimately humanity as a whole.

Along with this, despite his very real differences with the reactionary, and truly fascist, religious fundamentalists, Lerner's insistence on the promotion of the same religious traditions and scriptures cannot help but contribute to the strengthening of reactionary religious-based ideological and political viewpoints and programs, and actions flowing from them. This is so because, regardless of how Lerner might seek to "reinterpret" these traditions and these scriptures, they do, after all, stand for what they stand for—they do say what they say and mean what they mean. And, ironically, Lerner's limitations are also bound up with why he does not recognize the depth of difference and, yes, the antagonism that objectively exists between even what he is seeking to do and what is represented, not so much by particular individuals who may be drawn to be the rank and file of this fascist movement, but by the basic character and content of that movement, and where it is seeking to take things.

In other words, it is important to come to grips—to confront— what is the real nature of the "Religious Right": its character as a *Christian Fascist* movement, *aiming for a theocratic fascist form of capitalist-imperialist rule* within the U.S. and *domination on this basis throughout the world*. As has been examined here, this Christian Fascist movement is not only powerfully built around, and has as a major engine, the forceful reassertion of an absolutist kind of patriarchy, but also white supremacy, with a potentially genocidal dimension. And this movement is an ardent advocate of militarism and the military marauding of U.S. imperialism throughout the world.

This movement is waging a fanatical battle against the recognition—not just by individuals, but by society and its educational institutions—of the scientific fact of evolution. Why? Because it is necessary, in order to further its program, to promote an epistemology that causes people to move away from rational thought, to reject and ridicule the scientific method, and to be enslaved to an anti-rational ideology which fosters and insists upon unthinking obedience to the dominant forces and relations in society and to the absolute authority of powerful figures wearing the mantle of religious righteousness and proclaiming a special, covenanted relationship with the Almighty.

The battle around evolution is important in its own right, *and* it has a great deal to do with the battle for *revolution*. It is, first of all, a battle in the realm of epistemology—over questions of what is truth and whether and how human beings can acquire a true understanding of reality. Are we going to proceed according to a scientific approach—investigating reality, to accumulate experience and evidence about reality, and then drawing rational conclusions? Or, are we going to blindly adopt an outmoded way of understanding how the world works and what its driving forces are, and insist upon *superimposing that on reality* and on smashing down anything which conflicts with that non-rational (or irrational) approach? Are we going to insist on *a priori* notions of truth—dogmatic assumptions which are not drawn from reality and not testable in reality—and rule out of order things which *are* drawn from reality and have been tested and shown in reality to be true?

This battle over epistemology is a profound one, with very great stakes and implications. There is, in the U.S. in particular, a fierce political struggle being waged around evolution, but this is a political battle that not only involves the particular question of evolution, as important as that is, but concentrates the contention between two fundamentally opposed epistemologies. There are, of course, more than a few people who hold religious beliefs but accept the scientific fact of evolution and try to reconcile the fact of evolution with their religious worldview. In the final analysis, these are not reconcilable, but at any given time many people are capable of embracing at least the basic realities that are concentrated in the scientific theory of evolution, even while they cling to religious beliefs. But we're talking about something radically different than that, with the Christian Fascist outlook and approach. We're talking about something that defines truth *a priori*—in advance of and divorced from investigating reality and synthesizing what's learned from reality. And this is not just an *apriorism* in a general sense, but is an *apriorism* that serves a comprehensive reactionary political program, aiming to impose and enforce a theocratic-fascist capitalist dictatorship in the U.S., together with waging a crusade to impose—even more extensively, forcefully and mercilessly—the hegemony of America, as God's chosen nation, throughout the world.

It is in this context that evolution has become a concentration of such sharp struggle. The scientific fact of evolution—and the scientific method which leads to the very clear and firm conclusion that evolution is a fact, and which demonstrates this truth ever more comprehensively—all this is a great obstacle to mobilizing people behind the kind of worldview that is expressed in slogans like: "God said it, I believe it, that settles it." That is a self-contained worldview which cannot be penetrated by reality, unless and until the assertion of reality becomes so forceful that it explodes this worldview in one way or another. But, while it remains important to "assault" this worldview with rational and logical arguments about reality, such arguments, simply by themselves, will not really penetrate this worldview. And it can be seen how promoting such a worldview, and galvanizing a forceful political movement around such a worldview, is extremely important for particularly the core of the ruling class in the U.S. now (which has been grouped around the Bush regime) in the context of what they are setting out to do in the world, and how, together with that, they are determined to radically remake the U.S. itself in a fascist direction. A blindly fanatical religious fundamentalism can, they hope, act as a kind of steel band, tightly holding things in place in a situation where what they have set in motion in the world, and within the U.S. itself—all of which is far from under their control—has the potential to cause things to fly apart in sharply opposed directions.

It is in this light that the attempts to impose a "self-contained world"—and how and why evolution has become such a major focal point of struggle in relation to that—can be more fully understood. As things stand now, one of the key elements in having something accepted as a valid scientific theory is what's called "peer review," where work that has been done and conclusions that have been drawn are subjected to critical review by people who are knowledge-able in the relevant field (or fields) of science, to see if, in effect, they can punch holes in it. Although this, in itself, does not and cannot determine the validity (or lack of validity) of a scientific theory, it is a *crucial part* of any legitimate scientific process and of determining whether or not something should be accepted as scientifically valid. Well, besides continually employing their unscientific—and in fact *anti-scientific*—methods to attack scientific theories such as evolution (for example, claiming that gaps in the fossil record render the theory of evolution invalid, and then every time one of these "gaps" is filled by a new fossil discovery, turning around and claim-ing that this has simply created more gaps![36]), the Christian Fascists are now working both to set up their own spurious educational institutions, even on the university level (such as the Pat Robertson-founded Regent University, graduates of which have been brought into the Bush Administration in very large numbers) as well as to have people get advanced degrees, including in fields such as biol-ogy, from more legitimate and even prestigious universities, so that they can then use these degrees as credentials to lend credibility to their attacks on evolution (and other well-established scientific truths which conflict with fundamentalist religious dogma).

In all this, the Christian Fascists are facing some sharp contradic-tions when it comes to the realm of education. There is a significant

36. For important exposure and analysis of not only this particular tactic of the Creationists (in relation to the fossil record) but of the Creationist assault on evolution overall, including Creationism's recent incarnation as "Intelligent Design"—and the larger ideological and political implications of this—see *The Science of Evolution and The Myth of Creationism—Knowing What's Real And Why It Matters*," Ardea Skybreak, Insight Press, 2006.

movement among them to home-school their children in order to "quarantine" or "inoculate" them against things they would learn in public schools that would conflict with fundamentalist dogma and a more literalist reading of the Bible. At the same time, with assistance from wealthy individuals and institutions (right-wing foundations, etc.), they are building and financing Christian fundamentalist schools as an alternative to public schools. But then they run into a problem when the students finish high school: the parents don't want their kids to be stuck in the lower tier of society, they want them to have successful careers, and to have enough education, and educational credentials, to pursue those careers. And in this regard, although they are working to change this, the Christian fundamentalist universities still do not yet have enough prestige and "cachet" in society at large. At the same time, if you go into the mainstream, non-fundamentalist universities all across the country and you take biology, at this point evolution will be taught as a fact...for the simple reason that it is: it is not really possible to teach biology without teaching evolution as a well-proven theory—it is that foundational to all of biology. Here arises the contradiction that the young people who have been "educated" in the Christian Fascist tradition, and indoctrinated with that worldview, then go to mainstream universities and run right up against the fact that evolution is presented to them as a thoroughly established and proven theory. So the Christian Fascists are developing ways to try to work around this. They have summer camps where they send high school graduates to prepare them for college: "This is all the secular propaganda you are going to hear when you go to the university—all that sec-a-lar hoomanist stuff, and all these lies about eee-vo-lution. [Laughter] So here is what you need to learn to say in order to do well on the tests and get a good grade...but remember: Genesis is the real and absolute truth, and the rest of this is all lies and nonsense. You go to that exhibit in the museum in New York about Darwin and evolution—that's all lies." Along with this, fundamentalist groups organize tours where they take people to these creationist museums (one recently opened in the state of Kentucky, for example) where you learn such things as: the Grand Canyon was formed by the great flood associated with Noah.

Once again, the point of all this is to create, as much as possible, a self-contained world which will be ideologically sealed off from and impervious to the penetration of the larger world and a fact-based, rational and scientific understanding of reality.

For those in the ruling class who support and promote this Christian Fascist movement—and fundamentally for the ruling class as a whole—there is also an acute contradiction, in that they need some science to do what they're seeking to do in the world—economically and militarily. But, in the society at large, they increasingly need a population that is trained to not think critically and to accept an absolutist worldview that is not based on engaging and actually understanding reality. If you are trained and conditioned to believe that there is a higher truth than scientific truth founded in reality, then you can say, as some of these people do: "Never mind that there were no weapons of mass destruction in Iraq. Bush didn't lie, because he is carrying out God's will in the world, and that is a higher and greater truth than any fact you can cite about some statement Bush may have made on some occasion. It doesn't matter. There's a higher truth involved." And when you get people thinking in that kind of way, then—short of a major eruption in their lives and in the larger society and world they're a part of—that is relatively (not absolutely but relatively) impenetrable to facts, scientific analysis and rational discourse.

This goes along with a whole other dimension to the assault on critical thinking, and dissent, which is particularly focused on the universities at this point. Led by individuals and organizations with ties to the highest levels of the U.S. government, there is a concerted drive to target and silence, and/or drive out of academia altogether, professors whose work and teaching run counter to, or even raise significant questions about, policies and actions of the government— and particularly those who challenge the "official narrative" on the nature of this country, its history and its role in the world today. This is a spearhead of a broader move to purge out of public life any basis from which to call into question the whole juggernaut of war and repression which has been unleashed by the Bush regime, and to create a self-contained and self-reinforcing world, within society overall. As an article in *Revolution* newspaper recently put it:

> On one level, these right-wing forces are setting out to forge university administrations into *instruments of coercive enforcement and control* over faculty and students—intimidating, threatening, and "cleaning house" of dissident thinkers when called on to do so, while leaving scholars under attack to fend for themselves.
>
> On another level, they are setting out to turn the university into a *zone of uncontested indoctrination*, where severe limits would be placed on permissible discourse—in terms of professors speaking out, writing, or encouraging engagement over controversial issues in the classroom, etc.; and in terms of restricting and gutting programs like African American studies, women's studies, etc., that challenge and refute the official narratives and explanations of U.S. history and present-day inequality and global lopsidedness.
>
> And on a very basic level, they are setting out to *break the commitment of the university to rational and scientific discourse* and to undercut its ability to influence society in that direction. The attempt by Christian fascist forces to insinuate "intelligent design" into the universities, to blur and overwhelm the boundary between science and religion, and to train, accredit, and mobilize a generation of "creationist science" advocates is a signal and ominous development. ("WARNING: The Nazification of the American University," *Revolution*, issue no. 99, August 26, 2007, emphasis in original; available at revcom.us)

This is a sharp illustration of the links, and the fundamental unity, between the drive to suppress dissent and critical thinking in academia, the role and aims of the Christian Fascists, and the larger ruling class interests to which this is connected and which it ultimately serves.

Besides its overall importance, the reason I have gone into this at some length here, in the context of discussing *The Left Hand of God*, is that Lerner's epistemology incorporates in some important aspects—and makes significant concessions to—ways of thinking which are ultimately not rational but in fact irrational. This has to do with how Lerner understands—or fails to fully and correctly understand—what is represented by, and the extent and depth of the danger represented by, the Christian Fascists. Lerner even falls into attributing much of the growth of this reactionary fundamentalist force to not only the mistakes but the arrogance of "the left," as he conceives of it—in which he includes the Democratic Party in a general sense. And, according to Lerner, the fact that "the left" has made no room for religion, and has insisted on secularism, has contributed to and fostered an atmosphere in which people searching for spirituality and higher meaning are driven to the right. This is, in large part (though not entirely), Lerner's explanation for the growth of the "Religious Right."

In reality, this Christian Fascist movement is, to a large degree, an ideologically and politically reactionary response to challenges to certain entrenched privileges and to the traditional ways in which the oppressive and exploitative relations of this system have taken shape and been reinforced in American society, as well as in America's role in the world. Once again, this focuses to a very significant extent around patriarchy. Changes in the role of women in society—and now, for god's sake, all these gay people making demands for legal recognition and equality!—and the ways in which the traditional values that are associated with, and to a significant degree concentrated in, patriarchy are being challenged and undermined, even though this has ultimately remained within the framework and confines of the capitalist system—this is all too much for those who are drawn to Christian Fascism. Along with that, American exceptionalism (to refer back to the formulation employed by Kevin Phillips), that is, the notion of America's unique goodness, based on its special relationship with god, and its manifest destiny and divine mission in the world—this is a fundamental and essential part of the Christian Fascist belief system. And this, too, is being challenged in the practical realm, in struggle throughout the world, and ideologically and politically it is being rejected by significant sections of American society itself—large numbers of people who, for a variety of reasons and coming from different viewpoints, do not accept this vision of America and its relation to the rest of the world. Among the large numbers of people in the U.S. who have opposed the American invasion and occupation of Iraq, the sentiment has been broadly expressed that American lives are not more valuable than the lives of other people; and even though, for the most part, this does not yet represent a full and radical rupture with American imperialism, and as such is not a revolutionary viewpoint, it is nonetheless completely alien and antagonistic to the traditionalist, absolutist Christian Fascist worldview and those who are galvanized around that worldview.

These people are being mobilized around a fascist-imperialist program—this is something that Lerner does not really come to grips with, or even fully recognize—an orientation which is absolutely determined that the only way the rightful and righteous order of things, in American society and America's role in the world, can be reasserted and reestablished is through the imposition of a theocratic form of government in the U.S. itself: "This is a Christian nation. It's those sec-a-lar people that got God and prayer taken out of the schools, who insisted on teaching eee-vo-lution in the schools, who got us away from the word of God—that's why we're in the trouble we're in today and why people are attacking us and blowing up buildings in New York City, and why we gotta go get 'em in the world before they get us."

While one can point to real mistakes and shortcomings on the part of the "left," broadly speaking—including a paralyzing influence of rampant relativism, linked with identity politics—it is fundamentally misguided and disarming, ideologically and politically, to attribute the rise of this Christian Fascist movement, and its powerful connections to and support from the highest levels of government, to mistakes or arrogance on the part of the left. Now, there is a way in which, despite the widespread revolutionary sentiments and mood among large sections of American society that was manifest by the late 1960s, the reality that there was no revolution at that time has actually been turned into a factor that has contributed to the rise of some of this religious fundamentalism. Through the upsurge of the '60s, many things were called into question—not just in the realm of ideas, although that was extremely important, but in practice, in the realm of political struggle—things that are foundational to this society. And many changes were brought about, partly as a result of mass political struggle and partly because of the changing features and needs of the economy. Once again, one of the most important dimensions of this was in relation to the role of women, particularly among professionals and other sections of the middle class, where it became both possible and necessary for women to work full time, in the effort to maintain a middle class standard of living. When you combine that with political and ideological expressions of feminism, and other movements that came forward out of the '60s, this did pose a very direct challenge to traditionally institutionalized forms of oppression in this society.

But this didn't go all the way it didn't overthrow the political structures and power that enforce this oppression and exploitation—and so it was not able to reach to the root and foundation of those relations. As that movement receded, and in the context where there was a regrouping by the ruling class and an assault on many of the things that characterized the political movement and "counter-culture" of the '60s, there was a retreat on the part of many, particularly in the middle strata, who had been part of that movement. With regard to many of the spheres of society in which the movement of the '60s (and into the early '70s) had taken a radical expression, the orientation and objectives of much of the "left" increasingly became much more limited, narrow, reformist. To a significant degree, this devolved down into and got reduced to identity politics—sometimes, yes, in rather narrow and petty forms which didn't get to the essence and the foundation of what the oppression of different groups was rooted in, and instead often turned into a form of narrow commodity competition ("the oppression of the group with which I identify is the special province—and, in effect, the property—of people like me, and no one else has the right to say anything about, to make any demands or to negotiate for any concessions in relation to this").

So, in a very secondary way, *this* has contributed to a backlash against the very legitimate and necessary movements of opposition to various forms of oppression and exploitation which are in fact an integral part of the capitalist-imperialist system; and in this sense, it has contributed—again, very secondarily—to the growth of Christian Fascism in particular. But this is in no way the essential or defining reason why this reactionary movement has grown. This is a movement which is being led from on high—and here I am referring not to some non-existent god but to powerful sections of the ruling class, which have made the determination that such a movement, and quite possibly even a theocratic, Christian fundamentalist, form of capitalist dictatorship, is necessary, given what they are setting out to do in the world, how they envision the role of the U.S. in the world and what the corresponding character of U.S. society needs to be. And these Christian Fascist forces are absolutely relentless in pursuit of their objectives. The foot soldiers of this movement, whether "good people" or not, are being trained in a fanatical spirit of "onward Christian soldiers," right now largely in a political and ideological sense, but already as a potential military force, should that be deemed necessary at some point by those who head these forces.

Perhaps, ironically, we could say that Rabbi Rudin (author of *The Baptizing of America: The Religious Right's Plans for the Rest of Us*) has a better understanding of this than Rabbi Lerner, even though in an overall sense Lerner's views are more alienated from and in opposition to much of the character of American society and America's relation to the rest of the world, and the whole direction this is now taking. But Rudin (who is more of a "mainstream liberal") has grasped very clearly, even with his limitations, that the "Religious Right" is an unrelenting movement that is determined to change the character of American society and how it's ruled—to change, in important ways, some of the forms and some of the particular instrumentalities through which the oppressive nature of the system is carried out and enforced. In *The Baptizing of America* Rudin makes it very clear—and it is frankly quite refreshing to read this in a book by an author with Rudin's viewpoint—that attempting to compromise with these Christian Fascists will not work, and will only lead them to be more aggressive.[37]

For example, around the crucial and pivotal issue of abortion, many liberals—and in this they are "led" by the likes of the Clintons—promote the idea of seeking "common ground" with the Christian Fascists, with arguments like: "We can all agree that it is desirable to limit the number of abortions and make abortion rare, so let us unite together to make sure that birth control is widely and easily available." Yet experience has already shown that the Christian Fascists are determined to eliminate not only abortion but birth control as well, and that such pleas for "common ground" only make them

---

37. This basic point on the need to uncompromisingly confront and oppose what is represented by the Christian Fascist movement is also strongly argued, from his own point of view, by Chris Hedges in the conclusion of *American Fascists*: "All Americans—not only those of faith—who care about our open society must learn to speak about this movement with a new vocabulary, to give up passivity, to challenge aggressively this movement's deluded appropriation of Christianity and to do everything possible to defend tolerance....Tolerance is a virtue, but tolerance coupled with passivity is a vice." (p. 207) Overall, there is much of value and importance in Hedge's arguments here, and throughout *American Fascists*, even while it is limited by his own outlook, which includes a progressive interpretation of Christianity and, unfortunately, is significantly influenced by the erroneous and anti-communist views of the 20th century philosopher Karl Popper, as embodied in his work *The Open Society and Its Enemies*, as well as by Hannah Arendt and her unscientific theories of "totalitarianism."

more fanatical in seeking to do away with both. As Rudin plainly states, with a clarity and decisiveness that is all too rare among liberals and progressives these days:

> For Christocrats [Christian theocrats], the battle to ban abortions in the United States is their Gettysburg or Stalingrad, the turning point in the war they are waging to gain dominance over our society. Abortion is their overriding passion and for them, it is a fight to the finish.
>
> If they succeed in banning legal abortion in America, Christocratic leaders and their followers will be even more energized and empowered to press forward in the campaign to baptize America. (*The Baptizing of America*, pp. 205–06)

This is one important thing that the Rabbi Rudin grasps much more fully and correctly than the Rabbi Lerner.

And, as their determination to eliminate birth control, along with abortion, makes clear, what lies at the heart of the issue of abortion, and of the Christian Fascist's unrelenting attempt to make it illegal, is not the killing of babies (which is scientifically wrong in the first place) but is **the chaining of women in oppressive relations in which their essential role is reduced to that of being the property of men and the breeders of their children, according to "god's plan" and the dictates of theocratic interpreters of "god's will."**

The fact is that you are not going to defeat this Christian Fascist force—everything it represents and everything bound up with it—*and* you are not going to win significant numbers of people away from it, without taking it on in a very direct and forceful way—and, yes, offending people. In the fullest sense, it is necessary to challenge this movement, and those who are now a part of it, fundamentally and foundationally, in the context of building a movement that is not only opposed to this Christian Fascism but is increasingly being won to the objective of overturning and transforming society as a whole and uprooting all the outmoded, exploitative relations which this Christian Fascist movement is seeking to reinforce in extremely oppressive and repressive forms.

And it has been shown that in the course of challenging—and, yes, even offending—people, they can change. Not just individuals but masses of people. This was experienced on a grand scale in the '60s. I personally knew many people in the course of the '60s movement who had previously been "Goldwater Republicans" but who ruptured with that and became very radical, in a positive way, in the '60s. This kind of transformation "from reactionary to revolutionary" took place on a very large scale in the course of that whole upsurge. It is true, and important to recognize, that there is a particularity to this religious fundamentalism and its epistemology which has a tighter hold on people than more secular "conservative" politics, but this is also, in profound ways, crashing up against the way the world really is. That provides an important material basis for wrenching people out of this. But that is what will be required—wrenching them out of it. In building the kind of struggle that needs to be developed against the crimes and atrocities being committed by the Bush regime—and the whole system of which it is a key part and is now a leading force— winning over people who are currently caught up in the Christian Fascist movement is not, and should not be, the focus and main objective; but it should be an aim to win over as many as possible, as part of a broader effort to repolarize society, politically and ideologically, in a more positive direction and ultimately in a way that is more favorable for a revolution that can in reality transform society as a whole to uproot relations of exploitation and oppression.

Instead, and in opposition to this, we see that Lerner's position ideologically interconnects with and finds expression in an ultimate and essential political reformism. Throughout *The Left Hand of God* Lerner repeatedly talks about how the "left" can get back into power—as though it's a question of whether the "right" or the "left," in some classless sense, holds power—rather than grasping that what exists is *a system* that is *ruled by a class*, a system whose nature is *rooted in the underlying production relations* and which takes expression in the superstructure, in terms of political rule, as one or another form of *bourgeois dictatorship*. In relation to this, the following three sentences—which are found, among other places, in "Bringing Forward Another Way"—are very relevant and capture some essential reality in a concentrated way:

> In a world marked by profound class divisions and social inequality, to talk about "democracy"—without talking about the class nature of that democracy and which class it serves—is meaningless, and worse. So long as society is divided into classes, there can be no "democracy for all": one class or another will rule, and it will uphold and promote that kind of democracy which serves its interests and goals. The question is: which class will rule and whether its rule, and its system of democracy, will serve the continuation, or the eventual abolition, of class divisions and the corresponding relations of exploitation, oppression and inequality. (See "Bringing Forward Another Way" at revcom.us)[38]

As noted above, Lerner often identifies the "left" with the Democratic Party, which is objectively *a party of the ruling class*. While he does make valid, and at times sharp, critiques of policies, and even of the orientation, of the Democratic Party, it is clear that Lerner actually believes that it is possible to influence a section of the ruling class, as represented by the Democratic Party, to adopt the kind of program he advocates. He recognizes that people are going to accuse him of being unrealistic—to which he answers that

---

38. More extensive discussion of questions related to what is contained in the three sentences above, on democracy and class rule, and on the transition from all systems of class rule to a communist society—without class distinctions, exploiters and exploiters, and without dictatorship of any kind—is found in other works by this author, including *Democracy: Can't We Do Better Than That?*; *Phony Communism is Dead...Long Live Real Communism* (Second Edition, 2004); and the pamphlet *Dictatorship and Democracy, and the Socialist Transition to Communism*.

the way things are now is neither positive nor realistic in the sense of bringing about a better world. But there is no recognition on Lerner's part that the Democratic Party—and, for that matter, the "left" as he identifies it, a "left" that is situated well within the confines of the capitalist system, even while opposing some of its more egregious injustices—is a superstructural expression of underlying production and social relations, and of the dynamics of capitalist accumulation taking place through those production relations; and that these production relations and this process of accumulation fundamentally and ultimately establish the framework, and the limits, within which struggles in the realm of politics take place within this system. *For these essential reasons* it is not possible to win the Democratic Party to the kind of viewpoint and program that Lerner argues for, passionately. Taking Lerner's program as he himself puts it forward—and leaving aside for the moment the fact that, from the standpoint of the complete abolition of relations of exploitation and oppression, Lerner's program falls far short, and even in some significant aspects works against this goal—the truth is that in light of, and so long as things remain within the confines of, the fundamental relations and processes of capitalism, this program of Lerner's *is* totally unrealistic and unrealizable.

The severe limitations of Lerner's ideological viewpoint, as well as political program, come through very sharply in relation to the oppression of women. Now, I have to admit that I am tempted here to say: Never trust somebody religious when it comes to patriarchy. [Laughter] Never trust them, at least, to have a thoroughgoing stand in opposition to this oppression and in support of the complete emancipation of women. Maybe it is unfair to make such a sweeping generalization, but it is not incidental that Lerner's ideological and political limitations take very stark and concentrated expression around the question of abortion, where he puts forward—really to be honest—quite horrific positions, which in turn reflect, in a concentrated way, some of the fundamental weaknesses of his overall outlook and approach.

In a chapter entitled, significantly, "The Family, Sexuality, and Personal Responsibility," in *The Left Hand of God*, Lerner starts right out, in a section on abortion, with the, by now all-too-familiar, formula (or mantra): "make it safe, legal, and rare." (*The Left Hand of God*, p. 267) In this, and overall, it can be seen how Lerner's position on this question is closely in line with that of bourgeois politicians like Bill and Hillary Clinton, Al Gore, and the Democratic Party leadership in general. Now, Lerner does say that, "Spiritual progressives should be unequivocal in opposing any attempts to make abortion illegal." However, he then immediately adds: "But we should be equally unequivocal in recognizing abortion as a tragic loss." And things go further downhill from there.

Lerner makes the claim that, "Most women who have gone through abortions will tell you how very emotionally painful it has been to experience this loss of life." (p. 267) There are two things—two essential things—wrong with this. First of all, it is not true. It is far from the truth that "most women" who have had abortions would agree with Lerner on this. And, second, to the degree that there is any truth to it—to the degree that this does apply to some women who have had abortions—this cannot be divorced from the larger social context in which there has been a whole right-wing assault around the question of abortion, politically and ideologically, an assault in relation to which liberals and progressives—including people like Lerner, as well as ruling class politicians like the Clintons and Gore—have been ceding the moral ground and joining in the chorus declaring abortion a tragedy, even if people like Lerner do not believe it should be made into a crime.

Listen to this language from Lerner, and keep in mind that he is talking here about abortion: "The miracle of life flowing through us deserves to be treated with sanctity and care, and when life is snuffed out, this is an occasion for communal sadness and mourning." (p. 267) Note: not even just individual but *communal* "sadness and mourning." Here I feel like invoking the old joke about the Lone Ranger and Tonto. The Lone Ranger is out with Tonto, and suddenly they're surrounded by Indians, who pin them down and shoot at them; and, as the situation becomes more and more grim, finally the Lone Ranger turns to Tonto and says: "Well, it looks like we're in bad shape, Tonto". And Tonto replies: *"What do you mean* **we**, *white man?"* [Laughter] So here, in the same spirit, I would say to Lerner: *What do you mean "the miracle of life flowing through* **us**,*" white man?"* [Laughter]

And let's look further at this statement that begins: "The miracle of life flowing through us deserves to be treated with sanctity and care." Note the choice of words "when life is *snuffed out*" to refer to an abortion: this does very much sound like a description of the wanton taking of human life—something akin to, if not literally, murder. And even the more benign, or supposedly joyful-sounding, word "miracle" insinuates into the discussion a feel of mysticism about the process of reproduction. Childbearing—if it is wanted, intended and planned for—may well bring great joy, but there is nothing "mystical" about the process. Identifying it with notions of the miraculous—and especially when phrases are employed like "the miracle of life flowing through *us*"—fosters a sense that childbearing is somehow a *duty*—one imbued with a sense of *religious obligation*. Note also how Lerner makes the "tragedy" of abortion one that involves not only the woman but also the whole community; and in line with the view of this as a kind of communal experience, note again how Lerner speaks, with very deliberate language, of "the miracle of life flowing through *us*." This, as we will see, is not accidental or incidental phrasing.

Just a minute ago, when I quoted Lerner saying that abortion is a "tragic loss," I deliberately did not cite his whole statement there, but held part of it back. The full content of what Lerner says in characterizing abortion as a "tragic loss" is that this is so "not only for the individual woman who has chosen to undergo it but also for *the entire community*." (p. 267, emphasis added here) And things become even worse as Lerner continues his discourse on this: a little later he goes so far as to argue that with an abortion "this loss of life affects not only the woman, but *the man who was a part of the conception, and the community in which this woman lives, and the entire global community.*" (p. 268, emphasis added here)[39]

Lerner's view is that the position he advocates "does not relieve one of the burden and moral responsibility of making those choices," and he is careful to add: "nor does it empower a community to intervene and make our choices for us" and that he would "caution against anyone trying to pressure a woman to be part of this community process." (pp. 268–69) But, Lerner argues, such a communal process is positive because it "situates us as fundamentally linked to one another and as having some responsibility to check in with others about the impact of our actions on them." (p. 268) Now, he does say that this is not a checking in that can or should be legally mandated. And he goes on:

> I talked above about building a movement that creat-
> ed an ethos in the liberal and progressive culture that
> was disapproving of the demeaning of sexuality. So,
> too, we should seek to create an ethos in which women
> feel invited to consult and receive support from oth-
> ers affected by their decision to abort, and conversely
> for those involved to offer support and comfort should
> such a decision be taken by the pregnant woman. *At
> every stage of this process, the relevant community needs
> to be involved in a caring and supportive way.* (p. 269,
> emphasis added here)

One of the main forms of "support and caring" that Lerner advocates is that, as he puts it: "A spiritual community should be there to provide emotional and spiritual support, to make it possible for the woman to really grieve the loss [in the case of abortion], and to affirm a shared vision of the sanctity of life." And Lerner even goes so

---

39. Recent moves, for example in the state of Ohio, to pass laws that would effectively give "the man who was part of the conception" *veto power* over the woman's right to abortion, bring into sharper relief how truly terrible Lerner's position is on abortion.

far as to call for ceremonies to formalize this individual and communal grieving; he calls for—get this—"rituals of mourning and purification to acknowledge what is, in the absence of these rituals, usually experienced only as a personal tragedy." (See pp. 267–68, 272.)

It has to be said, straight out, that—despite the language of caring, community, nurturing and support, and despite disclaimers about not trying to pressure a woman into taking part in these community processes—these views of Lerner's, and the implications of what he advocates, will very rightly cause shudders among people with a deep understanding (or even a basic sense) of how, for thousands of years, not only the force of the state, but also social customs and traditions—and, yes, the pressure of the community—have been used to maintain women in an oppressed condition, and to punish them, often in the harshest and cruelest of ways, where they have sought to break out of these oppressive confines.

Here I'm reminded of Richard Pryor's remarks about how he didn't like to hear white people use the word "nigger." He said it made him respond in the same way as when he heard good ole boys shouting in the middle of the night: "YEEEE HAA!" It sent shivers down his spine—and not in a good way.

Whatever Lerner's intent, the fact is that what he calls for around abortion would in reality amount to nothing less than perpetuating patriarchal oppression—and even the worst horrors associated with it—and institutionalizing the communal enforcement of patriarchal traditions, values and relations, reinforced by wrapping women in a heavy shroud of guilt. And it must be said that what Lerner puts forward here is not that far removed from the bloody sheet of the wedding night. [Applause]

Not surprisingly, there is a very close link between these genuinely horrific views of Lerner's and his sentimentality about the family. He writes: "No matter what our own child experiences may have been, no matter how much we had to struggle later in life to repair some of the damage done by less-than-perfect parents, almost all of us recognize that the family is the only institution in our society whose explicit goal is to provide love and caring." (*The Left Hand of God*, p. 241) Here again, one has to ask: exactly what world is Lerner talking about? This is not to say that there aren't loving and caring parents; but what has been the actual experience, down through thousands of years, and up to the present time, especially for women in the context and confines of the family? It is far from this sentimental and romanticized view of the family. Right down to today, and in so-called "modern society," tremendous horrors have been perpetrated and perpetuated in the context of the family. Let's remember (as I pointed out in *Preaching From a Pulpit of Bones*) that it is only within the last few decades that the concept of marital rape has not been considered and treated, socially and legally, as a contradiction in terms; that "Well into the 1980s, in most states in the U.S. men could *legally* rape their wives"; and that it was not until nearly the end of the 20th century that this was declared a crime in all states, with North Carolina being the last state to do this, in late 1993. (See *Preaching From a Pulpit of Bones*, p. 20—emphasis in original.)

And let's not forget what I also pointed out in *Preaching*—which still has great relevance today:

> Women are more likely to be raped by their husbands—and children more likely to be sexually assaulted and molested by their fathers—than by strangers. It is only in recent years—and largely as a result of the social upheaval of "the '60s" (which actually carried over well into the 1970s), and in particular because of the women's movement that was brought forth out of that upheaval—that much light has been shed on *this* horrendous "domestic" violence. Before that, this was largely shrouded in darkness, behind the closed doors of "the home," protected by the "sanctity" of the "traditional family." (p. 19, emphasis in original)

So, to say the least—and in fact to wildly understate things—the statement I have cited here from Lerner on how the family is "the only institution in our society whose explicit goal is to provide love and caring" represents a highly romanticized, and distorted, picture of the family and the oppressive relations that still essentially and fundamentally define the family as a patriarchal institution and as an integral part of the overall oppressive relations of capitalist society—notwithstanding the intentions and efforts of many parents (including some fathers) to have some other kind of relationships within the family.

Now, Lerner is not entirely ignorant of, nor does he entirely ignore, the reality and history of oppression associated with the family. But in line with his overall views, he does not present this as something bound up, inextricably, with the division of society into antagonistic classes—something that is bound to exist as an integral and essential part of any society ruled by an exploiting class, most definitely including modern capitalist society.

Lerner's approach to this is, accordingly, one of reformism, which cannot and will not provide the means for getting to the root of—and finally abolishing—patriarchy and the oppression of women. Lerner puts it this way: "Of course, not all families live up to the ideal of being a place where genuine caring and nurturance are given." It would only seem fair to give Lerner some kind of award for understatement here. [Laughter] "Nor," he goes on, "have families always represented our highest values." Two times in a row he should get that award. [Laughter] "One great achievement of the twentieth century," he continues, "was our realization that the patriarchal family oppressed women and children and supported class divisions in the larger society, by legitimating the notion that inequalities of power are 'natural.'" "Spiritual progressives," he says, "seek to encourage the evolution of families from a structure based on domination to one founded on a spiritual partnership." (*The Left Hand of God*, p. 242)

Note first: *evolution*—not revolution—when it is revolution that is really required. And along with the other limitations of, and contradictions in, Lerner's position here, the unavoidable fact is that, as I have discussed here and elsewhere, the spiritual and religious traditions and related values that he wants to base things on are themselves powerful forces serving to rationalize and to reinforce patriarchy and the oppression of women. The failure to rupture with those traditions and values is completely interwoven with the failure to get to the root of—and with an inability to lead the way, or even to fully see the way, to rooting out—that oppression and, indeed, all oppression.

So it is not surprising that, once again, as with the question of abortion, Lerner fails to understand the essence of what is going on with the aggressive assertion of reactionary, patriarchal positions by the Christian Fascists; and this is bound up with the fact that Lerner's own views on this share certain basic assumptions with the religious fundamentalists. He fails to understand, or to agree, that there is absolutely *no good basis*—and that it is entirely wrong, in principle—to seek any common ground at all with people determined not only to outlaw abortion, but to forcibly assert absolute patriarchal authority and oppression.

To get a fuller sense of this, it is worth citing an article by Russell Shorto in the Sunday magazine section of the *New York Times*, May 7, 2006, entitled "Contra-Contraception." Among other horrors mentioned in this article, Shorto describes what the Christian fundamentalists call "Purity Balls." Shorto quotes Leslee Unruh, a sponsor of these "Purity Balls," where *fathers* attend, with their teenage daughters: "'We think the relationship between fathers and their daughters is the key,'" she says. Shorto recounts how at such "Purity Balls" a father "gives a 'purity ring' to his daughter—a symbol of the promise she makes to maintain her virginity for her future husband. Then, during her marriage ceremony, the daughter gives the ring to her new husband."

Among other things, the appropriate word for this is: "sick!" [Laughter] As a comrade commented when I read the above description to her: this conjures up visions of incest and cattle auctions, all at once. And once again, how far away is this from the bloody sheet of the wedding night—and the death penalty if the sheet is not bloody?

Along with this, although Lerner seeks to uphold the rights of homosexuals and to oppose the attacks on them from the "Christian Right," he is forced into some of the most astounding and ridiculous contortions in the attempt to reconcile this stand with the religious traditions with which he identifies and which he wants to promote. For example, many people who have been part of the debate around same-sex relations and gay marriage are familiar with the infamous statement in Leviticus 18:22, about a man not having sex with another man: "You shall not lie with a male as with a woman; it is an abomination." Well, Lerner claims, these words "allow for the interpretation that men should develop sexual behaviors appropriate for gay relationships that do not seek to imitate the behaviors appropriate for heterosexual relationships." (*The Left Hand of God*, p. 264) I'm not kidding—this is what Lerner actually says. [Laughter] It is frankly hard to believe that anyone, including Lerner, who is at all familiar with this passage, and in general with the scriptures it is a part of, could seriously believe what Lerner says here. But Lerner is, in a real sense, stuck, and cannot help going through these intellectual contortions, because he is determined to promote a "progressive spirituality" which is rooted in those scriptures and the religious traditions associated with them, and yet his sense of justice compels him to oppose the condemnation of same-sex relations. And matters become more strained because not only does any reasonable interpretation of the verse in question from Leviticus make clear that sex between men is being condemned in the strongest terms ("it is an abomination"), but a little later in Leviticus the penalty for sexual relations between men is spelled out in no uncertain terms: "If a man lies with a male as with a woman, both of them have committed an abomination; they shall be put to death; their blood is upon them." (Leviticus 20:13) And I am sorry, but Leviticus means what it rather obviously says—it means that a man can't have sex with another man, he is only supposed to have sex with a woman, within the proper confines of property relations—that is, within a marriage sanctioned by the religious and political authorities. There is no other *reasonable* interpretation of this. I don't believe there is any way you can truth-fully say that the Bible, in Leviticus, is merely insisting: "When you have sex with a woman, have it in the missionary position; but if you have sex with a man, you won't be able to do that, so naturally you'll have to do it in another position." [Laughter]

Next, I want to talk about Lerner's views of awe and wonder. This is a repeated theme in his book: the need of human beings for awe and wonder. Now, I do find significant areas of agreement with Lerner on this—it is something I have brought out in a number of writings and talks, including *Preaching From a Pulpit of Bones*. But there are two serious problems with Lerner's views on this.

First of all, while at times he just refers to awe and wonder, fre-quently he will formulate it as "awe and wonder at creation." So right away, he's brought a religious element, or the suggestion of a religious experience, into this. And if you understand, as a scientific viewpoint and method leads you to understand, that there is no creation in a religious sense—that is, there is no Creator, no supernatural being, but only matter in motion, existing infinitely and undergoing con-tinuous change—then you understand how, while awe and wonder are important, there is not and there cannot be awe and wonder "at creation," but rather awe and wonder at what is in reality the mani-fold forms and the changingness of nature, and the way in which this presents itself in many diverse and often unexpected ways.

Secondly, Lerner is one-sided on awe and wonder. Owing to the influence of his religious viewpoint—his philosophical idealism and metaphysics—he doesn't grasp the dialectical relation between, as we would say, materialism and romanticism; between the experi-ence of awe and wonder on the one hand, and solving mysteries on the other hand, which will be a continuous, never-ending process as long as human beings exist. To put this another way, we need awe and wonder—but not *superstitious* awe.

In *Observations on Art and Culture, Science and Philosophy*, I spoke to both sides of the picture, both aspects of the contradiction involved. As I put it there:

> Human beings do need to be amazed. You don't need religion to realize or appreciate that. In the motion of the material world and the interaction of human beings with the rest of reality, mysteries get resolved and new mysteries emerge. ("Intoxicated With the Truth," in *Observations on Art and Culture, Science and Philosophy*, p. 69)

I have also emphasized, for example in *Preaching From a Pulpit of Bones*:

> Communism—the real, vibrant communism of Marx, Lenin, and Mao, not the phony, lifeless "communism" of Khrushchev, Brezhnev, and Deng Xiaoping—does not weigh down on but gives the fullest flight to the "human spirit," to the imagination and the continual pondering of things which at any point are the source of mystery and of awe. Communism rejects the notion that mystery and awe must be identified only with things that cannot be known or understood; that the highest expression of this mystery and awe is belief in some unknowable and ineffable essence beyond material reality; and that we should obliterate the distinction between imagination and objective reality through the pretense that the supernatural forces and beings that human beings have created in their imagination are not only real but are the ruling and controlling forces of existence. (*Preaching From a Pulpit of Bones*, p. 87. This is also spoken to in "Materialism and Romanticism: Can We Do Without Myth?" which is included in the *Observations* book.)

Another way to put this is that materialism and mystery form a contradiction (in "Maoist terms," they constitute a unity of opposites). A materialist and dialectical method enables us to explore mysteries, sometimes to resolve them; it enables us to appreciate them even before resolving them, to appreciate them after we have resolved them, and to recognize that new mysteries will continually arise, including in relation to ones we resolve.

The communist world outlook is a *materialist* outlook. Now, that does not have the same meaning as the way in which "materialism" is commonly used: "materialism," in the popular sense, is associated with acquiring material possessions (you go to the mall and you get as many consumer goods as you can possibly buy). And one of the things that many people feel sick about and rebel against—often turning to religion as a result—is the never-ending quest for more and more material things. This is never ultimately satisfying. You always need more. But this is not what materialism means in the scientific, communist sense. In this sense it refers to the basic under-standing that all of reality consists of matter, in motion—that real-ity consists only of actually existing material things, which exist in many different forms and are constantly undergoing change—and anything that is not matter does not exist. The sun is matter, the stars are matter, energy is matter, we human beings are matter, the processes within our brains are matter—these are all real material things that are moving and changing. That's what all of reality con-sists of, and there is no reality that is something else than that.

Contrary to the claims of many—including 20th century philos-ophers Karl Popper and Bertrand Russell—Marxism is a science, a scientific approach to understanding and changing reality. It is not a religion.[40]

Here, I want to cite the following from *The Science of Evolution and The Myth of Creationism—Knowing What's Real And Why It Mat-ters*, by Ardea Skybreak, since it powerfully provides an answer to Lerner and to those who hold similar views concerning the funda-mental question of how to appreciate human existence and its rela-tion to the larger universe, to the rest of material reality:

---

40. See for example, Karl Popper, *The Open Society and Its Enemies*, es-pecially Volume II, *The High Tide of Prophecy: Hegel, Marx, and the Aftermath*, Princeton University Press, 1971; and Bertrand Russell, *Why I Am Not a Christian, and Other Essays on Religion and Related Subjects*, Simon & Schuster, Inc., 1957. In another work, *Making Revolution and Emancipating Humanity* (available at revcom.us), I speak to some of Popper's attempts to discredit Marxism and the distortions involved in this.

We now know that our own human evolution as well as the evolution of all living things can be explained by entirely *natural processes* and requires no super-natural explanations. But will our ability to increasingly understand life without god leave us feeling in some way adrift and empty? Why should it? We still can, and should, be duly amazed, sustained, and even humbled, by the recognition of the wonders of diversity and complexity that naturally evolving life can itself bring forth, and by both the limitations and ongoing potentials of our own humanity...Far from being a recipe for a grey, cold and passionless outlook, a truly materialist *scientific* method, systematically applied to uncovering the *actual* genuine wonders of the natural and social world, can uncork the imagination, the sense of purpose and the transformative consciousness and initiative of human beings in ways no reference to a presumed higher power ever could. Isn't that an outlook worth striving for? (See the last page of the centerfold pictorial section of *The Science of Evolution*, emphasis in original.)

Before moving on to the next section of this book, I want to examine a little further Lerner's views in relation to the question of epistemology—and more specifically what is, and is not, rational thought. Lerner critiques "scientism" but this critique of "scientism" involves a confusion and mingling of actual science and the scientific method, on the one hand, with *positivism*—the tendency to reduce things to their immediate physical cause (or to empirical evidence in and of itself and as a thing unto itself) and to argue that there is nothing else, no larger factors and processes, which are involved, or which interact with the immediate and instant phenomena, and no leaps from one state of matter to another, as a result of such often complex processes and their interactions.[41]

---

41. This positivism is an expression of *determinism*, since it embodies, or carries within it, the conclusion (or implication) that whatever *is* must *of necessity* be.

At times, Lerner treats science as the reduction of everything to what, as Lerner puts it, can be "observed and measured"; at other times he refers to "the tools of science—empirical observation and rational thought." (The *Left Hand of God*, pp. 131, 133) But his general tendency to conflate, or equate, positivism and reductionism, on the one hand, with the actual scientific outlook and method, on the other hand, creates a muddle which then serves to discredit science. In reality, the scientific outlook and method involves not simply empirical evidence, but also qualitative leaps to theory and conceptions, synthesizing facts and observations into a higher level of comprehension of reality; and it involves the testing of hypotheses and theories in practice and engagement with the larger objective world. And this is true, most of all, of the communist world outlook and methodology, which is a synthesis of materialism and dialectics and provides the most consistent, systematic and comprehensive scientific approach to all of reality.

This is qualitatively and radically different from scientism, from positivism and reductionism, which, among other things, are characterized by the notion of a linear connection, a more or less direct extension, between experience and concepts, instead of what actually happens in reality—where, as Mao Tsetung pointed out, there are, repeatedly, qualitative leaps from experience and perceptual knowledge to conceptual or rational knowledge. Rational knowledge, correctly understood, is...well, rational knowledge, which synthesizes what is learned through experience of various kinds—including scientific investigation and experimentation—into an abstraction which reflects reality in a more concentrated and higher way.

Lerner wants to argue that religion is no less a mode of rational thought than science. But the truth is that religion is *non*-rational thought. It involves and relies on leaps of faith, which are in opposition to—and represent a rupture with—rational thought and which do not and cannot involve leaps to correctly synthesize what is learned through experience of the objectively existing world. Religion puts forward as truths—even as essential and defining truths—things which are not derived from, and cannot in turn be tested in, the objective world of material existence. To identify the non-rational nature of religion is not a matter of hurling insults, but of speaking to the essential reality and character of religious thinking. And in reality, this non-rational way of thinking that characterizes religion cannot help but lend itself, in one way or another, to *ir*rational thinking.

From all this, it can be seen more fully that, on the one hand, there are important insights in Lerner's *The Left Hand of God*, and there is a significant scope for building unity with Lerner and those who hold similar views; but, at the same time, Lerner's worldview, and the political orientation and objectives that go along with it, cannot lead things where they need to go, even in terms of fully and thoroughly transforming and uprooting the ills in the world and in the relations among people that Lerner points to—sometimes quite incisively—and definitely in terms of uprooting and advancing beyond *all* relations of exploitation, domination and oppression, and the culture and ways of thinking that go along with and reinforce them.

The Myth of the Truthfulness and Positive Role of Religious Myth

Next, I want to briefly discuss Karen Armstrong's basic thesis about myth, and its social role, as put forward in her book *A Short History of Myth*, in particular in Chapter 1, "What is a Myth." She writes:

> Mythology is not an early attempt at history, and does not claim that its tales are objective fact....The Neanderthals who prepared their dead companion for a new life were, perhaps, engaged in the same game of spiritual make-believe that is common to all mythmakers: "What if this world were not all that there is? How would this affect our lives—psychologically, practically

or socially? Would we become different? More complete? And, if we did find that we were so transformed,
would that not show that our mythical belief was true
in some way, that it was telling us something important
about our humanity, even though we could not prove
this rationally?" (*A Short History of Myth*, pp. 8–9)

And she goes on:

A myth, therefore, is true because it is effective, not because it gives us factual information. If, however, it does
not give us new insight into the deeper meaning of life,
it has failed. If it *works*, that is, if it forces us to change
our minds and hearts, gives us new hope, and compels
us to live more fully, it is a valid myth. (p.10, emphasis
in original)

Once again we get back to the question of the difference—the
qualitative difference—between art, including myth, and reality, as
well as between art and science. At the end of *Preaching From a Pulpit of Bones*, I spoke to these questions and made the point that art,
as *distinguished from science*, generally does not ask us to believe
that what it presents is actually and literally true; rather, as a general
characteristic, art presents things about life which are not represen-
tations or mere reproductions of life as it is. Religion, too, presents
things which are other than the way reality actually is. That is what
art and religion have in common—and where they both differ from
science. Where the *difference* lies between art and religion—and it is
an essential difference—is that religion asks us to believe that what
it presents *is* actually true, and not only the truth but the defining
and essential truth about reality and its motive causes and forces.
As I put it in *Preaching*:

If religion were to present itself in the same way and
with the same expectations and requirements that art
typically does—if it were to allow and encourage people to have the ultimate recognition that its fantastic

creations are not real—then it would no longer be harmful and a hindrance to the all-around development of humanity in the way it is now. But it would also no longer be *religion*. In this era of world-historic transformation and in the future to come, humanity will never be able to do without the imagination and without art; it must and will do without—and do much better without—religion. (p. 88, emphasis in original)

To get into another dimension of this, we can discuss what there is in common, but also what is different, between beauty and truth. Both are important in their own right. And, in important ways, they are interconnected: there can be, and often is, an aspect of beauty in truth, and in the discovery of truth, and an aspect of the truth in beauty—beauty, or art in a more general sense, may reveal important truths, often from new angles. But beauty—or conceptions of beauty and what is and is not beautiful—are, unlike truth, *socially conditioned* and have social content, and in an overall sense correspond to and are part of one world outlook or another. Different viewpoints, which, in class society, ultimately correspond to different class outlooks (and it is important to stress *ultimately*, and not fall into reductionism), have different ideas of what is beautiful and not beautiful. There is not a scientific way to arrive at a universal consensus about what is beautiful and what is not. There *is*, by contrast, a scientific way to arrive at determining what is true and what is not true.[42]

Truths are important for changing the world—but not, again, in a narrow, utilitarian sense. They are important in and of themselves, in the sense that it is important to know what is true and what is not true, regardless of whether that has specific application to any particular endeavor or sphere of activity at a given time (and,

---

42. For a discussion of views which have points in common but also some differences over the question of beauty and truth, see Bob Avakian and Bill Martin, *Marxism and the Call of the Future, Conversations on Ethics, History, and Politics*, Open Court Publishing/Carus Publishing, 2005, chapter 3, "Ethics and the Question of Truth."

with regard to communists, whether or not it relates directly to our political objectives at any given time). Nonetheless, truth does have a universality which beauty does not: truth is *not* socially conditioned. Or to put it another way: truth does not have a class character. As I have emphasized previously,[43] so long as there are classes, truth (what is known to be true and truths that are continually discovered) will enter, in one way or another, into the overall struggle between classes; but truth is not reducible to and it is not determined—nor can it be determined—by how it relates to the class struggle. Truth is objective: truth is a correct—or more or less correct—approximation of objective reality, and does not depend on the class position of the person or persons who discover that truth; nor does the truth of something depend on its social impact.

All this is directly and fundamentally opposed to what Armstrong is putting forward about truth, specifically in terms of the relation between myth and truth. And, besides other aspects of what is wrong with her viewpoint, she is wrong in her essential assertion that the myths of religion do not present themselves as though they are to be taken as truth in a factual or historical sense. They certainly do and certainly have. What is the battle over evolution all about? Evolution cannot be true, argue Christian fundamentalists, because, they insist, the origin myth in the Bible is true—and this myth has, throughout history, precisely been intended as something to be taken as literally, historically true. The Bible says that God created the heavens, the earth and everything therein in six days, and on the seventh day He rested. That's presented as historical fact, that's not presented as a myth which is "true" merely because it is "effective." It is not presented, nor intended to be taken, as art that is not representing reality (in this case, historical reality) as it actually is (or was). It is not something that you are supposed to approach as

---

43. See *Observations on Art and Culture, Science and Philosophy*, in particular "Bob Avakian in a Discussion with Comrades on Epistemology: On Knowing and Changing the World."

some sort of "organizing experience"[44] which may have a useful role in getting people to act in certain ways but doesn't correspond to what really happened in history and in fact. Quite the contrary. And more generally throughout history, many religious myths have been presented as truth and historical fact—and have been fought for as such. That is not to say that there have never been myths presented, including in religion, which were not meant to be taken as literally true. But to put forward as a general statement and a general characterization of myths, particularly in the context of religion, that they are not intended to be taken as literal and historical truth—that is completely wrong.

What Armstrong presents is also an expression of pragmatism and instrumentalism, as shown in her concept of what makes myth valid. This is another expression of what Lenin called "truth as an organizing experience." Or, another way of more crudely formulating this—and this is in line with the pragmatic outlook that is so widely propagated and popularized in American society especially—is that if something is useful and helps achieve a desired objective, then it is true—that this is the meaningful definition and criterion of truth. This is what Armstrong is arguing for when she says that a myth is true "because it is effective, not because it gives us factual information." She is positing a subjective definition of truth: at least as applied to myth, according to Armstrong truth is determined by whether or not it "works"—and what "works" is, in turn, determined by whether "it forces us to change our minds and hearts, and gives us new hope, and compels us to live more fully."

To underscore what is wrong with this view, and the epistemology

---

44. The formulation "truth as an organizing experience" was utilized by Lenin (in his major philosophical work *Materialism and Empirio-Criticism*) as part of his critique of various philosophical viewpoints that treated truth as a subjective rather than an objective phenomenon. "Truth as an organizing experience" is expressive of a viewpoint which today we would generally describe as "instrumentalist," in the sense of making reality an "instrument" of subjective desires and aims—and attempting to torture reality to make it conform to those desires and aims.

it embodies, it need only be said that more than a few people in Nazi Germany would have said—and in fact acted as if—the murderous mythology propagated by the Nazis fulfilled all the criteria Armstrong mentions here with regard to the truthfulness—that is, the usefulness—of myth. And the question also poses itself: once one agrees to criteria of this kind with regard to myth, then what basis is there for refusing to apply the same criteria to *anything* which is asserted, by someone, to be true? And where does that lead?

Let's examine another aspect of how Armstrong seeks to establish criteria for the validity of myth: whether or not it "gives us new insight into the deeper meaning of life." First of all, it should be pointed out that this is in essence a tautological argument whose conclusion is really a restatement of its initial assumptions. What is "the deeper meaning of life," except as that is defined by the same *a priori* notions with which Armstrong is approaching the question to begin with? Who is to say what is "the deeper meaning of life," if that is *divorced from the criterion of correspondence to reality*? If anyone can determine, by the use of subjective criteria, whether something provides greater insight into the deeper meaning of life, *regardless of whether or not that something corresponds to real life, to objective reality*, then "the deeper meaning of life" has in reality lost all meaning, except as part of *apriorist* and tautological reasoning. And, of course, this is concentrated, rather crudely, in the pragmatic and instrumentalist assertion: "if it *works*," then it is valid.

This is unvarnished subjective idealist epistemology (the notion that whether something is true or not is a matter to be determined by the subject, by a particular individual, without regard to whether it conforms to a larger, objective reality).[45] But this is a subjective

---

45. A fundamental dividing line in philosophy, as Engels pointed out (see, for example, *Anti-Duhring*), is whether it is understood that reality exists objectively and independently of the perception (or beliefs) of anyone (any subject), and that in fact people (as well as other conscious beings) and their thought processes themselves consist of matter, and nothing else—that *all of reality consists of matter in motion*—or whether, on the other hand, it is believed that ideas exist independently of matter, that ideas and matter are two separate categories (that

idealism in the service of *objective* idealism—that is, religion and belief in the supernatural as objectively true (or as functionally the same as objectively true). And we know where the viewpoint that it doesn't matter if something is factually true or not—it can be an illusion with regard to reality, but if it fulfills a function as defined by someone somewhere, *a priori*, then that's as good as the truth, if not literally the truth—we know where that kind of thing can lead, where it has led and will lead. Not only to all kinds of errors, but to all kinds of horrors. If everyone is free to choose what's valid and true according to whether it suits them, we're back to all the problems with relativism—including, ultimately, particularly when myths conflict with each other, the reduction of things to a contest of power relations to see which myth can be imposed over the other. In short, "might makes right"—this is where things can go, and have often gone, when there is no objective criterion to determine whether something is true and valid or not.

This leads me to the more general question of certitude, scientific and moral certitude—what is the same and what is different about them. In science, and through the application of the scientific method, we can arrive at certitude. Or, to invoke what perhaps seems like an oxymoron, we can arrive at certitude, relatively: relatively, in the sense that reality is constantly changing and our best approximations of it are taking place in that context; and relative in the sense that whatever part of reality we understand is interconnected with other parts of reality, as well as with all the changingness

---

ideas and consciousness constitute something other than matter in motion) and that the reality that is perceived by an individual is the extension of the mind, or ideas, of that individual and is therefore in essence subjective (in which case there can be different realities for different individuals or subjects) or is the extension of the mind of ONE TRANSCENDENTAL AND UNIVERSAL BEING, which of course is a way of saying (or of positing something equivalent to) GOD. The former outlook (recognizing that all of reality consists of matter in motion and that reality exists independently of the mind or ideas of any particular being) corresponds to a *materialist* understanding of reality; the latter to philosophical *idealism*, in one form or another (broadly speaking, either "subjective" or "objective" idealism).

of reality. But nonetheless, while relative, this (scientifically based) certitude is *real*. This is another way of formulating a fundamental philosophical principle that Lenin emphasized. Lenin pointed out that Marxism rejects relativism philosophically—it recognizes, and insists upon the recognition, that there is in fact objective reality and that things that are objectively true have the quality of absoluteness in their being true. But, Lenin added, while rejecting relativism, Marxism also recognizes that there is an element of the relative in the absolute. For example, that human beings are born and then die is objectively true, and this truth has the quality of absolute truth (it is definitely true and not true only in a relativ*ist* sense—not only in relation to and as determined by subjective criteria, such as whether or not someone believes it, regardless of whether it has an objective basis, that is, whether or not it corresponds to objective reality). But because, as Lenin also stressed, boundaries in nature and society, while real, are also conditional and relative (or, as Mao put it, the range of things is vast and there is the interconnectedness of things); because once again any particular aspect of reality is part of, and interconnected with, a larger reality; and because all of reality is undergoing constant change; for these reasons, whatever we have correctly understood about a part of reality is objectively true—corresponds to objective reality, and has the character of absolute truth—but at the same time it contains an aspect of the relative. This basic Marxist understanding is crucial in maintaining the objective, and fundamental, distinction between a scientific, materialist (and dialectical) outlook and approach, on the one hand, and a relativist (and philosophically idealist) outlook and approach, on the other hand.

So, yes, it is possible to be, on a correct basis, *certain* about certain things. Evolution—we can be certain about that. It has stood the test of, not just time in the abstract, but of repeated attempts to disprove it, and in fact it has been reinforced rather than undermined by the continuing accumulation of evidence and the leap from evidence to the synthesis of further knowledge. So we can say with *certitude* that evolution is a scientifically established fact. Or, in simple and basic terms: it is true. And we can say, with *certitude*, that the account of creation in Genesis is *not true*.

Now, when you get to the question of morality, things are more complex. Arriving at the truth through scientific means can often be complex; but with questions of morals, things are complex in a different way. Science deals with what *is*—and also with what has been and what is coming into existence. But science by itself cannot answer all the questions of "ought." It can tell us what is, but it cannot by itself answer the question of what *ought* to be. Does that mean, therefore, that we cannot have any moral certitude? No, we can have moral certitude—relatively. We can, to take a crucial example, scientifically determine what the communist revolution aims for and will achieve, and the changes this revolution will bring about in human society, in human social relations and in the thinking of people. We can scientifically establish that with certitude (but with a relative aspect within that certitude, as spoken to here). We can say that the advance to communism represents an emancipation, the bringing into being of a better world, for the great majority of people and ultimately for humanity as a whole. And we can say, therefore, that in making this leap we are acting in correspondence with the interests of the great majority of humanity and ultimately humanity as a whole. About this, we can have a moral certitude.

Of course, people representing the bourgeoisie can, and will, say: "that ought not to happen," [Laughter]. And they will argue that in fact this is not good for humanity. So, let's sort this out further.

Is the argument that communism is good for humanity merely a relative—or relativist—argument, and can there be no objective determination of whether this is true? No. We can objectively determine this. However, to make the leap to say it *ought to happen* requires something beyond merely science—it does require and involve a partisan standpoint. All this is related to points I've discussed previously about communist universalism—universalism in the sense that we can say that communism, as a world outlook and methodology, embraces all the various spheres of knowledge and endeavor of human beings, while not replacing them, and universalism in the sense that communism, as a political objective, embraces the interests of the great majority of humanity.[46] About that we can have moral certitude, and from that standpoint we argue that achieving communism, and being guided by the communist outlook and method, *ought* to be done.

Once more, of course, the defenders of the present order, who passionately oppose the advance to communism, would argue that what goes on in capitalist society and under the rule of imperialism does not constitute exploitation, oppression and domination but is in fact in the best interests of those who are subjected to this; they would insist that all this is non-exploitation, non-oppression, and non-domination. But what happens to people under this system constitutes *an objective reality* that is *reflected accurately in the concepts* "exploitation," "oppression," and "domination"—and calling this something else (even *non*-exploitation, non-oppression, and non-domination) would not change the essence of that objective reality (it would only involve employing words and terms in a way that is very different from, and in fact conveys the opposite of, what has evolved as the socially agreed upon meaning of those words and terms). The same is true with regard to concepts such as "the interests of the masses of people, and ultimately humanity as a whole" and "emancipation" from exploitation and oppression: these, too, correspond to a reality that exists objectively. And, while it is possible to argue that the advance to communism does not represent

---

46. This point is made, for example, in *Preaching From a Pulpit of Bones*:

"Thus, while communist morality—like all other morality—is not transcendental, in the sense of being independent of any historical and social basis and being applicable in any era, it *does* have the quality of universality precisely for this era: it corresponds to the leap that humanity must make in this era and to means for making that leap." (p. 80, emphasis in original)

"Communist universalism" is also discussed in *Great Objectives and Grand Strategy*. Regarding the principle that Marxism embraces, but does not replace, the many different spheres of human knowledge and endeavor, see *Observations on Art and Culture, Science and Philosophy*.

these interests (and that it does not constitute an "advance" or an "emancipation"), making that argument does not negate the objective reality to which the statements—the advance to communism is in the interests of the masses of people, and ultimately humanity as a whole, and this will constitute an emancipation from exploitation and oppression—correspond.

This relates to the basic principle, and fundamental truth, that communism as a world outlook and method is *both* objective *and* partisan. It is both a thoroughly, systematically, and comprehensively scientific outlook and method for engaging reality—for understanding and transforming reality—and it corresponds in the largest sense to the interests of a class, the proletariat, in leading the struggle to transform all of society, achieve the "4 Alls" that Marx spoke of, and bring forth the era of communism all over the world.[47]

Here enters in the importance of my statement that, "Everything that is actually true is good for the proletariat, all truths can help us get to communism." As I have also recently emphasized:

> contrary to the way in which it is often, even generally, presented in this society, ideology does not necessarily mean an instrumentalist approach to "organizing reality" in pursuit of desired ends, which bears little or no relation to how reality actually is. Communist ideology is definitely a worldview and set of principles to live by, on the one hand; at the same time it is, in fundamental

---

47. The "4 Alls" is a characterization of a statement by Marx that was popularized during the course of the Cultural Revolution in China. This is referred to earlier in this text, where it speaks of "the elimination of all class distinctions, all the production relations on which these class distinctions rest, all the social relations that correspond to those production relations, and the revolutionization of all the ideas that correspond to those social relations." The original statement by Marx, from which this is drawn, is as follows:

"socialism is the *declaration of the permanence of the revolution*, the *class dictatorship* of the proletariat as the necessary transit point to the *abolition of class distinctions generally*, to the abolition of all the relations of production on which they rest, to the abolition of all the social relations that correspond to these relations of production, to the revolutionizing of all the ideas that result from these social relations." (*The Class Struggles in France, 1848–50*, emphasis in original)

terms, in accordance with reality and its motion and development, and is a means for scientifically engaging reality. This is why we say that communist ideology is both *partisan*—it stands with and for a definite side among the contending social forces in the world, the side of proletarian revolution and the advance to communism—and it is *objective*: it seeks an objective, scientific understanding of reality, in order to transform it in accordance with the advance to communism, and since that advance is objectively possible and its possibility is expressed in the way the fundamental contradictions in human society are tending, on a world scale, there is no need for communists to distort reality, or contort it, to make it fit their aims and objectives—and, on the contrary, any such distortion and contortion will actually work *against* the advance to communism. Of course, it has not always been the case that communists have acted in accordance with this fundamental truth—there have been marked tendencies in the history of the communist movement to fall into adopting various forms of "political truths"—in other words, stating as truths things which are in reality *not* true but which seem convenient at the time (an approach Lenin identified philosophically and criticized as "Truth as an organizing principle" or "organizing experience"). But the fact remains that, as a matter of basic principle, communism as a worldview and method rejects such instrumentalist approaches and recognizes the fundamental epistemological principle that, as I have put it in another discussion: "Everything that is actually true is good for the proletariat, all truths can help us get to communism." (Footnote by the author to "Bringing Forward Another Way," emphasis in original; the statement cited at the end here is from "Bob Avakian in a Discussion with Comrades on Epistemology: On Knowing and Changing the World", in *Observations on Art and Culture, Science and Philosophy*.)

Reason Has *Not* "Failed Us" — Reason Is Absolutely Necessary — Though, In Itself, It Is Not Enough

This leads me to the next point I want to discuss, before moving to a conclusion. And that is the question, which is of great importance overall and specifically in terms of the relation, or the contrast, between science and religion, and which is frequently posed in today's world: Has reason failed us?

To begin to get into this, we can say: The truth will not set us free, in and of itself, but we will not get free without the truth. This is closely bound up with the statement that "Everything that is actually true is good for the proletariat, all truths can help us get to communism."

The fact is that reasoning and science and the results of science can, in certain aspects and certain dimensions, be used not only by the proletariat, but also by the bourgeoisie and other reactionaries—they can be used for very different purposes and be employed to promote radically different ends and objectives. As with truth, reason—or the process of rational thought—will not by itself, and in and of itself, necessarily lead to a radically different and better world. But we can never achieve the emancipation of humanity without reason and the process of rational thought—and, above all, reason and rational thought as this is applied as part of the most comprehensive, systematic and thoroughly scientific outlook and method, the outlook and method of communism.

Bound up with this is the question of two radically different kinds of leaps: the leap from perceptual to conceptual (or rational) knowledge about reality, on the one hand; and, on the other hand, "a leap of faith." In this connection it would be helpful to cite some passages from an article I wrote, within the last few years, dealing with this subject:

> As Mao Tsetung pointed out in his important philosophical works, such as "On Practice," in the gaining

(or accumulation) of knowledge by people, there are two basic stages: The first is the stage of *perceptual* knowledge, and the second stage is that of *rational* knowledge. And arriving at the second stage, of rational knowledge, not only involves and requires building on what is learned through the first (perceptual) stage but also making a *leap* in *systematizing* what is perceived: identifying the "patterns" in what is perceived and the essential character and basic identity of things that lie beyond the outward appearance of things....

As Mao also pointed out, when we first encounter anything, we see it in only a partial and scattered way, observing some of its features but not what "ties them together"—what is the essential character of something, which gives to that thing its identity as such—and how it is both different from and at the same time relates to *other* things. This is the stage of simply *perceiving* something, of *perceptual* knowledge....

The understanding of reality that is gained, through the leap from perceptual to rational knowledge, becomes, in turn, the basis, the foundation, from which further perceptual knowledge that is accumulated is analyzed and synthesized to make *further leaps* of this kind (from perceptual to rational knowledge yet again...and then again...). So the acquiring of knowledge—by individuals and by society and humanity overall—is not a "one-time" thing, but an ongoing process. This applies to "everyday life" and it applies in a concentrated way with regard to the conscious and systematic application of the scientific method. This relates to another point Mao emphasized: beyond the leap from perceptual knowledge to rational knowledge, there is a further leap—from rational knowledge to practice, in the course of which material reality is changed and further perceptual knowledge is gained, laying the foundation for a further leap to rational knowledge...and on...and on. ("A Leap of Faith' and a Leap to Rational

Knowledge: Two Very Different Kinds of Leaps, Two
Radically Different Worldviews and Methods," *Revolution* #010, July 31, 2005, posted at revcom.us, emphasis
in original)

As that article (and its title) emphasize, "a leap of faith" is the
opposite of a leap from perceptual to *rational* knowledge of reality: a
"leap of faith" is a leap *away from reality* and to conclusions or inferences which are *in conflict with reality*.

The article cited several examples which illustrate the fundamental contrast between those two kinds of leaps: viewing a football
game; weighing evidence as part of a jury; and a child learning to
determine when it is, and is not, safe to cross the street. In each of
these cases—and the many others from everyday life that could be
examined—the contrast can, and must, be drawn between, on the
one hand, learning more about the realities of something and then
systematizing that into a higher level of understanding which *concentrates* what is essential in this reality ("identifying the 'patterns'
in what is perceived and the essential character and basic identity of
things that lie beyond the outward appearance of things"), which is
what takes place in the leap from perceptual to rational knowledge;
and, on the other hand, a leap of "faith," which involves rupturing
away from the process of learning about reality and systematizing
what is learned, and adopting instead an approach of relying on a
belief which is not drawn from but rather is superimposed on the
reality that is taking place (for example: telling a small child, "don't
worry about the traffic, god will protect you"; or insisting, "I know
the defendant is guilty, because the Lord revealed that to me"). In
short, a scientific outlook and method involves and requires rational
thought, while a religious worldview, with its "leaps of faith," involves
and embodies *non-rational* thought. And, as I pointed out in discussing Michael Lerner's viewpoint, and his epistemology in particular,
such non-rational thought cannot help but lend itself to *ir*rational
ways of approaching things.

Now, speaking of rational thought, one important element of

this is formal logic.[48] For example, it can be clearly determined that if something happens *after* something else, the second thing was *not*, and could not have been, *the cause* of the thing that happened before it. (It is true that when you get to certain levels of matter that are investigated by theoretical physics, things become more complicated in regard to time and causality. But, in terms of the more limited realm of reality with which we normally deal in everyday life, formal logic can and does lead to the valid conclusion that something which happens after something else cannot be the cause of that previous thing.) But, even aside from questions posed by theoretical physics, formal logic has its limitations, and that is important to understand as well.

Pointing to these limitations, Mao—in his typically "Mao-esque" way—observed that, with regard to syllogisms, every affirmation is also a conclusion. (This is another illustration of the dialectical interconnection of things, which Mao also emphasized). But what does this mean, that in syllogisms every affirmation is also a conclusion?

Well, a syllogism is a kind of logical construct which starts with a primary premise, or affirmation; then states a second premise, in relation to the first; and then draws a conclusion. For example: Everybody in Texas is brilliant; all the people in Lubbock are in Texas; therefore, all the people in Lubbock are brilliant.

Now, that follows logically. You have an affirmation, or a major premise, followed by a secondary premise, and then a conclusion— and it is *all logically consistent.* The question is: *Are the premises (or affirmations) accurate and true?* To answer that, it is necessary to step outside of the particular syllogism and the formal logic involved

---

48. In *Anti-Duhring* Engels said that, once the philosophical breakthrough had been made by Marxism which established materialism on a firm, scientific basis, all that was left of previous philosophy was dialectics and formal logic. While I have some significant disagreements with this argument by Engels, there is a continuing importance to formal logic, correctly understood. For a discussion of differences with Engels on this point, see *Observations on Art and Culture, Science and Philosophy,* especially "Marxism Is a Science, It Is Not 'The End of Philosophy.'"

in it. That was Mao's point about how, already in the first premise, or affirmation, there is a conclusion. The conclusion in this example is that everybody in Texas is brilliant. But where did that conclusion derive from, how was it arrived at? To determine that, and to determine if the conclusion is valid, you have to step back and make an analysis, and synthesis, by applying scientific methods that are more all-encompassing than formal logic. Was this first (major) premise, or affirmation, arrived at by scientific methods and can it be verified and validated by scientific methods? No, in this case (speaking of Texas, and the city of Lubbock).

Or take another example. Richard Pryor had this routine where he said: "All Italians are not in the Mafia, but most of them work for the Mafia." [Laughter] Well, in reality, that is not true. But let's examine this more closely. And let's make his second statement more "universal," so that it says: "All Italians work for the Mafia." Let's make that the major premise of our syllogism. Then we can go on: Giuseppe is Italian; therefore Giuseppe works for the Mafia. Well, to know if this is actually true, we have to determine whether the first affirmation, the first premise, is true? Do all Italians in fact work for the Mafia? (Once again, in reality, that is not true.) And then we would also need to know if the second(ary) premise—that Giuseppe is Italian—is actually true, before we could determine whether the conclusion is valid. So not only the first affirmation but also the second premise has to be tested in a larger context of engaging and drawing rational conclusions about reality. Formal logic can—and in fact must—be a part of this, but in and of itself it cannot tell us what is true and not true. This is important to understand in relation to formal logic: what is valid about, and what are the limitations of, formal logic?

We could go on endlessly playing around with examples. "All Black people are good at basketball; James is Black; therefore James is good at basketball." Well, we have to test whether the first two premises are true. Are all Black people good at basketball? In reality, this is not the case. Is James actually Black? I don't know, we'd have to go find out who James is and discover what his background and his "race" (or nationality) is. [Laughter] Still, despite its limitations—and with an understanding of its limitations—formal logic is important, in the context of, and on the basis of, an overall and all-around scientific approach (and this, once again, is most fully expressed in the outlook and method of communism: dialectical materialism).

Formal logic, like rational thought (or reason) more generally, is necessary but in itself is not enough.

Religious "Faith"—Let's Call It What It Is: *Irrational*

In contrast to logic and reason, let's talk some more about faith. In the Bible, in the words of Paul (or words that in any case are attributed to Paul) we find the following: "Now faith is the assurance of things hoped for, the conviction of things not seen"; and "we look not at what can be seen but at what cannot be seen; for what can be seen is temporary, but what cannot be seen is eternal." (See Hebrews 11:1 and 2 Corinthians 4:18.)

This is very similar, frankly, to the (non-rational) reasoning of Karen Armstrong about myth. What is being argued is that faith has its owns standard of validity, which is not the standard that science would establish. In fact, the claim of faith to validity is explicitly excluded from the realm of science, because faith is the conviction—of what? Of things not seen—things which not only are *not* seen, but which *cannot* be seen, by definition. And why is that important? Because, as we see in Second Corinthians: "What can be seen is temporary"—it is of this world, in other words—"but what cannot be seen is eternal."

Here we find another tautology. A realm, beyond the actual world, has been invented—and, by definition, things pertaining to this realm cannot be tested—and then it is declared that, given the "other worldly" quality of this realm, whose existence cannot be tested, it is more important than that which can be experienced, and tested, and from which rational conclusions can be drawn. This is logically no different than arguing: A is greater than B, because B is lesser than A.

This is why faith is, by its very nature, thinking that is removed from the realm of rational thought. It doesn't even necessarily involve consistent formal logic, but more fundamentally than that—and even where there may be expressions of religious faith that are consistent with formal logic—the premises of faith do not conform to reality and to a rational approach to reality: They can be shown by scientific methods to be untrue, or can be shown to have no foundation in anything which could even be tested to determine if they are true. So let us remove faith from the seemingly lofty place to which it has been assigned by the ruling interests and dominant institutions of contemporary capitalist society (and previous societies), and assign faith its rightful designation: Faith is nothing more than *irrationality*.

God Does Not Exist—And There Is No Good Reason to Believe In God

Here we get to the whole question of burden of proof. You often hear religious people arguing: "Despite what you say, you haven't disproved and you can't disprove the existence of God." Well, you can play that game forever. You can't disprove that right now there is an invisible dinosaur hovering in the sky above us. [Laughter] If I declare "by faith" that there is such a dinosaur but you simply cannot see it—can you disprove that? By definition you cannot, because I am not putting forward any attributes of this alleged dinosaur that are testable in the real world.

Or, if I were to inform you that my (invisible) friend James, here—who by the way exists—is going to rob and murder you later today, you would demand of me some proof of this. [Laughter] And if I couldn't provide any proof, other than my insistence on this—or by quoting some "holy scripture" that I wrote to back this up ("And James appeared in a glorious blaze of light, and the light shone all about him, so that others could not see him; but James was evil and had determined to rob and murder all those about")—if that is what I offered, by way of proof, you would say that maybe I needed some help from a mental health professional. [Laughter] In that case, you would quite correctly insist: "If you are going to say that something exists, which no one can see, and there's no material reality to demonstrate its existence, *you* have to provide the proof of that."

If I tell you about a god that is different from the god that you have come to believe in, and I say that this god is more powerful than your god, that terrible things are going to happen to you if you don't follow this god, and that your god can't offer you any protection from this more powerful and awful god—you are going to say to me: "Prove it."

In situations of that kind it can be readily seen, and people will readily agree, that the onus is, correctly, on me to prove something for which there is no evidence, in the real material world. The reason people respond this way in these circumstances is because they have *not been socially conditioned* to believe in this particular god that is alien to them—it is not the case, with this particular god, that the dominant relations, structures, institutions, ideas and culture in the society in which they live have been working to make them feel as if belief in this god is simply "natural" and it would make you somehow "odd," or worse, *not* to believe in this god. But, when it comes to a god that people *have* been taught and conditioned to believe in, all of sudden they want to argue that it is up to those who do *not* believe in the existence of that god to prove that it does not exist, even though there is no more evidence, in the real material world, for the existence of that god than for any other gods. This calls to mind an observation I made a number of years ago: "Every religion in the world believes that every other religion is superstition. And they're all correct."

Sometimes people will argue, "God may not exist for you, but god definitely exists for me." [Laughter] Well, then, that's just a god you invented. [More laughter] Because if god really exists, then god exists for everyone—including me—even if I don't believe in god. In reality, it is only because, for reasons spoken to earlier, belief in various gods has been institutionalized—because the dominant institutions of a given society insist that this or that god exists—it is only for that reason that many people believe in this or that god, and that they insist: "If you deny the existence of this god, it is up to you to prove it does not exist." This is turning reality upside down. It is not up to those who do not believe in god to prove the non-existence of something which does not exist—and for the existence of which no valid proof has been provided. [Laughter]

To those who continue to insist, despite all the evidence to the contrary, that the imaginary gods that have been invented by people *do* really exist, it is necessary to say: *You* provide the evidence for it. And this evidence must be something other than round-in-a-circle arguments such as: "The Bible says that god exists; the Bible is The Truth; therefore God exists." Provide some actual evidence of this god in the real world—how this god (and not just *belief* in this god) has manifested itself in the real world and has had an effect on things in the real world. Provide arguments and evidence about the existence of this god which can be *tested in the real world.*

It is necessary to insist that the same standards and criteria that are applied to other things also apply to assertions about the existence of god: If someone posits something, it is up to that person to provide proof for what they are positing. If I predict that a hurricane will strike a city, somewhere a thousand miles from any ocean, in the middle of winter, it is up to me to provide evidence for this assertion. Or, if I claim that in the next year a human being will be born who will be able, all on its own, to fly around the equator of the earth in ten minutes, it is up to me to provide the evidence for this. And if anyone posits the existence of a god whose existence can be known only through "faith," then it is up to that person to provide evidence—other than the tautological arguments of faith—for the existence of that god. Merely saying, "I choose to believe it is so, as a matter of faith," does not make this anything other than a subjective notion on your part—which there is no valid reason to embrace or believe, if you cannot provide any evidence for it in the real world. And to say, "Well, I believe it, and it's true because it's important to me" is not evidence of its actual existence. It is only evidence of your psychological need to believe this. Nothing beyond that psychological need has been established by your assertion that this thing exists because it makes you feel better to believe in it, or that you know it as a matter of faith. That only tells us something about you, not about the existence of this thing that you are calling god.

So, the "substance of things not seen," which is faith, *has no* substance. This is *not* rational thought. This is *non*-rational thought which inevitably verges on and lends itself to *ir*rational thought and leads to *ir*rational action—action that is qualitatively and essentially out of line with reality.

As emphasized before, calling this irrational is not a matter of insult, but of scientific analysis. And, while there is no scientific or rational basis for belief in any god or supernatural beings of any kind, there *is* a rational and scientific basis for grasping the very harmful effects of *belief* in gods and the supernatural, and the negative role of religion, in the history of human society and in this era of human history especially.

Here, the following passage from *The Science of Evolution and The Myth of Creationism—Knowing What's Real And Why It Matters*, answering the claim that religion is outside the realm of scientific inquiry, is highly relevant:

> *In my view it is actually very unscientific to claim that "science doesn't have anything to say about religion."* It is of course true that science cannot test for the presence of any supernatural force or power, which *by definition* (and believers admit to this) has no tangible existence in the natural material world. But what about human *ideas* about gods and other supernatural forces or

powers? Doesn't science have anything to say about *that*? Can't *scientific methods* be applied to uncovering where such ideas came from, and how they have been given material expression by human beings? What about the *social history* which concretely records when and how human beings in different parts of the world started to tell or write down stories about various supernatural realms (the social origins of the many different kinds of creation myths and religious scriptures from all around the world)? What about the *roles* that religious belief, rituals and practices have played, and the *purposes* they have served, at everything from the personal individual level to the larger societal (and world) level? And what about the *history* of how religious beliefs have *changed* over time (whatever happened, for instance, to the ancient Egyptian, Greek or Roman gods that people used to believe in as firmly as many modern-day people now believe in the God of the Jewish, Christian, or Islamic scriptures)?

Can't the same kind of scientific methods which are used to investigate questions in any other *historical science* (evolution, cosmology, archaeology, comparative linguistics, and so on) be applied to investigating the history of human belief in supernatural powers? And can't the methods of science be applied to gaining a better understanding of why some religious beliefs have at times been officially encouraged and promoted or, alternatively, severely restricted or even targeted for annihilation? All these phenomena—and the various human beliefs in a supernatural realm themselves— undeniably have real, tangible, material existence even if the objects of such beliefs (gods or other super-natural powers) by definition have no such tangible material presence....

In short, I would argue that applying a scientific methodology—and in particular the outlook and methodology of dialectical and historical materialism—to arrive at an understanding of what is represented by religion, and how it actually leads away from systematically understanding and changing reality, *is* both possible and necessary. (Ardea Skybreak, *The Science of Evolution and The Myth of Creationism—Knowing What's Real And Why It Matters*, pp. 291–92, emphasis in original)

Religion as an Opiate of the People— And an Obstacle to Emancipation

This leads us back to the question: What is the role of religion—and is it really harmful? A lot of people say: "Alright, maybe it's not true, but what harm does it do? It makes people feel better—a loved one dies and they want to believe that the loved one went to heaven, and when they die they'll be reunited with that loved one. Or something terrible happens in someone's life, and she wants to take comfort and solace in the belief that there is some larger purpose, directed by some god, that makes this have meaning in some form. How can that do any harm?"

Well, let's paraphrase Stevie Wonder's song "Superstition": "When you believe in things and they don't exist and you suffer, superstition's in your way. [Laughter] (Actually he says, "When you believe in things that you don't understand..."—but it's the same point.) You do suffer when you believe in things that you not only don't understand, but that, by definition, you *can't* understand. And whether or not Stevie Wonder had religion in mind in saying this, it definitely applies to religion.

Now some might argue: "You're not Stevie Wonder, so who are you to say that it applies to religion?" [Laughter] How can I say that? Well, it's simple and basic: I'm someone who sees very clearly that if you believe in things that you don't understand and you suffer, then superstition is indeed in your way. And this is all the more true when you believe in things that you don't understand and they *don't even exist*.

When you shape your life and determine the course of your life, or try to, by belief in these things, you are going to suffer. You may seek, and even achieve in a short-term sense, some temporary consolation, but you are going through life in a way that is fundamentally out of keeping with reality, to the degree that this belief guides how you act and how you see things. The consolation will never be long-lasting, because life will keep asserting itself. And under a system like this, for the great majority of people in the world, it will continually bring forth horrors.

As I have discussed, some people—good-hearted, well intentioned people—try to use the Bible, especially the New Testament and more particularly the words of Jesus himself, as the basis for promoting tolerance and diversity, being against discrimination and injustice, fighting oppression and promoting peace, and even as a way of trying to provide an inspiring vision of a better world. But the fact is: this will not work, and it will not do.

Now, it is important to understand why many people, especially oppressed people in a world that seems so crazy and intolerable, often turn to religion in the hope of finding something solid that can hold things together amidst all this madness. Marx spoke of religion as "the opiate of the people." But Marx didn't approach this in a simple-minded way. He also said that it is "the heart of a heartless world." This world of capitalism *is* heartless. It does treat people as things to be used and then cast on the junkpile—it does this even to children, on a massive scale and in the most horrific ways. And this, spontaneously, strengthens the impulse in many people toward religion, toward seeking an *illusory* way out of this heartlessness.

In regard to the narcotic ("opiate") role of religion, I like to use the following example. Many people turn to religion, especially an absolutist kind of religious fundamentalism, as a way of trying to deal with all the afflictions, and even some addictions, that they experience. This reminds me of the situation where someone gets deeply into debt—they are in debt everywhere they turn, they owe this, they owe that—and then there are the companies that advertise: "We'll consolidate all your debt into one debt. We'll pay off all your debts, and you can just pay us (with interest of course), instead of trying to pay all these other creditors." Well, the role of religion, especially fundamentalist religion, is to take everybody's afflictions and addictions, and consolidate them into *one big affliction and addiction*. [Laughter, Applause] But, along with offering people no real way out, what this ends up doing is blaming people for their own suffering, oppression and miserable conditions.

Many people, feeling that their hopes have been crushed for a better life in this world, have fallen back on hoping for a better future in *another*, future existence, and seek to organize their lives around preparing for that supposed "future life." The problem, once again, is that this is an illusion. And this quest for happiness, or relief from suffering in this way, cannot bring about the satisfaction that people are seeking. Like a narcotic, the relief or escape provided by this kind of religious belief is never sufficient. You always need another "fix," and this soon turns into yet another chain on people.

And, more fundamentally, the point is that we do not want—and, beyond that, we no longer have any need—to be imprisoned within a heartless world. We need and can bring into being a world with heart: a world freed of the oppression and misery that is imposed and enforced by the way human society is structured and controlled. A world in which people do not think of each other—and do not treat each other—as mere objects to be used and profited from. Religion, at least as practiced by more truly compassionate and progressive-minded people today, may aim at providing consolation—a salve for people in their agony and torment—but we can bring into being a world in which people no longer *need* this kind of consolation, because poverty and oppression, and all the needless suffering bound up with that, will have been eliminated and uprooted forever, along with the ideas and culture that reinforce this.

But in order to do that, we need to confront reality as it

actually is. We need to engage and transform reality, the reality of human society as well as nature, with a consciously and consistently scientific outlook and method. And the point is this: **For the first time in human history, there is the possibility to do that**. Measured against that, religious doctrine and tradition, and the religious way of conceiving reality, fall way short—and, in fact, lead away from what, for the first time, has become possible for humanity.

Closely connected with this is the question of "sin." This concept of "sin" is a big part of the religions I've been speaking about. Sin is defined as deviation from the way of God. This notion of "sin" is a tremendous weight on the masses of people. It is accompanied by—it gives rise to and continually reinforces—a sense of shame, guilt and fear; and, as we have seen, it even promotes the idea that things like disease are caused by sin, or possession by evil beings ("something's wrong with that boy, the devil got in him"). This keeps people from understanding and dealing with what is actually going on and what is actually the problem with individuals and, more fundamentally, with society and the world.

As I pointed out in "Putting an End to 'Sin'" (the second essay in *Preaching From a Pulpit of Bones*), there are two things involved here. One, there is no such thing as "sin"—here's a syllogism of formal logic that is valid, because its premises are true: "Sin" is defined as deviating from the way of God; there is no God; therefore there is no sin. That is objectively true, and obviously important, but what is also objectively true is that there is *the concept* of sin, which weighs heavily on the masses of people. And, again, what is the effect, and to a large degree the purpose, of preaching about this notion of sin? It is to promote the idea that an individual who is in torment, and generally the masses of oppressed people, are responsible for their own suffering. *You* must have done something wrong, *you* must have made God angry, *you* must have gone away from the right way.

This is what is promoted with the concept of "sin"—instead of looking to the real causes. And if you don't look to the real causes, if you don't look to the real problem, how can you eliminate the real causes, how can you find the real solution? If you think the problem resides in you, all you can do is be weighed down. This is adding insult to injury. It is an additional burden of oppression on people. Think how terrible it is to suffer every day as a result of the workings of this system, and then to have it drilled into you that *that's* not why you are suffering—you are suffering because of something wrong with *you*, and some way in which *you* did something wrong.

Don't tell me that religion doesn't do any harm. It does tremendous harm.

There Is No Such Thing As Unchanging, and Unchangeable, Human Nature

Tied in with religious notions is the idea of "human nature"—and specifically some essential, and unchangeable, nature of human beings that causes them to do wrong, to do things that are harmful to themselves and to other human beings. How often have we heard: "Human nature is just this way; people are just naturally sinful?" Or "people are naturally selfish—it's just 'human nature' to want to get over on everybody else." In fact, these are not qualities that are part of some unchanging and unchangeable "nature" of human beings. These inclinations in people are a reflection, and an extension, of the production and social relations, and the corresponding culture, as well as the political rule, of a *system*—a system that encourages and coerces people into acting in this way. People are thrown into competition and even into antagonism with each other all the time—both by the conscious policies and actions of the ruling class and by the underlying dynamics and workings of the capitalist-imperialist system. Under this system, even to get a job, even to have a means to live, you are thrown into conflict with other people. And this also happens in many other ways, through the workings of the capitalist system, as it has in previous systems founded on exploitation, domination and oppression of the many by the few. This has characterized human society, not since "time immemorial," but since the time that early communal societies, for very material reasons, gave way to and were supplanted by societies based on the monopoly of wealth (and the means to produce wealth), as well as the monopoly of political power and of intellectual life, by a small part of society.[49]

In *The Poverty of Philosophy*, Marx made an extremely important observation in this regard: "All history," he noted, "is nothing but the continuous transformation of human nature." Concentrated in that sentence is a tremendous amount of wisdom, if you will. This draws from—and concentrates in a profound way—Marx's analysis of how, in any given set of circumstances, people in a society enter into relations with each other in order to meet the material requirements of life. These *relations of production* are in turn historically determined—they are not chosen, at will, by the people who enter into them, but are, at any given time, and in any particular society, fundamentally determined by the character of the productive forces at hand (resources, technology, etc., as well as people and their knowledge). The prevailing production relations are accompanied by certain social relations. And arising on the basis of the mode of production—embodying the prevailing relations of production—there exists a superstructure (forms of political rule and institutions and ways of thinking and culture) which stem from and *reinforce* the underlying relations of production and the corresponding social relations. Further, and of decisive importance, Marx showed how the development of human society does not consist only in incremental

---

49. Reasons for the replacement of early communal societies by societies built on class exploitation—and characterized by oppressive social relations, including very importantly and pivotally the oppression of women—are discussed in my talk *Views on Socialism and Communism. A Radically New Kind of State, a Radically Different and Far Greater Vision of Freedom*, an edited version of which was printed in *Revolution* and is available at revcom.us. Important analysis of and insights into these and related questions, with a particular focus on the oppression of women, are also provided in *Of Primeval Steps & Future Leaps, An Essay on the Emergence of Human Beings, the Source of Women's Oppression, and the Road to Emancipation*, by Ardea Skybreak, Banner Press, 1984.

evolutionary change but is driven forward by the constant dialectical interplay between the forces of production and the relations of production, and between the economic base and the political-ideological superstructure; that this repeatedly involves radical leaps and ruptures from one form of society to another, qualitatively different one; and that in circumstances where the prevailing relations of production have become more a fetter on the productive forces than an appropriate form for their further development, the need for the radical transformation of society, for revolutionary change, in the economic base and the superstructure, will increasingly find expression in the realm of the superstructure—in the formulation of ideas and programs seeking to bring about, or to prevent, revolutionary change, and in the political struggle to determine the direction of society, which will ultimately take its most concentrated expression in military struggle to determine who (which class, representing which way of carrying out production, through which production relations) will exercise power in society. To boil things down to a single sentence: When the productive forces are fettered by the production relations, there will be a need for a revolution in the superstructure, to bring about a new form of political rule; and representatives of the class which represents the new, rising relations of production will formulate ideas and programs, and mobilize masses of people around them, in order to carry out the struggle to seize political power and, on that basis, to transform society in accordance with the interests and viewpoint of that class, bringing into being a qualitatively new economic base and superstructure.

To a great deal, all this is concentrated in Marx's pithy formulation: "All history is nothing but the continuous transformation of human nature." And, accordingly, **what seems "natural" in one era, seems very unnatural in another**. Marx made this statement about the future of communism—that in that future era, it will seem as ridiculous and outrageous for one person to own one part of the globe, as it now seems for one person to own another. But for thousands of years, it did not seem at all ridiculous and outrageous, at least in terms of the viewpoint of the ruling class and the ruling ideas in society, for one person to own another. That was considered very "natural"—it was "in accordance with human nature" that things were that way—such were the dominant relations and the corresponding ideas.

In this era, when human society has moved to a point where the capitalist mode of production has largely taken hold—or at least wherever this capitalist mode of production has more or less thoroughly taken hold—the idea and practice of some human beings owning others, and exploiting them in outright, literal slavery, is not in accord with the accumulation of profit by the capitalists. Capitalism needs a class to exploit that is not literally enslaved: because of the motion of capital and the way in which different capitalists compete and proceed through competition to accumulate more wealth, there are times when it is in their interests to lay off some (or even many) workers. If you buy a slave, and you don't get back your initial investment, plus an additional amount, you will be in trouble economically. If you get rid of that slave before you've made back what you've invested in buying the slave, you've lost on your investment. But if you are a capitalist, you don't pay in one lump sum to own somebody—you pay them by the hour, by the day, by the week, or whatever, and as soon as it's not profitable for you to employ them in this way, you let them go and you're not responsible for paying them anything any more. You haven't laid out an investment in advance to buy them, which you have to recoup by working them for a certain period of time. So it's not profitable, generally, under the capitalist mode of production—wherever it has more or less thoroughly taken hold—to buy and own people as slaves, have them literally be your property, and exploit them in that way. It's more profitable to be able to hire them and let them go, and have them be more mobile, free to be employed or discharged according to the dictates of capitalist accumulation. Therefore, according to the "human nature" that corresponds to the capitalist mode of production, slavery doesn't make sense and is contrary to what's good and right and natural.[50]

All of this is an illustration of the fact that *there is no such thing* as "human nature" in the sense of some unchanging and unchangeable essence of human beings (which, however, just happens to conform to whatever, at the time, embodies and serves the prevailing forms of exploitation and oppression). Just as there is no such thing as sin, there is no such thing as "human nature" in the sense in which this is propagated by the dominant class and popularized through its institutions of rule and of molding public opinion.

Human beings do have certain qualities as a species, broadly defined, including the capacity for rational thought—a relatively high level of consciousness and ability to synthesize concepts— which distinguish humans as a species. But one of the things that most distinguishes human beings, including in their ability to think, is their *plasticity*: the ability to change with changing circumstances, *and* to change circumstances by consciously acting upon them. This is, perhaps, the most essential quality that distinguishes human beings from other species.

The notion of "unchanging human nature" is completely erroneous, and the idea that people are naturally selfish is nothing but another tautology. As Marx and Engels pointed out in the *Communist Manifesto*, this amounts to nothing other than saying that, with the domination of the bourgeois mode of production, the dominant thinking and ways of acting will be in accordance with the dictates of the bourgeois mode of production. As the *Manifesto* also puts it,

---

50. It is true that capitalism has been able to make use of, and integrate into its overall process of accumulation, exploitation that is carried out in "pre-capitalist" forms, including not only feudalism but outright slavery. It is also true that some forms of slavery continue to exist in the world today and that, in an overall sense, the results of this form of exploitation feed into the overall process of capitalist accumulation, especially on a world scale. (See, for example, "21st Century Slavery Under Global Capitalism," in *Revolution* #102, September 23, 2007, also available at revcom.us.) But this manner of exploitation is not characteristic of capitalist production/exploitation as such, nor is outright slavery openly advocated and defended as "natural" ("in accordance with human nature") in capitalist society.

the ruling ideas of any age are ever the ideas of the ruling class—and these ideas are spread and have great influence not only within the ruling class itself but also among other sections of the population, including the class (or classes) most brutally exploited and oppressed by the ruling class. But, as spoken to earlier, from era to era in human history, and even within the confines of the era of capitalist rule, when there are upsurges of mass struggle people undergo great changes in their ways of thinking and of relating to each other. In a basic sense, this is, and can only be, temporary and partial, as long as there is not a successful revolution and a radical qualitative change in society as a whole. Nonetheless, especially in circumstances of great social upheaval and struggle against the established order, people go through great changes in their thinking and their way of relating to each other. If this were not so, revolutions could never be made and social relations could never be changed by people consciously reacting back upon them. Yet, looking at the history of human beings and their society, this has happened frequently—radical changes in society as a whole have been brought about repeatedly—and this will happen again, in a far greater and more radical way, with the communist revolution.

In light of this, it is all the more possible to recognize the great harm that is done by religious worldviews and associated notions of sin, of unchanging human nature and the "fallen nature" of humanity: "It all goes back to Adam and Eve. That's where a-l-l-l the trouble bogan. Eve convinced Adam to eat that apple, and that's why we're in the position we're in today." [Laughter] No. This has nothing to do with reality. But the notion that this is so does a great deal of harm and keeps people from understanding why we're really in the position we're in today, and what to do about it.

So, on the one hand, it is necessary to struggle, boldly and vigorously, against religion in all its forms—and especially against fundamentalist religious obscurantism and absolutism and its expression politically as Christian Fascism in the U.S. It is crucial not to in any way underestimate the importance of the struggle in the realm of thinking, of ideology, and specifically struggle against the religious worldview in all its manifestations, because of the way in which this interferes with and leads people away from really understanding reality, and therefore being able to engage it and transform it in accordance with their own fundamental interests. At the same time, and for a long time, it will also be crucial to unite with a broad diversity of forces, including many people who hold religious views. In terms of the basis of unity in the political struggle, the dividing line should never be whether or not people believe in god and are religious, but whether they are willing to unite, and can be won to unite, in ways that are objectively in the interests of the masses of people. To the degree that they do so, it is necessary to build unity with them, and to struggle with them to do so more fully and consistently, even while struggle is also carried out with them, in the ideological realm, over the question of which worldview actually corresponds to reality and will lead to emancipation. In order to forge the broadest unity, it is important to recognize and act on the understanding that among those who have carried out and are capable of carrying out self-sacrificing and inspiring acts in the fight against injustice and oppression are many people who hold religious beliefs and are motivated in significant ways by those religious beliefs. But religion, and a religious view of the world, cannot lead us where we need to go. As important as unity in the political struggle is, and as important as it is to build it as broadly as possible at every point, the striving for such unity must not involve avoiding or downplaying the importance of the profound struggle that must be waged in the ideological realm, including over the question of religion; and the fact is that, the more and the better this ideological struggle is waged, the stronger, not the weaker, the basis will be for building broad unity in the struggle against oppression and exploitation and for a new world.

In sum, to achieve, through the course of the overall struggle, the leadership that is necessary in order to thoroughly and consistently take on all the pillars of oppression weighing on the masses of people and finally uproot them through the revolutionary transformation of society, and ultimately the world as a whole—to achieve communist leadership, practically and ideologically—will require working to unite as broadly as possible on a principled basis with many and diverse people and forces, including progressive religious people; but it will also require bringing forward and struggling consistently, systematically and vigorously to win people to the communist program and to the communist world outlook and method—to grasping and applying materialism and dialectics—and specifically, as a key part of that, *atheism.*

The understanding—not the opinion but the scientific understanding—that there is no god, and that belief in god and the organized ignorance and superstition that is embodied in religion does great harm and is a direct obstacle to the struggle for a radically different and better world: this is crucial to actively and boldly put forward and struggle for.

At the same time, among those who do seek to build unity in the political struggle, this process should involve honest wrangling and, yes, the confrontation of views, around decisive questions of politics and ideology, such as the basic issue of reform vs. revolution, as well as fundamental principles of epistemology and philosophy. This should include:

- What is the actual content, as well as the historical influence and effect, of the major religions and religious traditions in the world, and where does following the teachings and traditions of those religions actually lead?

- What is the actual content of communism and what is the real and essential nature of the experience of socialist countries ruled by the proletariat and led by its vanguard party (the dictatorship of the proletariat)? What lessons can and should be drawn from this?

- What is the correct understanding of what the ills of society are, what they stem from, *and* what is necessary to put an end to them and to bring a better society and world into being?

- What are the correct means and methods for understanding the development of human society, including in the realm of ideas, as well as in terms of economic, social, and political relations and institutions, and the broader question of the nature of human beings and their relation to the rest of reality?

- What is the best way to understand, and what are fullest implications of the principle, that while meeting the basic material requirements of life for all of humanity is one of the bedrocks of a just society and world, this is not all that human beings need, that people cannot live by bread alone; and how do we understand the role of awe and wonder and the need of human beings to be amazed, in relation to the material world and to the realm of ideas and philosophy?

Liberation Without Gods

In concluding, then, let's pose the question: As opposed to being enslaved to things seen, and "things unseen," what would it really feel like, and what would it mean, to be free?

To a significant degree, especially as things are posed in U.S. society (and more broadly in the world) today, this involves the questions not only of whether brutal and powerfully entrenched oppressors can be uprooted from power but also whether the masses of people can themselves be transformed in order to carry out a revolutionary struggle that would really result in a better world. Can this be led by communists, who reject religion and belief in the supernatural, and insist that people themselves must, and can, understand and change the world in essential ways, through their own conscious efforts and in their own highest interests, in the interests of humanity as a whole?

Can we be good without god? Well, as I spoke to in *Preaching From a Pulpit of Bones*, we can be—and we have to be—for two reasons. First, and fundamentally, there is no god. So if we're going to be good, if we are going to bring into being a good society and a good world, we have to do it without god. But also, and very importantly, for all the reasons that have been spoken to here, a new—radically different and better—world can in the final analysis *only* be brought into being by people increasingly casting off belief in god (and the supernatural in general) in the process, and as a crucial part of the process, of ever more consciously confronting reality as it actually is, and transforming it in a revolutionary way.

Can there be meaning to human existence without god? The answer that communism gives to this is definitely yes. But the meaning there is to human existence is **only the meaning that we human beings give to it.** For those who are ruthlessly exploited, oppressed, dominated and demeaned, under the rule and according to the dictates of the capitalist system—and for all those who are deeply concerned about the future of humanity and recognize the need and the potential for a radically different world—the greatest meaning that can be given to existence is to be part of the struggle to bring that new world into being, and to take up the scientific world outlook and method of communism, which can illuminate the way and provide the basis for forging, through struggle, the means to advance, through all the twists and turns, to the realization of that goal.

So in conclusion: For generation after generation—not only in those parts of the world where the "Judeo-Christian tradition" has held sway, but among the billion or so people who live in lands where Islam is the dominant religion, and in places where other religions and religion-like traditions and notions have been dominant—for thousands of years in this way, human society and the great majority of humanity have literally groaned, not only under the weight of material relations of exploitation and oppression, and the accompanying agony, poverty and violence, but also under the weight of religious notions of "sin," and similar concepts such as "karma," which have served to confuse people as to the source of their suffering, and indeed have served to convince people that they themselves are responsible for this suffering, since they must have somehow acted in a way to displease some supernatural being or beings, or other supernatural forces, which ultimately determine the destiny of humanity.

As it is put in *Preaching From a Pulpit of Bones*:

> With communism will come the end of "sin." If "sin" is defined as deviation from the way of god, then objectively there is not and never has been any such thing, because there is not and never has been any god. But, beyond that, when the point is reached where the material and ideological conditions exist for humanity to voluntarily and consciously change itself and the world, then there will also be no (subjective) basis for "sin," because there will no longer be a need or a basis for belief in god. At that point and into the future, there will still be right and wrong, good and bad—in the sense of what does and does not conform to objective reality and does and does not contribute to forging freedom out of necessity and enhancing the ability of society and the individuals who comprise it to continue developing in an all-around way. But there will no longer be the notion of "sin." (p. 81)

When we have reached that point, great burdens will have been lifted from people; and all this will be a true, a great, an unprecedented liberation.

> The communist revolution and the communist world it will bring into being will give flower and give flight to art and to the imagination—to the "human spirit"—on a far broader basis and far higher level than ever before in human history, and it will remove the shackles of religion and all superstition. It will, in the words of *The Internationale*, "free the spirit from its cell" and allow it to soar to heights unseen, and unimagined, before. (*Preaching From a Pulpit of Bones*, p. 89)

This is what it will mean to live in a world where it will be possible to give flight to the imagination without being caught up in the illusion that the imaginary is real; where people will not go through life fearing the supposedly awesome power of supernatural beings, which in fact do not exist; where religion and superstition no longer stand in the way of consciously engaging and changing reality in the interests of humanity; where there will be no need to search desperately for some other "next" life in which the endless night of suffering and anguish, mental as well as physical, which is the experience today of the vast majority of humanity, will finally come to an end—no need, because that suffering and anguish will have been ended in *this* world.

This is what it will mean to be free in a qualitatively new and far greater way than ever before in the history of humanity.

SELECTED BIBLIOGRAPHY

Ali, Tariq. *The Clash of Fundamentalisms.* London; New York: Verso, 2002.

Alterman, Eric. *What Liberal Media? The Truth About <u>Bias</u> and the News.* New York: Basic Books, 2003.

Anonymous. *Imperial Hubris: Why the West is Losing the War on Terror.* Dulles, VA: Brassey's, 2004.

Arendt, Hannah. *The Origins of Totalitarianism.* New York: Harcourt Brace Jovanovich, 1973.

Arkin, William M. "The Pentagon Unleashes a Holy Warrior," *Los Angeles Times,* October 16, 2003.

Armstrong, Karen. *The Battle for God.* New York: Alfred A. Knopf, 2000.

———. *A History of God: The 4000-Year Quest of Judaism, Christianity, and Islam.* New York: Alfred A. Knopf, 1993.

———. *A Short History of Myth.* Edinburgh: Canongate Books, 2005.

Arulraja, M.R. *Jesus the Dalit—Liberation Theology by Victims of Untouchability, an Indian Version of Apartheid.* Hyderabad: Volunteer Centre, 1996.

Avakian, Bob. "Bringing Forward Another Way." Chicago: RCP Publications, 2007. Also available online at http://www.revcom.us/avakian/anotherway.

———. *Democracy: Can't We Do Better Than That?* New York: Banner Press, 1989.

———. "Dictatorship and Democracy, and the Socialist Transition to Communism," *Revolutionary Worker,* Aug. 22, 2004 through Jan. 16, 2005. Also available online at http://www.revcom.us/avakian/avakian-works.html#democracyspeech.

———. *For a Harvest of Dragons: On the "Crisis of Marxism" and the Power of Marxism—Now More Than Ever.* Chicago: RCP Publications, 1983.

———. "Great Objectives and Grand Strategy," *Revolutionary Worker,* November 18, 2001 through March 10, 2002. Also available online at http://www.revcom.us/avakian/avakian-works.html#gogs.

———. "'A Leap of Faith' and a Leap to Rational Knowledge: Two Very Different Kinds of Leaps, Two Radically Different Worldviews and Methods," *Revolution,* July 31, 2005. Also available online at http://www.revcom.us/a/010/avakian-leap-faith-leap-rational. htm.

———. "Making Revolution and Emancipating Humanity," *Revolution,* October 21, 2007–serialization continuing. Also available online at http://www.revcom.us.

———. *Observations on Art and Culture, Science and Philosophy.* Chicago: Insight Press, 2005.

———. *Phony Communism Is Dead...Long Live Real Communism.* 1992. Second ed. with appendix, *Democracy: More Than Ever We Can and Must Do Better Than That.* Chicago: RCP Publications, 2004.

———. *Preaching from a Pulpit of Bones: We Need Morality but not* Traditional *Morality.* New York: Banner Press, 1999.

———. *Revolution: Why It's Necessary, Why It's Possible, What It's All About,* DVD. Chicago: Three Q Productions, 2004.

———. "The Truth About Right-Wing Conspiracy...And Why Clinton and the Democrats Are No Answer," *Revolutionary Worker,* October 17, 2004. First published *Revolutionary Worker,* November, 1998. Also available online at http://www.revcom.us/a/1255/avakian_clinton_right_wing_conspiracy.htm.

———. "Views on Socialism and Communism: A Radically New Kind of State, A Radically Different and Far Greater Vision of Freedom," *Revolution,* March 5–April 9, 2006. Also available online at http://www.revcom.us/avakian/Avakianviewson.html.

Avakian, Bob, and Bill Martin. *Marxism and the Call of the Future: Conversations on Ethics, History, and Politics*. Foreword by Slavoj Žižek, preface by Raymond Lotta. Chicago, IL: Open Court, 2005.

Bacevich, Andrew J. *The New American Militarism: How Americans Are Seduced by War*. New York: Oxford University Press, 2005.

Barber, Benjamin R. *Jihad vs. McWorld*. New York: Times Books, 1995.

Bennett, William J., ed. *The Book of Virtues: A Treasury of Great Moral Stories*. New York: Simon & Schuster, 1993.

Berlet, Chip. "The Right Rides High: Dogmatism and Religious Fundamentalism in U.S. Republican Party," *The Progressive*, October, 1994.

The Book of Mormon: Another Testament of Jesus Christ; The Doctrine and Covenants of The Church of Jesus Christ of Latter-day Saints; The Pearl of Great Price. Salt Lake City, UT: The Church of Jesus Christ of Latter-day Saints, 1981.

Bowden, Mark. *Black Hawk Down: A Story of Modern War*. New York: Atlantic Monthly Press, 1999.

Brock, David. *Blinded By the Right: The Conscience of an Ex-Conservative*. New York: Three Rivers Press, 2002.

———. *The Republican Noise Machine: Right-Wing Media and How It Corrupts Democracy*. New York: Crown Publishers, 2004.

Brooks, A. "God the Original Fascist," *Revolution*, September 25, 2005–November 20, 2005. Also available online at http://www.rovcom.us/a/series/god-original-fascist-all.htm.

Carroll, James. *Constantine's Sword: The Church and the Jews: A History*. New York: Houghton Mifflin, 2001.

Chomsky, Noam. *Hegemony or Survival: America's Quest for Global Dominance*. New York: Metropolitan Books, 2003.

Cleveland, William L. *A History of the Modern Middle East*. Boulder, CO: Westview Press, 2000.

"Cold Truth, Liberating Truth: How This System Has Always Oppressed Black People, and How All Oppression Can Finally Be Ended," *Revolutionary Worker*, Special section, August 14, 1989. Also available online at http://www.revcom.us/coldtruth.

Conason, Joe. *Big Lies: The Right-Wing Propaganda Machine and How It Distorts the Truth*. New York: Thomas Dunne Books, 2003.

Crier, Catherine. *Contempt: How the Right is Wronging American Justice*. New York: Rugged Land, 2005.

Crossan, John Dominic. *Jesus: A Revolutionary Biography*. New York: HarperCollins, 1994.

——. *Who Killed Jesus? Exposing the Roots of Anti-Semitism in the Gospel Story of the Death of Jesus*. New York: HarperCollins, 1995.

Davis, David Brion. *Inhuman Bondage: The Rise and Fall of Slavery in the New World*. New York: Oxford University Press, 2006.

Davis, Mike. *Planet of Slums*. London; New York: Verso, 2006.

Dean, John W. *Worse than Watergate: The Secret Presidency of George W. Bush*. New York: Little, Brown and Company, 2004.

Ehrman, Bart D. *Misquoting Jesus: The Story Behind Who Changed the Bible and Why*. New York: HarperCollins, 2005.

——. *The New Testament, Part I*. VHS. Chantilly, VA: The Teaching Company, 2000.

——. *The New Testament, Part II*. VHS. Chantilly, VA: The Teaching Company, 2000.

Engels, Friedrich. *Anti-Dühring*. 1878. Peking: Foreign Languages Press, 1976.

Everest, Larry. *Oil, Power & Empire: Iraq and the U.S. Global Agenda*. Monroe, ME: Common Courage Press, 2004.

Falwell, Jerry. Transcript of Pat Robertson's interview with Jerry Falwell from the Sept. 13, 2001 edition of *The 700 Club*, printed in Press Release of People for the American Way, Sept. 17, 2001. Also available online at Common Dreams NewsCenter, www.commondreams.org.

"Falwell Apologizes to Gays, Feminists, Lesbians." Posted Sept. 14, 2001 at www.cnn.com/us.

Finkelstein, Norman G. *Beyond Chutzpah: On the Misuse of Anti-Semitism and the Abuse of History*. Berkeley and Los Angeles: University of California Press, 2005.

———. *The Holocaust Industry: Reflections on the Exploitation of Jewish Suffering*. London; New York: Verso, 2003.

Garbus, Martin. *Courting Disaster: The Supreme Court and the Unmaking of American Law*. New York: Times Books, 2002.

Gibbon, Edward. *The Decline and Fall of the Roman Empire*. 3 vols. New York: Modern Library, 1995.

The Glorious Qur'an. Translated by Muhammad M. Pickthall. 10th ed., Des Plaines, IL: Library of Islam, 1994 (originally translated, 1930).

Goldberg, Michelle. *Kingdom Coming: The Rise of Christian Nationalism*. New York: W.W. Norton & Company, 2006.

Grayling, A.C. *Descartes: The Life and Times of a Genius*. New York: Walker & Company, 2006.

Greene, Brian R. *The Elegant Universe: Superstrings, Hidden Dimensions, and the Quest for the Ultimate Theory*. New York: Vintage Books, 2000.

———. *The Fabric of the Cosmos: Space, Time, and the Texture of Reality*. New York: Alfred A. Knopf, 2004.

Hamid, Mohsin. *The Reluctant Fundamentalist*. Orlando, FL: Harcourt, 2007.

Hamilton, Marci. *God vs. the Gavel: Religion and the Rule of Law*. New York: Cambridge University Press, 2005.

Hardisty, Jean V. *Mobilizing Resentment: Conservative Resurgence from the John Birch Society to the Promise Keepers*. Boston: Beacon Press, 1999.

The HarperCollins Study Bible: New Revised Standard Version, with the Apocryphal/Deuterocanonical Books. Gen. ed., Wayne A. Meeks; assoc. eds. Jouette M. Bassler, et al. New York: HarperCollins, 1993.

Harris, Sam. *The End of Faith: Religion, Terror, and the Future of Reason*. New York: W.W. Norton & Company, 2004.

———. *Letter to a Christian Nation*. New York: Alfred A. Knopf, 2006.

Hedges, Chris. *American Fascists: The Christian Right and the War on America*. New York: Free Press, 2006.

Herrnstein, Richard J. and Charles Murray. *The Bell Curve: Intelligence and Class Structure in American Life*. New York: Free Press, 1994.

Hersh, Seymour M. *Chain of Command: The Road from 9/11 to Abu Ghraib*. New York: HarperCollins, 2004.

Hitchens, Christopher. *God Is Not Great: How Religion Poisons Everything*. New York: Twelve, 2007.

Hollinger, David A. *Science, Jews, and Secular Culture: Studies in Mid-Twentieth-Century American Intellectual History*. Princeton, NJ: Princeton University Press, 1996.

Hourani, Albert Habib. *A History of the Arab Peoples*. New York: Warner Books, 1992.

Jacoby, Susan. *Freethinkers: A History of American Secularism*. New York: Metropolitan Books, 2004.

Kaplan, Esther. *With God on Their Side: How Christian Fundamentalists Trampled Science, Policy, and Democracy in George W. Bush's White House*. New York: New Press, 2004.

Katznelson, Ira. *When Affirmative Action Was White: An Untold History of Racial Inequality in Twentieth-Century America*. New York: W.W. Norton & Company, 2005.

Kautsky, Karl. *Foundations of Christianity: A Study in Christian Origins*. 1908. Authorized Translation from the Thirteenth German ed., New York: Monthly Review Press, 1972.

King, Martin Luther, Jr. *Where Do We Go From Here: Chaos or Community?* New York: Harper & Row, 1967.

King, Noel Q. *Religions of Africa: A Pilgrimage Into Traditional Religions*. New York: Harper & Row, 1970.

Kinzer, Stephen. *All the Shah's Men: An American Coup and the Roots of Middle East Terror*. Hoboken, NJ: John Wiley & Sons, 2003.

Koonz, Claudia. *The Nazi Conscience.* Cambridge, MA: Belknap Press, 2003.

Krakauer, Jon. *Under the Banner of Heaven: A Story of Violent Faith.* New York: Anchor Books, 2004.

Kramnick, Isaac, and R. Laurence Moore. *The Godless Constitution: A Moral Defense of the Secular State.* New York: W.W. Norton & Company, 2005.

Lanternari, Vittorio. *The Religions of the Oppressed: A Study of Modern Messianic Cults.* Translated by Lisa Sergio. New York: Alfred A. Knopf, 1963.

Lapham, Lewis H. *Gag Rule: On the Suppression of Dissent and the Stifling of Democracy.* New York: Penguin Press, 2004.

Lenin, V.I. *Materialism and Empirio-Criticism.* 1908. Peking: Foreign Languages Press, 1972.

Lerner, Michael. *The Left Hand of God: Taking Back Our Country from the Religious Right.* New York: HarperCollins, 2006.

Levine, Amy-Jill. *The Old Testament, Part I.* VHS. Chantilly, VA: The Teaching Company, 2001.

———. *The Old Testament, Part II.* VHS. Chantilly, VA: The Teaching Company, 2001.

Linker, Damon. *The Theocons: Secular America Under Siege.* New York: Doubleday, 2006.

Lloyd, Brian. *Left Out: Pragmatism, Exceptionalism, and the Poverty of American Marxism, 1890-1922.* Baltimore, MD: Johns Hopkins University Press, 1997.

Locke, Dr. Hubert. "Reflections on the Pacific School of Religion's Response to the Religious Right." Talk at the Pacific School of Religion in Berkeley on May 17, 2005. Reprinted in *Revolution*, January 29, 2006. Also available online at http://www.revcom.us/a/032/religious-against-christian-fascism.htm.

Lotta, Raymond with Frank Shannon. *America in Decline: An Analysis of the Developments Toward War and Revolution, In the U.S. and Worldwide, in the 1980s, Vol. One.* Chicago: Banner Press, 1984.

Luttwak, Edward. *Turbo-Capitalism: Winners and Losers in the Global Economy.* New York: HarperCollins, 1999.

Mamdani, Mahmood. *Good Muslim, Bad Muslim: America, the Cold War, and the Roots of Terror.* New York: Three Leaves Press, 2005.

Mann, Jim. *Rise of the Vulcans: The History of Bush's War Cabinet.* New York: Viking Penguin, 2004.

Manschreck, Clyde Leonard. *A History of Christianity in the World.* Englewood Cliffs, NJ: Prentice-Hall, 1985.

Mao Tsetung. "On Practice." 1937. *Selected Works of Mao Tsetung,* Vol. I. Peking: Foreign Languages Press, 1967.

Marx, Karl. *The Class Struggles in France, 1848 to 1850.* 1850. New York: International Publishers, 1964.

———. *The Poverty of Philosophy.* 1847. Peking: Foreign Languages Press, 1977.

Marx, Karl, and Friedrich Engels. *The Communist Manifesto.* 1848. New York: Verso, 1998.

Marx and Engels On Religion. Moscow: Progress Publishers, 1975.

Mayer, Arno J. *Why Did the Heavens Not Darken? The "Final Solution" in History.* New York: Pantheon Books, 1988.

McChesney, Robert Waterman. *Rich Media, Poor Democracy: Communication Politics in Dubious Times.* New York: New Press, 2000, with new preface. Originally published by University of Illinois Press, 1999.

Merriam-Webster's Encyclopedia of World Religions. Consulting ed., Wendy Doniger. Springfield, MA: Merriam-Webster, 1999.

Nafisi, Azar. *Reading Lolita in Tehran: A Memoir in Books.* New York: Random House, 2003.

Peters, F. E. *The Harvest of Hellenism: A History of the Near East from Alexander the Great to the Triumph of Christianity.* 1970. New York: Barnes & Noble Books, 1996.

Phillips, Kevin. *American Theocracy: The Peril and Politics of Radical Religion, Oil, and Borrowed Money in the 21st Century.* New York: Viking, 2006.

Popper, Karl R. *The Open Society and Its Enemies. Volume II - The High Tide of Prophecy: Hegel, Marx, and the Aftermath.* Princeton, NJ: Princeton University Press, 1971.

Raskin, Jamin B. *Overruling Democracy: The Supreme Court Versus the American People.* New York: Routledge, 2003.

Revolution. Available online at http://www.revcom.us.

Revolutionary Communist Party, USA. *Notes on Political Economy: Our Analysis of the 1980s, Issues of Methodology, and The Current World Situation.* Chicago: RCP Publications, 2000. Also available online at http://a/special_postings/poltoc_e.htm

Ricks, Thomas E. *Making the Corps.* New York: Scribner, 1997.

Robertson, Pat. *Answers to 200 of Life's Most Probing Questions.* Toronto: Bantam Books, 1987.

———. *The New World Order.* Nashville, TN: Thomas Nelson, 1991.

Rodinson, Maxime. *Muhammad.* New York: Pantheon Books, 1980, with new Introduction and Foreword by Maxime Rodinson. Translation by Anne Carter, 1971. Originally published in France as *Mahomet* by Club français du livre, 1961.

Roediger, David R. *Working Toward Whiteness: How America's Immigrants Became White: The Strange Journey from Ellis Island to the Suburbs.* New York: Basic Books, 2005.

Rose, Steven. *The Future of the Brain: The Promise and Perils of Tomorrow's Neuroscience.* New York: Oxford University Press, 2005.

Rudin, A. James. *The Baptizing of America: The Religious Right's Plans for the Rest of Us.* New York: Thunder's Mouth Press, 2006.

Russell, Bertrand. *Why I Am Not a Christian, and Other Essays on Religion and Related Subjects.* Edited with an Appendix on the "Bertrand Russell Case" by Paul Edwards. New York: Simon and Schuster, 1957.

Set the Record Straight. Available online at http://www.thisiscommunism.org.

Shorto, Russell. "Contra-Contraception," *The New York Times Magazine,* May 7, 2006.

Skybreak, Ardea. *Of Primeval Steps and Future Leaps: An Essay on the Emergence of Human Beings, the Source of Women's Oppression, and the Road to Emancipation.* Chicago: Banner Press, 1984.

———. *The Science of Evolution and the Myth of Creationism: Knowing What's Real and Why It Matters.* Chicago: Insight Press, 2006.

Smolin, Lee. *The Life of the Cosmos.* New York: Oxford University Press, 1997.

Stewart, Matthew. *The Courtier and the Heretic: Leibniz, Spinoza, and the Fate of God in the Modern World.* New York: W.W. Norton & Company, 2006.

Suskind, Ron. *The Price of Loyalty: George W. Bush, the White House, and the Education of Paul O'Neill.* New York: Simon & Schuster, 2004.

Tabor, James D. *The Jesus Dynasty: The Hidden History of Jesus, His Royal Family, and the Birth of Christianity.* New York: Simon & Schuster, 2006.

"21st Century Slavery Under Global Capitalism," *Revolution*, September 23, 2007. Also available online at www.revcom.us.

Wallis, Jim. *The Soul of Politics: A Practical and Prophetic Vision for Change.* New York: New Press, 1994.

"WARNING: The Nazification of the American University," *Revolution*, August 26, 2007. Also available online at www.revcom.us.

West, Cornel. *Democracy Matters: Winning the Fight Against Imperialism.* New York: Penguin Press, 2004.

Wilmore, Gayraud S. and James H. Cone, eds. *Black Theology: A Documentary History, 1966–1979.* Maryknoll, NY: Orbis Books, 1979.

Wolff, Lenny. *The Science of Revolution: An Introduction.* Chicago: RCP Publications, 1983.

Index

A

Abiathar, 65
abortion, 14, 181–182, 185–189, 192
Abraham, 124, 129
abstinence. *See* virginity.
Abu Ghraib, 42
Adam and Eve, 49, 122–123, 130, 231
adultery, 23, 66, 151
affirmative action, 143
Afghanistan, 42, 99, 107, 110
Africa, 40, 55, 102–103, 113
African-Americans. *See* Black people;
   slavery; Black religious
   tradition.
Afrikaners, 142
Ahemilech, 65
Allah, 85–86, 89–95. *See also* Qur'an
American chauvinism, 104n, 168
"American exceptionalism", 39, 141, 178.
   See also U.S. imperialism.
Angel Gabriel. *See* Gabriel
apriorism, 172, 204
Arab nationalism, 107
Arendt, Hannah, 181n
Armstrong, Karen, 199–210
art, 200–201, 236
Arulraja, M.R., 19n
awe and wonder, 194–197, 234

B

Babylon, 13
Barber, Benjamin R., 100
beauty, 201–202
Bennett, William, 30
Bible. *See also* Jesus; New Testament;
   Old Testament; sin.
   and adultery, 22–24, 66, 151
   and children, 12, 29, 34, 132–135
   errors and discrepancies in, 5–6, 27,
      31, 62–63, 65, 124
   and homosexuality, 15, 151

Bible *(continued)*
   political decisions about scriptures
      in, 63–65
   and polygamy, 129–130
   reflecting society, 6–7, 51, 123
   and slavery, 7–8, 17, 18, 26, 30, 143
   and women, 9, 11–14, 17, 19–24, 34,
      49, 83n, 122–123
Bible Belt, 136–149
birth control, 181–182
Black people, 136–154. *See also* slavery.
Black religious tradition, 144–149
Blackwater, 99n
Bonaparte, Napoleon. *See* Napoleon
Book of Mormon, 55–56
bourgeois democracy. *See* democracy
Bowden, Mark, 99n
Boykin, General Jerry, 45
Brock, David, 36–37
Brooks, A., 7–11
Brown, John, 138, 140
Bush, George W., 35, 37, 44–45, 97, 128
Bush regime, 42, 96, 172, 176, 183

C

Canaan, 9–10
capitalism/capitalism-imperialism
   accumulation under, 162–163, 185,
      229
   and bourgeois-democratic transfor-
      mation, 98
   and bourgeois dictatorship, 184
   fundamental contradiction of,
      114–117, 162
   as heartless world, 223
   and "human nature", 226–231
   Marx's critique of, 166–167
   and slavery, 229
   and spiritual malaise, 162n
Carlin, George, 134n
Carroll, James, 64n, 71

ABOUT THE AUTHOR

Bob Avakian is a veteran of the Free Speech Movement and the revolutionary upsurges of the 1960s and early '70s. In 1975 he led in founding the Revolutionary Communist Party, USA, and has been its Chairman ever since.

Bob Avakian has an extensive body of work, including numerous books, other writings and talks. Among these works are:

From Ike to Mao and Beyond: My Journey from Mainstream America to Revolutionary Communist [a memoir]

Marxism and the Call of the Future: Conversations on Ethics, History, and Politics [co-authored with Bill Martin]

Observations on Art and Culture, Science and Philosophy

Revolution: Why It's Necessary, Why It's Possible, What It's All About [a video/DVD of a talk by Bob Avakian]

Democracy: Can't We Do Better Than That?

Phony Communism is Dead...Long Live Real Communism! [2nd edition, includes Appendix: *Democracy: More Than Ever We Can and Must Do Better Than That*]

Reflections, Sketches & Provocations

Recent talks by Bob Avakian include *"Communism and Jeffersonian Democracy"* and *"The NBA: Marketing the Minstrel Show and Serving the Big Gangsters."* [available as audio files]

****

For audio downloads and recent works by Bob Avakian, see www.bobavakian.net

Praise for Other Works by Bob Avakian

From Ike to Mao and Beyond: My Journey from Mainstream America to Revolutionary Communist, **a memoir**

"Bob Avakian is a long distance runner in the freedom struggle against imperialism, racism and capitalism. His voice and witness are indispensable in our efforts to enhance the wretched of the earth. And his powerful story of commitment is timely."

Cornel West, Class of 1943 University Professor of Religion, Princeton University

"A truly interesting account of Bob Avakian's life, a humanizing portrait of someone who is often seen only as a hard-line revolutionary. I can understand why Bob Avakian has drawn so many ardent supporters. He speaks to people's alienation from a warlike and capitalist society, and holds out the possibility for radical change."

Howard Zinn, Author of *A People's History of the United States*

"Beyond the compelling ideological and philosophical ruminations from the book's early chapters, when all the fun of football vanishes and he struggles with a dreadful sickness, rests the evidence of Avakian's fortitude and resilience that are hallmarks of his character and integrity."

Herb Boyd, author, journalist

Preaching From a Pulpit of Bones: We Need Morality, but not Traditional Morality

"For this clergyman who has struggled with the relevance of the Biblical faith in the face of the crises in our society, the critique of Bob Avakian comes as an urgent challenge...There is insight and truth-speaking in this vital book which those of us of religious faith need to hear and to which we need to respond."

Reverend George W. Webber, President Emeritus, New York
Theological Seminary

"Avakian points the way toward what some doubt is possible, a materialist ethics. Like Mao's, this is a Marxism that aims at a social analysis that is clear and systematic but not 'cold'—a Marxism with heart."

Bill Martin, Associate Professor of Philosophy, DePaul University, Chicago

Marxism and the Call of the Future: Conversations on Ethics, History and Politics (co-authored with Bill Martin)

"At this dark time in the history of our country and of the world, we need some new conversations about Marx and the socialist tradition —conversations free of dogmatism, open to ideas from all sides, but oriented in a progressive direction and eager to learn from thinking critically within the Marxist tradition. This book provides us with one model of what those kinds of conversations can be like."

Allen Wood, author of Karl Marx and Kant's Ethical Thought

"...so important that it should stand on the shelf of everyone who cares about the destiny of the political Left...marks the beginning of a new approach."

Slavoj Žižek (from the Foreword)

Revolution: Why It's Necessary. Why It's Possible. What It's All About. A talk by Bob Avakian (video/DVD)

"Avakian...lucidly explains concepts ranging from dialectical materialism to irony without condescending to his audience...He's no less sharp when he's answering questions than when he's outlining his revolutionary program."

Jonathan Rosenbaum, Chicago Reader

"Just like landmark art work or historically seminal music, Bob Avakian's delivery and timing is truly inspiring. The only thing more inspiring is the vision and message he presents to us. Avakian is a revolutionary leader whose voice must be heard far and wide today."

Wil-Dog, Jiro and Uli from Ozomatli